Journey Towards Holiness

Journey Towards Holiness

A Way of Living for God's Nation

Alan Kreider

Foreword by Howard A. Snyder

HERALD PRESS
Scottdale, Pennsylvania
Kitchener, Ontario
1987

Library of Congress Cataloging-in-Publication Data
Kreider, Alan, 1941-
    Journey towards holiness.
    Bibliography: p.
    Includes index.
    1. Christian life—Mennonite authors.   2. Holiness.
I. Title.
BV4501.2.K7   1986   248.4'897   86-22838
ISBN 0-8361-3423-0

JOURNEY TOWARDS HOLINESS
Copyright © 1987 by Herald Press, Scottdale, Pa. 15683
    Published simultaneously in Canada by Herald Press,
    Kitchener, Ont. N2G 4M5. All rights reserved.
Library of Congress Catalog Card Number: 86-22838
International Standard Book Number: 0-8361-3423-0
Printed in the United States of America
Cover by Ann Graber
Cover photo from Streano/Havens
Design by Paula Johnson
Graphics by London Mennonite Centre staff with Priscilla Trenchard

87 88 89 90 91 92 93 94 95 12 11 10 9 8 7 6 5 4 3 2 1

For
Andrew

Quotations from the Bible

I have used the Revised Standard Version of the Bible as the basis of my study (copyrighted 1946, 1952, © 1971, 1973). Where I have supplemented this with other translations, I have indicated this.

Scripture references marked NIV are from *The Holy Bible: New International Version*. Copyright © 1973, 1978, 1984 by the International Bible Society. Used by permission of Zondervan Bible Publishers.

Scripture references marked TEV are from the *Good News Bible*. Old Testament copyright © American Bible Society, 1976; New Testament copyright © American Bible Society, 1966, 1971, 1976.

Scripture references marked JB are from *The Jerusalem Bible*, copyright © 1966 by Darton, Longman & Todd, Ltd., and Doubleday & Company, Inc. Used by permission of the publisher.

Scripture references marked NEB are from *The New English Bible*. Copyright © by the Delegates of the Oxford University Press and the Syndics of the Cambridge University Press, 1961, 1970. Reprinted by permission.

I have occasionally made changes in the RSV text. At times this is to avoid sexist language (e.g., "all people" instead of "all men"); and at times it is to render more faithfully the force of the original text. For instance, in one case, I prefer "justice" over "righteousness" (see chapter 2, note 3). Other alterations include: "Yahweh" for "the Lord"; "Lord of armies" for "Lord of hosts"; "shalom" for "peace"; "nations" for "gentiles"; and "holy ones" for "saints."

—Alan Kreider

Contents

Foreword

Once in awhile a book comes along which breaks new ground or makes new connections, helping us see more clearly. *Journey Towards Holiness* is such a book.

Wesleyans have often been intrigued by John Wesley's words that the gospel "knows of . . . no holiness but social holiness." But what *is* "social holiness"? Wesley meant that one can experience true Christianity only in fellowship with other believers. The ideal of holiness is not solitary saints, Wesley argued, but a holy community.

It is this theme which Kreider explores with insight, passion, and high interest. The book develops in some depth this aspect of holiness which Wesley alluded to—and practiced—but which has received inadequate attention from Wesleyan scholars.

As a Mennonite, Kreider writes (as he makes clear) from an Anabaptist perspective. The Anabaptists, embodying what is sometimes called the Radical Reformation of the sixteenth century, felt that true reformation and renewal must include holiness—not only what Christians *believe* but also how they *live*, and specifically how they live together as a community. Many Anabaptists died for their faith at the hands of both Protestants and Roman Catholics, but their witness has impacted subsequent "believers churches." Wesley himself, in his theology and practice, showed a close affinity with this tradition as I have shown in my book, *The Radical Wesley*.

But this book is no mere restatement of the Anabaptist view of the church. Kreider breaks fresh ground both in his overview of biblical history and in his application of social holiness to the contemporary church. In his excellent summary of the Bible story, Kreider shows what it means today to be a *people* who live according to the biblical way of holiness.

Contemporary readers will find much here to ponder and digest. The "manna principles" of sufficiency and equality will help us examine our lifestyles. The ways God provides our basic needs of provision and protection raise questions about the sources of our security. And the discussion of holiness in terms of living force, separateness, godlikeness, and dynamism help us see holiness in fresh ways.

Kreider is writing primarily about the social experience of God's holiness in the Christian community and in the world, not about how one personally experiences holiness of heart. But the two are part of one great truth, not conflicting emphases. I hope this book will help many believers today—Wesleyans, Anabaptists, and those from other traditions—become more fully and authentically part of God's "holy nation" in the world today.

—Howard A. Snyder
Irving Park Free Methodist Church

Author's Preface

I never thought I'd write a book on holiness. A book on church history, yes. Or one on Christian discipleship or even on the debate about nuclear weapons. But on holiness?

Holiness was real to me, alright. I think back especially to experiences in prayer groups in the early 1970s. Or, more recently, I recall an occasion on which, together with a dear friend, I was in a special place, a place of prayer. My friend turned to me and said simply, "This is a holy place." We were both moved to be in the presence of the Holy One.

Some English Baptist friends must take responsibility for my beginning to think seriously about holiness. When they asked me to give an address on "social holiness" at the 1984 Mainstream Conference, I pondered, prayed, and accepted. Little did I know that by taking on this assignment I would be dealing with something that would integrate my life and thinking in a new way. Holiness, I began to discover, is about life. Every area of life. It is supremely about God, but then God is involved in the world.

As I proceeded to study what the Bible had to say about holiness, a suspicion of mine was confirmed—that every major Christian doctrine, if looked at carefully, has to do with life in the world. It is not only holiness that is social.

In writing, I have been conscious that my insights are often not new ones. Sometimes I have felt like a cardplayer shuffling a familiar pack! I also am aware of how much I have had to leave out. In my attempt not to write an endless book I have had to omit important doctrines and favorite Bible passages. But then, I have reminded myself, I am not writing a book of systematic theology. I am trying to retell the Bible story in such a way that I, and anyone who reads this, will feel called into new dimensions of holy living.

What is it then that I have to offer? One thing, I hope, is simplicity. I have tried to write so that the majority of Christian readers can understand what I'm saying. Christian social strategy—how we live our workaday lives as disciples of Jesus—is not something for the "professionals" alone. It is for us all. I want to communicate with laypeople who are so busy with job and family that it is hard to find time for church, to say nothing of time for reading. Equally, I have tried to write in such a way that busy pastors, who are besieged by funerals and growth groups, will be able to read this in bed!

Second, I want to write primarily, not about the contemporary world, but about the Bible. Most people who write about Christian involvement in the world assume that their readers will know the Bible's story inside out. Most of them also assume that their readers will have a basic knowledge of Christian theology. After developing a particular biblical image or theme, such as justice, peace (shalom), or salt and light, they then proceed to analyze the world's problems and to present a Christian approach to them. I would like to start farther back. It's not that I doubt that many of you will know biblical history or teaching. But I think there is value in retelling the story of God's dealings with men and women.

Not the whole story, of course. There isn't enough space for that. But all of us tell the story. We tell it to our children and inwardly we tell it to ourselves. And as we do this, we are standing in a tradition of biblical storytellers who have retold the story to emphasize significant themes and developments. That is what Moses did as he prepared to say good-bye to the Israelites (Deut. 29). It is what Joshua did in his farewell speech (Josh. 24). It is what the scribe Ezra did as he challenged the repatriated Jewish exiles to faith and faithfulness (Neh. 9). It is what Stephen did as he defended himself before the Sanhedrin (Acts 7). None of these people told the whole story. But they told enough to make sense of what God had done so that his people could respond faithfully to his next actions. I hope it is not arrogant of me to try to stand in their tradition.

Third, I am writing as a historian, not as a formally trained theologian. In a book about practical theology this has its obvious drawbacks, but it can have its advantages as well. The historian's perspective, it seems to me, is not a bad one when it comes to studying the Bible. Historians, like biblical scholars, are trained in the analysis of texts. But more importantly, we are taught to tell a story—and to see significant blocks of time in it. All of us recognize these time-blocks in our own lives. Before I got married my life was different from what it's been like since. Moving from one job to another changed what I do with my time and how I think about things. So it is with history—biblical and secular. The historian calls this "periodization" (I won't mention the word again!). And as we proceed through this book, we will see, in the ebb and flow of the faithfulness and faithlessness of God's people, distinct patterns which can teach us a great deal.

Fourth and finally, I am writing, not as a member of one of the dominant Christian traditions (Reformed, Catholic, Orthodox, Anglican, etc.), but as a representative of a 450-year-old renewal tradition, the so-called "Anabaptist" (re-baptizer) tradition. This movement began in 1525 in Switzerland and

Germany as a result of a search for a more consistently renewed form of Christian discipleship. The Anabaptist leaders thought that European Christians, through their alliance with state power, had developed some bad habits which had departed from the convictions and lifestyle of the Christians of the first three centuries. They felt that God was giving them some insights about how things might be changed to return to those early patterns of faith-filled living.

Partly because the Anabaptist leaders themselves were at times stubborn in their new insights, they encountered a lot of defensiveness from the leaders of the established churches. Not only defensiveness but also—despite their desire for dialogue—excommunication and persecution. Across the European continent in the sixteenth century thousands of Anabaptists were either banished or executed. Even in England, at Smithfield in London where many Protestants had earlier been executed, two Anabaptists in 1575 were burned on the orders of Protestant Queen Elizabeth I. Ever since then, most theologians and church historians have ignored the Anabaptists or dismissed them as sectarians.

Things are changing today, however. Within the past seventy-five years lineal descendants of the Anabaptists (Mennonites, Brethren in Christ, Hutterites) have spread, through mission, persecution, and migration, to over fifty countries. In rediscovering their history, many of these people have regained a sense of purpose and peoplehood. They have also experienced spiritual revitalization. Many of us twentieth-century Anabaptists, while understanding why our forebears withdrew from the "world" in response to persecution, do not want to go that route ourselves. In many places we have emerged as participants in the life of the secular world and the wider Christian church, being committed to service, mission, scholarship and professional involvement.

But among today's Christians there are many "nonlineal" relatives of the Anabaptists as well. Around the world many believers are encountering ideas which the Anabaptists held dear: the church as the body of Christ, simplicity of lifestyle and economic sharing, nonviolence and enemy love, and Jesus as the heart of God's revelation of an appropriate lifestyle for God's people. Moreover, they are adopting these ideas, not because the Anabaptists held them, but because they are discovering their own roots—in the early church. In a world in which traditional answers seem explosively irrelevant, many Christians are willing to consider "new" alternatives.

It will be obvious to those who stay with me throughout this book that I, as a modern Anabaptist Christian, cannot stand alone. I have learned much from Anabaptist-Mennonite men and women—from parents, pastors, and friends, and also from scholars, most notably from John Howard Yoder, Willard Swartley, Ron Sider, Larry Miller, and Millard Lind. The latter two are especially dear friends, and their biblical vision and expertise have been an inspiration to me. Repeatedly over the years Wilbert Shenk of the Mennonite Board of Missions has provided me with a theological vision for mission. This time his comments at an early stage helped me to see the way forward in writing this book. And the Board's financial support made it possible. But much though I owe to Mennonites, I hope that my debt to Christians of other traditions will be equally apparent. Some of these I have never met. With others I have shared life and worship. Jim Punton, Kim Tan, Lesslie Newbigin, Stanley Hauerwas, Neil Summerton, Jim Wallis, Jeanne Hinton, Richard Mouw, Herbert Butterfield, Andrew Kirk, Bob Goudzwaard—how much my life and thinking owe to them!

Christian communities are said to be poor places to write. "You've got to get away to get anything done," I've been told. This is to some extent true. As I have written this book, sisters and brothers have helped to protect me from interruptions. I have enjoyed these times of solitude. But in many ways, this book is a product of my involvement with serious Christians who have come together to hunt for alternative forms of church life. Spiritually I have been stretched by these people and by the experiences of God's grace that we have had together. From them I have also learned a lot about the world and the Bible. Without my experiences in a number of Christian communities, I would never have written this book, for I would have had nothing to say.

It was in a community in Switzerland that I began work on the book. The Sisters of Grandchamp, a community of Protestant sisters near Neuchatel, taught me much about worship, work, and living in genuine unity. The next stages of work took place in York, England, under the umbrella of the church of St. Michael-le-Belfrey, who provided me and my family with housing and with inspiration and ministry. My debt to Graham Cray and Sharon Stinson is immense. In nearby Leeds, members of the Aslan Education Unit have also been helpful. Bill Phelps, Paul Langley, and Cathy Magnall have read chapters and made suggestions. The support of Pippa Julings, friend and spiritual and intellectual comrade, has been magnificent.

Most of the writing, however, I have done in London, England, within the sphere of support of my home church—the London Mennonite Fellowship. Many members have helped me. Over the years, I have learned much through conversations with Wally Fahrer. Will Newcomb and Peter Olsen have helped in innumerable ways. Some members have read each chapter as I have written it and made perceptive criticisms. Judith Gardiner, David Nussbaum, Kathy Nussbaum, Andy Potter, Sally Welch, Chris Marshall—all have been helpful to me. My most long-suffering critics have been Eleanor Kreider and Andrew Kreider, my wife and son. Both have read the manuscript with painstaking attention to detail. Both have suggested new ways forward when I was in a mental cul-de-sac. And Andrew has prepared the index. I am grateful.

—Alan Kreider,
London Mennonite Centre,
Highgate, London, England, July 1986

Part I
Surveying the Territory

Holiness:
Three Snapshots

Holiness, Snapshot 1

The scene, a refugee camp on the eastern shore of the Red Sea. Date, approximately 1280 B.C. Documentary evidence, Exodus 15.

It is a scene of some confusion. People of all ages are milling about, intermingling with animals. In most ways their life is pretty primitive. They've got a few leaders, but very little organization. And they have practically no possessions. As refugees they have only what they can carry with them. They don't even know very well who they are or what their history is.

But they do know two things. They used to be slaves on the western side of the Red Sea, in Egypt. But now they are free. And they are free, not because of anything they have done, but because something amazing has just happened.

When they had been pursued by the mightiest military machine of their day; when they had found themselves pinned in between it and the deep blue sea; when they had been powerless, utterly out of ideas, and full of fear—Someone Else had acted. A God whose name they had just learned, whose character they had just begun to discover, had saved them from forced labor in the brickyard.[1] He had kept them from being wiped out as a people. The Sea, which had parted to allow them to pass through dry-shod, had swallowed their pursuers. What an act! It boggled their minds. And it frightened them (Exod. 14:31), for they sensed that an Awesome Power had been unleashed in their experience which they couldn't begin to understand. They had no categories into which to fit acts of concrete, tangible grace. But, despite their fear and bewilderment, they were immensely relieved.

So they gathered in thankful disarray to sing a new song—so new in fact that they were learning it as they sang. Moses, their leader, led the singing. The prophetess Miriam, his sister, was in charge of the rhythm section, brandishing her tambourine and leading the women in an unrehearsed dance.

What were they singing about? They were singing about their King. Indeed, they were singing *to* their King, whose name they had just learned.

> I will sing to Yahweh, for he has triumphed gloriously;
> the horse and his rider he has thrown into the sea.
> Yahweh is my strength and my song,
> and he has become my salvation. . . .
> Yahweh is a man of war;
> Yahweh is his name. (Exod. 15:1-3)

Why sing? Because of what their King had done. When the enemy, with his chariots, his army, and his picked officers, had said, "I will pursue, I will overtake . . . I will draw my sword, my hand shall destroy them," their King had acted.

> You blew with your wind, the sea covered them . . .
> Who is like you, O Yahweh, among the gods?
> Who is like you, majestic in HOLINESS,
> terrible in glorious deeds, doing wonders? (Exod. 15:10-11)

In their rejoicing, they were given a vision, an inspired premonition of the place of their rescue, and of their own existence as a people, in a much larger story.

> You have led in your steadfast love the people whom you
>   have redeemed,
> you have guided them by your strength to your HOLY
>   ABODE. . . .
> You will bring them in, and plant them on your own mountain
>   . . . your sanctuary, O Yahweh, which your hands have
>   established. (Exod. 15:13, 17)

The implications of this were more than they in their exuberance could anticipate. They could not know that they would be called to be a holy nation. They could not comprehend that their national lifestyle would be one of *holy deviance* which would set them apart—not just from the Egyptians but from all peoples. They could not know that this holiness would require them to go on living precariously, trusting in their Deliverer for their protection and provision.

But they did sense one thing—that their experience was not random or meaningless. History was going somewhere. Although it was out of *their* control, it was not out of control. They were in the hands of their own King—one who was invisible but tangibly powerful.

"Yahweh," they shouted. "Yahweh [not Pharaoh, not any Canaanite or Israelite king] *will reign for ever and ever.*"

Holiness, Snapshot 2

The scene, the temple in Jerusalem. Date, over five hundred years later, 742 B.C. Documentary evidence, Isaiah 6—7.

Isaiah, an educated man, was in the temple—the focal point of his nation's religious life. The evening sacrifice was taking place, but Isaiah's attention was far from the liturgy. Intensely concerned about politics, his mind kept flitting to plans which were being made elsewhere in the capital city.

It was a time of political crisis. Two centuries earlier, the Israelites had, despite Yahweh's protest, chosen to have kings. Since then, things hadn't gone very well most of the time. Within less than a century, the kingdom had split in two. Many of the kings of both Israel and Judah had done (in the recurrent phrase in the books of Kings) "what was evil in the sight of Yahweh."

Uzziah, king of Judah, had been a better king than many. "He was marvelously helped, till he was strong" (2 Chron. 26:15). But his strength had made him proud, and he had just died as a leper, excluded from the temple. His son, Jotham, was untried, and the storm clouds of multinational warfare were gathering. Judah was a tiny state, alienated from Israel and Syria to the north. In her weakness, she was inclined to look around for allies, perhaps to the great power, Assyria, which was amassing its forces to the East. Everyone, including Isaiah, was uncertain what would happen next.

Suddenly Isaiah's political musings were interrupted. In a terrifying moment, he saw Yahweh. At any rate, he saw Yahweh's vestments (his "train"). He observed the actions of his celestial courtiers and heard his voice and those of his courtiers. The experience was overwhelming. The seraphim flew, calling to one another,

> Holy, holy, holy is Yahweh Sabaoth (the Lord of armies);
> the whole earth is full of his glory. (Isa. 6:3)

The glorious space was filled with smoke, and the temple's monumental foundations were shaken.

So were Isaiah's. In his fear, he almost came unstuck. In the face of holiness, he knew that he was unwhole. "What a wretched state I'm in. I am lost!" More acutely than ever before, he knew that he was a sinner. He was unable to enter into the angels' song, unable with his unclean lips to speak to the political situation of his time. His fellow countrymen were as sinful as he was, confused and mute in the face of crisis. His understandings, his very being, had been called into question by what he had seen. For in the year that King Uzziah had died, Isaiah had seen the King, the Lord of armies. The King did not leave Isaiah cringing on the floor of his throne room. At his command, one of the seraphim took a live coal from the altar. With it he touched Isaiah's lips. Isaiah's sin was forgiven. His unclean lips became holy, fit to be a mouthpiece for the message of the King to his people. "Here I am!" said Isaiah. "Send me."

The message which the King gave him was an uncomfortable one. It was not a general call to withdraw to the temple, where all the people could experience the static sanctity of God's holiness. Instead, it was a word of judgment. God's people had forgotten their calling to be a holy nation. No longer were they living in holy nonconformity, trusting in God to protect and provide. Instead, their lifestyle had come to be one of unholy conformity to the patterns of life of the surrounding nations.

Like their bellies, their ears had become heavy. Not only were they unable to speak the word of God; they couldn't even hear it. On no account would they turn around and be healed (become holy again). As a result, the military forces that were building up would sweep over them. Their "large and beautiful houses" (Isa. 5:9) would be devastated. Their cities would be depopulated. When they ceased to be a holy nation, God's people were on course for catastrophe.

Unless . . . unless they would trust in their King Yahweh again. They could still turn to "the Holy God [who] shows himself holy in justice" (5:16). They could still trust in God instead of in military alliances, as Isaiah (7:9) shortly thereafter said to King Ahaz, "If you will not believe, surely you shall not be established." If his people would live in holy trust, relying on him instead of the Assyrians, Yahweh would once again demonstrate his power in world events.

Holiness, Snapshot 3

The scene, a room in Jerusalem. Date, early 30s, A.D. Documentary evidence, Acts 4.

There is tension in the air. A small room in Jerusalem is packed with men and women, many of them unsophisticated villagers from the North Country (Galilee). The people are tense for good reason. Their movement is a new one and the authorities have decided that it is dangerous. Interrogations and sudden arrests have followed. Rumors of systematic persecution have been rumbling. And now, while the people are having their evening gathering, two of their leaders—Peter and John—are being interrogated by the authorities. Will they be released? What future is there for their movement which is constantly under threat?

Despite these uncertainties, the people in the room knew that in the brief time since their movement had begun, they had experienced a new dimension of reality. It was a dimension so earth-shaking that they had left the petty securities of their former life and come to their present position of risk. It is less than a year after the disappearance of Jesus, the builder-rabbi from Galilee. Although the ruling regime's party line is that he is dead, his bones stolen by his disciples, the people in this room knew better. For they had seen him. They had touched his risen body. They had eaten with him. They had heard him reinterpret the Scriptures in light of himself and God's kingdom. They watched as he had ascended to be with the Father. And, most important of all, they were all "together in one place" when holiness burst in upon them. Jesus had kept his promise: the Spirit had enveloped them and equipped them with dynamic power.

Things had not been the same since. They had been living in hope, not in confusion and despair. They had been worshiping with renewed eagerness, both in the temple and in homes. The apostles had been teaching them, and the kind of wonders and signs which God's "holy servant" Jesus performed had been occurring in their midst. In their love for each other, they had been overcoming their fear and greed, and had been redistributing their goods according to need. And because they couldn't keep quiet about the Lord and Messiah who had loved them so much and was turning their lives around, they had repeatedly been in the bad books of the authorities.

Suddenly Peter and John enter the room. Everybody clamors to hear their story. "The authorities tried to impress us with their sophistication. Then they tried to bully us with threats. But they couldn't argue against the facts. Here, standing with us, was this aging blind man who could now see as well as any Pharisee. He was *evidence*—evidence of God's power at work. It was wonderful. Some of them even commented that there was something about us that looked like Jesus. But, brothers and sisters, what should we do? We responded to their threats by saying that we couldn't—literally couldn't—stop speaking about Jesus. He's made our lives completely different. But was that the right thing to say? After all, the stakes are pretty high, and we all know what happened to Jesus."

The gathered company did not discuss these questions. Instead they turned to the one who was in charge. "Sovereign Lord," they addressed him. Their minds, steeped in Scripture, were drawn to Psalm 2: "Why do the nations rage? . . . The kings of the earth set themselves in array, and the rulers were gathered together, against the Lord and his Messiah." It was so clear that the rulers and nations had done their worst against God's "holy servant Jesus." And now they were threatening to do the same to his disciples. With the Scriptures ringing in their hearts, the company began its intercessions.

> And now, Lord, look upon their threats, and grant your servants to speak your word with all boldness, while you stretch forth your hand to heal, and signs and wonders are performed through the name of your holy servant Jesus. (Acts 4:29-30)

Suddenly the same mysterious, overwhelming thing that Isaiah had experienced in the temple happened to them in their domestic setting. The room was shaken, and they with it—but in joy, not fear. They were filled with God's Holy Spirit and their tongues were loosened to speak with boldness the good news about Jesus.

As God acted, their lifestyles changed. Unlike the Jerusalemites of Isaiah's time whose lives were imprisoned by materialism and militarism, these early Christians were being freed by the Holy Spirit for a new kind of living. The holy impetus which they received from worship expressed itself in economics. The reality which they were experiencing in the Spirit was the reality of Old Testament Jubilee, in which lands were redistributed and poverty was abolished. What the Law had required (Lev. 25) and Jesus had reinstated (Luke 4:16-18) was being lived. And "great grace"—concrete, tangible grace—was the experience of them all.

These early believers had much to learn. They had not yet met the challenge of the outsider and the enemy, whom the Holy Spirit would soon bring into their midst. They hadn't worked out fully what their identity was as a new people. It would take time for their teachers to come to an understanding of "new creation" and the "holy city."

But they did know that God was their King and sovereign Lord, for they had experienced the dynamic greatness of God's holiness. They knew that Jesus, God's "holy servant," was alive. And they knew that the Holy Spirit was shaking their lives and overcoming all the barriers—even economic ones—which prevent people from being "of one heart and soul."

CHAPTER
2

Towards
the Holy City

Our three snapshots are fascinating, aren't they? Each one shows a meeting between individuals and their King. In each the King is revealing himself as no ordinary ruler. He is mystery and power, someone who fits into no neat categories. To describe him, ordinary vocabulary simply won't do.

The King's behavior is unpredictable. In two of our snapshots, he was shaking the foundations of his people and sending them out into conflict. In the third, he was rescuing them from their enemies. But in each he was showing something of himself. And what he showed is unlike any other reality. Meeting him is therefore unlike any other human experience. From a very early date, his people came to call his reality *holiness.* Often they have called him the Holy One. And they have responded to him in awe and worship.

In these snapshots other things strike us as well. One that immediately seizes our attention is that holiness is not at all private or otherworldly. In fact, the holiness in these episodes is practical. It relates to people's immediate, "unreligious" needs.

As the people experienced his holiness, God invaded their lives as individuals and communities. He began to change them. His presence could be pretty terrifying, as he shook the people's spirits and jarred their approaches to life. When God touched them, their attitudes and their economics began to take on a distinctive character. Their lifestyle became unconventional. Their ways of doing things became different from the ways "normal" people did them. But somehow what they were becoming and doing bore the stamp of the Holy One. By living a life of holy nonconformity, they were coming to "share his holiness" (Heb. 12:10).

Holiness, however, was not only social. It was also on the move. The people in our snapshots didn't have the choice of staying where they were and basking in holiness. For holiness was dynamic. When people experienced it, God invited them—indeed, propelled them—into a new kind of living, a kind of living that was risky.

What was the way ahead? Much though the people in our snapshots might have wondered, it was impossible for them to know. Their King was inviting them to set out on a journey—a journey into the unknown. He didn't provide them with any maps. Would there be oases in the wilderness? What would happen when powerful, heavy-eared people rejected the King's message? How could God's people go on living a life of economic sharing when the authorities kept harassing them because they couldn't keep quiet about King Jesus? Our snapshot people could not be sure.

But one thing they were sure of. In each case they knew that meeting the Holy One had thoroughly upset their "business as usual." Not only that. The Holy One had also led them into situations of uncertainty and danger. They could survive in these, but only if they kept rediscovering something absolutely basic—trust in the concrete, everyday grace of God.

These snapshots, of course, have their limitations. The events which they record are "frozen" and out of context.

Naturally we want more detail than they reveal. But to begin to get a feel for holiness, they are pretty useful, for they provide a record of important events in a family history. They mark points of progress in a long journey. They give us general impressions about the kind of people who are on the road. And, most important, they give us glimpses of the only one who can keep them going—their King.

But one thing the snapshots don't tell us. Where is the road going? The snapshot people themselves didn't know and can't tell us. The goal always remained a mystery.

God's Project

It's a mystery to us, too. The Holy One invites you and me to be fellow walkers on the road. But what is its destination? The rest of the Bible doesn't give us a map, either. But it does give us some clues.

The Bible makes it clear, for example, that God is a critic of the way things are. God knows that we humans have distorted creation. God is intensely aware of how much we suffer as a result. And God grieves. Not only for the spoiled creation. Also for—and with—oppressed, hurting humanity. When the prophets wailed "O, my people" one can hear God's anguish. And when Jesus wept over the Holy City (Jerusalem), bewailing that because it did not know "the things that make for shalom" (Luke 19:42) it would be smashed by the Roman army, he was in tune with the cry of God's heart.

But God doesn't simply empathize with suffering men and women. Our departures from what was intended in creation haven't paralyzed God. In fact, the Bible makes it clear that God is determined to change things. Precisely *how* God is going to change things it doesn't make clear. But from one end to the other a message of hope blazes out: God has not given up on the creation that we humans, in our rebellion, have spoiled. And God is determined to restore it.

The Bible's word for this is a modest one—God's *project* (or "plan" [Eph. 1:10]).[1] But there is nothing modest about the project. It is not one of bringing individuals to heaven. Its purpose and time scale are vastly greater than that. The last two chapters of the Bible, Revelation 21—22, depict the goal of history as an act of re-creation. In this great act, God is redoing everything: "Behold, I make all things new" (Rev. 21:5). All things!

To begin, there is a new heaven and a new earth. And a holy city—a holy social order—is given to men and women. From it, God has abolished suffering and eradicated death. Even the areas in which humans have most persistently resisted God's authority—wealth and power—have been brought under the unchallenged control of the Holy One. The city is therefore a place of complete wholeness. And of healing. By its river there is a tree whose fruit heals the nations. And throughout the city, as creatures respond to their Creator and Re-creator, there is worship.

Our glimpse of the holy city is important, for it lets us see how large, how life-embracing, and how beautiful holiness is. But it is important for another reason as well. It helps us put ourselves and our experience of life into perspective. If we're at all in touch with what is going on about us, we know that our world is in agony.

But the holy city shows us that it doesn't have to be like that. God is not the god of no alternative. God's project is specifically to say "no" to the deforming status quo and to say "yes" to an alternative social order.

So God's project is big. God is aiming at nothing less than a "new creation" (2 Cor. 5:17; Gal. 6:15), a reconciliation of *all things* (not just all people) in Christ Jesus (Col. 1:20). Unimaginable things will happen! Wolves and lambs will live side by side. Infants and snakes will play together (Isa. 11:6-8). God is going to complete his creation, which was marred by human rebellion. God will make all things new. God will make everything whole.[2]

Active Waiting

But how do we get to the holy city? Our cities are unholy. They are marked by brokenness, not wholeness. As Paul says in Romans 8:22, the "whole creation has been groaning"—and the more in touch we are with what is going on in the world, the more we know how right he was. Between the world that we experience as we walk the streets and watch our TVs— people lined up at soup kitchens, starving Africans, an epidemic of drug-taking, newer and better weapons—and the holy city, there is a great chasm. Nothing seems able to bridge it.

According to the Bible, this chasm *is* unbridgeable. Human engineering cannot catapult us across it. Nor are there maps to guide us down one side and back up the other. In short, we humans, for all our cleverness, can't engineer the holy city. Only God can establish the holy city. Only God can bring us there.

But how will God do it? Just when we would most like the Bible to be clear, it characteristically isn't! In fact, when it talks about future events it often sounds like our dreams—full of bizarre events, fantastic happenings.

> The day of the Lord will come like a thief, and then the heavens will pass away with a loud noise, and the elements will be dissolved with fire, and the earth and the works that are upon it will be burned up. (2 Pet. 3:10)

We can read too much into passages like this. But we will be in trouble if we ignore their central message. It is God's action, not ours, that will bring the holy city. He will do so on his day, when his Son Jesus will return in judgment and mercy. Might God allow us humans, by our perverted prowess, to bring about the day that will mark the end of the world as we know it? No one can say. But if so, it wouldn't have surprised Jeremiah, who understood God's judgment like this: "I am bringing evil upon this people, the fruit of their devices" (Jer. 6:19).

But the Bible is hopeful, not doom-ridden. Even when its writers were facing the destruction of their civilization, they were confident that God was going to do something new. God is judge. But God will also be the Re-creator. Peter knew that on the day of the Lord there would be burning and noise and colossal destruction. But immediately after recognizing that, he stated his hope: "According to his promise we wait for new heavens and a new earth *in which justice dwells*" (2 Pet. 3:13, my emphasis).[3]

The groaning of the old creation is not senseless pain. It is the groaning of "one great act of giving birth" (Rom. 8:22, JB). And the biblical writers had evidence for this: the Holy Spirit was equipping them with "the powers of the age to come" (Heb. 6:5). This, to be sure, was not conclusive evidence. But it was enough—enough to feed their faith and to convince them that they were not hoping in vain.

Until then, they waited. But what an active form of waiting it was![4] They often called this *patience* (Rom. 8:25). But it was a stance of vigorous commitment, not of resignation. They didn't know the way forward. Only God, they believed, knows that. They were not in control of events. God was. They were sure that there would be a lot of pain and turbulence before the holy city arrived (Acts 14:22). In the meantime, they were determined to *live their lives in light of the social order of the coming city.*

The coming city would be ruled in peace and justice. So they and their congregations would begin living in peace and justice *now.* Already they would experience reconciliation with national enemies and an eradication of poverty. Since the coming city would be a holy city, their life now would be marked by "the holiness without which no one will see the Lord" (Heb. 12:14). In political terms, these early Christians were weak. But they set about their life of active waiting, confident that they were participating in "an adventure which is nothing less than God's purpose for all of creation."[5]

Confidence in Weakness

The confidence of the New Testament writers is breathtaking. Weren't they realistic enough to tell that they were a fringe event, that the real performers were playing on the main stage? Surely what was really important was happening in the Sanhedrin and Praetorium, to say nothing of the imperial capital of Rome. How could they imagine that their fellowships were vital to God's project? Couldn't they sense their insignificance?

At times they could. The apostle Paul was candid about it. Not many of his Corinthian brothers and sisters, he admitted, "were wise according to worldly standards, not many were powerful, not many were of noble birth" (1 Cor. 1:26). But that didn't discourage him. For something momentous had been taking place among them. God had chosen "things low and contemptible, mere nothings, to overthrow the existing order" (1 Cor. 1:28, NEB).

This was nothing new. Time and again, the Hebrew Scriptures testified that God chooses to work through the weak. With that kind of history to look back to, the early Christians sensed that their congregations were just the kind of place that God would act.

But they knew that God would act elsewhere as well. For the Old Testament had made it clear that Yahweh was the God not just of "church history" but of world history. Indeed, he revealed himself through historical events. And to achieve his purposes of bringing life and freedom to the world, God used nations.

God Uses the Nations

God used two classes of nation, to be precise—the "nations" and his holy nation. On the one hand, God often employed "the nations" that didn't know him to do his work. Was judgment necessary? "I am rousing the Chaldeans, that bitter and hasty nation" (Hab. 1:6). Did exiles need to be returned to their native land? "Thus says Yahweh to his anointed, to Cyrus, whose right hand I have grasped, to subdue nations before him ... 'I will go before you ... I gird you, though you do not know me' " (Isa. 45:1-5). Yahweh called this pagan monarch his *anointed* (messiah, in Hebrew)—an exalted title and role.

On a number of occasions, God even commissioned the *enemy nations*—Assyria and Babylon—to do his task. Three times in the book of Jeremiah he called the Babylonian king Nebuchadnezzar "my servant" (Jer. 25:9; 27:6; 43:10).[6] To be sure, the Old Testament writers were wary of overstressing the importance of these nations in God's purposes. To God they were "like a drop from a bucket" (Isa. 40:15). And although the nations might be God's instrument of judgment, they themselves would be judged as well—and punished for their violence and injustice.

The early Christians were well schooled in these Old Testament understandings. The apostle Paul was at pains to remind them that the pagan nation occupying the Promised Land and oppressing the Christians in Rome was "God's servant" (Rom. 13:4). The Christians also recounted Jesus' response to the Roman governor Pilate—"You would have no power over me unless it had been given you from above" (John 19:11).

God's Holy Nation

But the early Christians also sensed that the real action was not taking place among the nations. The historian Luke reflected their attitude accurately. In the first sentence of chapter 3 of his Gospel, he mentioned five national rulers and two religious leaders. To each of them he gave a fraction of a sentence. But to John, the hairy man in the wilderness to whom the word of God came, he gave an entire chapter! The nations, therefore, were not unimportant. God could use them in his purposes. But God's most important work on his project was taking place elsewhere. By his Word and Spirit, God was forming a *new nation*.

In the Old Testament, it was this second class of nation—a class of one—that was the heart of the story. From Genesis 12 onward it was a solitary nation, the descendants of one couple, whom God was using to bring his blessing to "all the families of the earth" (Gen. 12:3). It seems bizarre. Why call a pair of well-heeled citizens of the Chaldean city of Ur to leave their comfortable homes and to head into the unknown? And why form their descendants into a "holy nation" (Exod. 19:6)?

The Old Testament writers do not explain fully why God should be so curiously selective. In Deuteronomy 7—9, however, Moses addressed himself to the subject. Yahweh had not chosen them, he told the Israelites, because there were so many of them or they behaved so well. It was because of something else: "Yahweh loves you" (Deut. 7:8). Because he loved them, he wanted them to live differently from the other nations. "Lo, a people dwelling alone, and not reckoning itself among the nations" (Num. 23:9).

But they were to be different from the other nations not just because differentness was beautiful! It was because God had a larger purpose for them. By being different, they would have something to contribute. Through their eccentric lifestyle, God would bring salvation and blessing to all of humanity. The prophet Isaiah gave this idea its classical expression: "I will give you as a light to the nations, that my salvation may reach to the end of the earth" (Isa. 49:6). In this vision of national distinctiveness there was nothing selfish, nothing introverted.

The "holy nation," it was clear in the Old Testament, was to be the primary vehicle of God's purposes in history. The New Testament writers knew this as well. To be sure, the events which they recorded introduced new dimensions in the story. The arrival of the long-awaited Messiah Jesus inevitably changed things. So also did the incorporation of the Gentiles (literally in Greek, "the nations") into the "new humanity" which God was forming (Eph. 2:15), and their empowering by the Holy Spirit. Yet, despite these changes, among both Jewish and non-Jewish Christians there was still a strong sense of being a "holy nation" (1 Pet. 2:9). "You are the light of the world," Jesus had told them, echoing Isaiah. Therefore "do not do as the nations do" (Matt. 5:14; 6:7). Peter put the same thought in different words:

> As obedient children, do not be conformed to the passions of your former ignorance, but as he who called you is holy, be holy yourselves in all your conduct; since it is written, "You shall be holy, for I am holy". (1 Pet. 1:14-15)

This is where the action is. Mysteriously but potently, God is using this puny but holy transnational nation to bless his entire creation. Other nations, including the mighty Roman Empire, could be his tools for a time. But he has entrusted his project to the "holy nation" that he has chosen. Through it he will prepare the way for the holy city.

CHAPTER
3

Fourfold Holiness

But what is holiness? I have been using the term quite freely because it is an essential part of the biblical story. But it is not a term whose meaning in the Bible can be stated—dictionary-fashion—in a phrase. Furthermore, its meaning quickly leads onto terrain where prophets have literally feared to tread. "Do not come any closer," God warned Moses. "Take off your sandals, because you are standing on holy ground" (Exod. 3:5, TEV). When I attempt to define holiness I am not therefore explaining an idea. I am trying to approximate in words the character of the Inexpressible One. As a result, I shall write the following paragraphs in trembling, and—because of my own encounters with the Holy—in humility.

Holiness (I): Living Force

What, I repeat, is holiness? To begin to answer this question we start, not with language or ideas, but with experience. From the beginning of time, humans have encountered a *living force,* unseen but very real. This force is a mysterious power, an awesome reality which fits into no normal human categories. To describe it, people have compared it to physical substances—light, fire, smoke, power. They have described its quality—powerful, pure, radiant, sublime. They have reported their own emotional responses to it—fear, joy, awkwardness, awareness of guilt, fascination, reverence. But the reality of holiness has always transcended language. It is "a mystery inexpressible and above all creatures . . . that which is beyond conception or understanding, extraordinary and unfamiliar."[1]

The Living Force, Jews and Christians have confessed, is the Holy One, the Yahweh of the Bible. He it is who has broken into the human story and graciously allowed his creatures to experience his character. We must never forget this. There are, as we shall see, other aspects of holiness, and these are indispensable. But the experience of God as Living Force—as light, power, joy-giver—is literally life-giving. This puts other things in perspective. How pure and loving God is! When we, like Isaiah, have seen the Holy One, we will also see ourselves as we are—both unholy and infinitely loved. Without this experience of God as Living Force, "holiness" can produce a religion that, although rational and moral, is cramped and dessicated.

All too often, Christians who have tried to follow Jesus radically have stumbled at this point. They have been unable to integrate moral zeal (with which they are at ease) with the awesome (from which they remain estranged). Indeed, I am convinced, on the basis of my reading of both the Bible and subsequent history, of a general rule: genuinely significant initiatives—initiatives which lead to new departures in faithful living—grow out of a powerful experience of God's awesome otherness. Francis of Assisi and John Wesley, like Isaiah, knew that an experience of God is the source of endless reserves of energy and imaginative power.

But there is more to holiness than personal experience. There are evil forms of otherness as well as life-giving ones. And many of these can be quite awe-inspiring. We must therefore define the holy by the measuring-stick of the Holy One. His character is revealed in the "holy writings" (Scripture; 2 Tim. 3:15). It is expressed perfectly in Jesus, who also is called the "Holy One" (Acts 3:14). And it is experienced, through the work of the Holy Spirit, as searing love.

Furthermore, the holiness revealed in the Bible is never an end in itself. How much we sometimes wish it were! There is something fascinating about the holy which tempts us to cling to it, to treat it longingly, aesthetically. As the twentieth-century English composer, Gerald Finzi, commented, "There is a great resemblance between the static and the ecstatic."[2] But no biblical writer would have approved of this statement. When Peter suggested something similar—building vacation cabins on the Mount of Transfiguration—Jesus strongly rebuked him (Luke 9:28-36). For holiness is *on the move*. It is a geyser of spiritual energy, transforming people into the image of the Holy One, and advancing his rule on earth.

Holiness (II): Separateness

This awesome otherness is basic to a second aspect of holiness—the status of *separateness*. The root of the Hebrew word for "holy," *qadosh*, means just that—set apart. Anything that is associated with the One who is the Living Force is unlike other things, which are common and unclean. These two categories—holy and common—were not to be mingled or confused. "You are to distinguish between the holy and the common," commanded the Levitical Law (Lev. 10:10). And to make sure that this happened, the Law established elaborate regulations to prevent contact between the two.

Some things, such as the Sabbath and the Jubilee, were holy simply because God decreed that they were. But other things, common things, could be made holy. By proper ceremony they could be "sanctified" or "dedicated" to him. They thus would belong absolutely to him and be suitable for his use. For

example, vestments and altars and priests were holy. Booty
captured in war and devoted to God was holy.

So also were God's people. In the Old Testament, they were
made holy by obeying God's voice, by keeping his covenant,
and by observing the prescribed rituals of atonement and purification (Exod. 19:5, 10ff; Lev. 20:7-8). After the coming of
the Messiah, things changed. God's people were sanctified by
Jesus' definitive sacrifice (Heb. 10:10). But in both Testaments
there is a sense that the status of holiness—and the separateness
which it entails—is something which God brings about. "You
are a people holy to the Lord your God . . . [who has] chosen
you to be a people for his own possession, out of all the peoples
that are on the face of the earth" (Deut. 7:6).

Holiness (III): God-Likeness

Holiness is not, however, simply an experience or a status. It
has a third aspect, a *distinctive God-reflecting quality*. True
holiness must always be more than oddity! It must never be ec-
centricity or deviance for its own sake. Instead, holiness is a
way of living which reveals the One who has called the holy nation into existence. "I am the Lord your God; consecrate yourselves therefore, and be holy, for I am holy" (Lev. 11:44). This
is a summons not just to be different, but to be different in a
certain way. It was a summons to become like God, to enter
into God's character.

There is something about the experience of God which
enables us to become like him, to be transformed. And it seems
especially to happen in worship. As Orthodox theologian Paul
Evdokimov observed, "The power of divine holiness is a
devouring flame that consumes all impurity; when it touches a
man it purifies him and makes him holy; it brings him into
harmony with the holiness of God—even into his likeness."[3]
This is a bold claim, but it is a biblical one. Through the Holy
Spirit, according to the apostle Paul, "we all . . . beholding the
glory of the Lord, are being changed into his likeness from one

degree of glory to another" (2 Cor. 3:18). The new creation is a display of the Creator's character.

As God's holy nation we have a long and exciting journey ahead of us. As we travel it, the Holy One will be changing us so that we more and more reflect his character. This is too large a reality, certainly, for me to describe. It is also something that no one can legislate. But it is rich and beautiful!

For God-likeness is wholeness, and God has a passion for wholeness in every area of life. From an early date, Yahweh was called "the God of *shalom*" (Judg. 6:24). In modern English translations, this word has generally been translated as "peace." The biblical writers, however, had something richer in mind than the English word can communicate. For them, *shalom* was "enjoyment in one's relationships," in all the dimensions of human experience—with God through worship and service, with other human beings in community, and with the natural world.[4] It is, therefore, not surprising that the all-embracing wholeness of shalom is behind a great deal of the Old Testament law (especially the "law of holiness," Lev. 11—26). Sacrificial animals were to be perfect specimens. Only unblemished priests could offer bread to God. Weights and measures were to be faultless (Lev. 23:18-20; 21:17; 19:36). After studying this legislation, anthropologist Mary Douglas observed, "To be holy is to be whole, to be one; holiness is unity, integrity, perfection of the individual and of the kind."[5] Holiness, in short, is the way things ought to be and—when the holy city comes—the way they *will* be.

Holiness (IV): Dynamism

Our definition of holiness will not be complete, however, until we mention a fourth aspect—its *dynamism*. Holiness, according to the Bible, is on the move. There is something propulsive, forward-looking about it. It is the realization of God's "unconditional will, his royal rule."[6] Holiness shows itself in action, shattering all resistances to his sovereignty and liberating

women and men from all forms of bondage. In the Exodus,
God showed himself to be "majestic in holiness" (Exod. 15:11).
The Exodus is a pattern for his people (Lev. 11:45). Just as God
invites his people to enter into his character, so also God calls us
to take part in his holy actions.

God's holiness is thus not something that is changelessly sublime. It is not legalistically separate. It is not self-preoccupied in
its concern for its own wholeness. Any of these on its own is a
distortion of holiness, for it is static and small-minded. God's
holiness, in contrast, is cosmic in scope and always in motion. It
is historical, in world as well as "church" history. It is under-
standable, therefore, that when the Holy One confronted
Isaiah, he did not just call him to be a missionary ("Here am I!
Send me." [Isa 6:8]). There was to be something distinctive
about his mission. He was to speak Yahweh's word in the
political realm where Yahweh would unfold his historical plan.
Similarly, when Peter had a rooftop vision of common and unclean foods, God was not simply trying to change Peter's diet.
God was doing no less than preparing him to be midwife at the
birth of a transnational, holy nation (Acts 10).

God's holiness is thus *en route*. It is an energizer of all actions
that point to the completion of his project, the coming of a re-
created cosmos.

What a vision! God, though transcendently "other," is revealing himself to men and women. God is calling us to occupy
a special place—that of a nation under his kingship. God is im-
planting in us the vision and reality of wholeness. And God is
energizing us to be participants in his own all-embracing historical plan. One is speechless at the magnificence of it.

Response (1): Worship

Awestruck we may be. But once we get a glimmer of true
holiness, our almost reflexive response will be praise and *worship*. In God's presence we will see ourselves as we are, as
flawed and finite, yet infinitely loved. And our spirits will leap
in response to God.

God's holiness will collide with the woundedness of the world. But in the midst of the struggle he will show himself to be healer and shalom-maker. Our worship will respond to what God is doing. Again and again we will tell the story of his actions. And we will constantly be adding new chapters! For the Holy Spirit will go on breaking down inner and outward barriers, bringing spirit to breathless persons and life to the despairing. In our worship we will get glimpses of the glory of God's presence—glimpses of the holy city to come. And we, unworthy though we are, will praise the King.

> All your works shall give thanks to you, O Lord,
>   and all your holy ones shall bless you!
> They shall speak of the glory of your kingdom,
>   and tell of your power,
> to make known to the sons of men your mighty deeds,
>   and the glorious splendor of your kingdom....
> My mouth will speak the praise of Yahweh,
>   and let all flesh bless his holy name for ever and ever.
>   (Ps. 145:10-12, 21)

Response (2): Change

A second response to what true holiness is like is also essential. It is the response of *transformation*. "You shall be holy; for I the Lord your God am holy." This phrase, repeated many times in both Testaments, is not simply a bit of advice. Nor is it a prediction of our ultimate perfection in the afterlife. It is a command—a command to allow ourselves to be changed into the likeness of the One who will change us.

God himself has taken the lead in changing us. By Jesus' pouring out of his lifeblood (Heb. 9:13-14; 13:12), by the Father's pouring out of the Holy Spirit (Rom. 15:16; 1 Pet. 1:2), God has already sanctified us. He has made us holy. But we have a part to play, too. We are called to live in a new way, to obey Jesus. To be like him.

Holiness, in fact, is what Jesus was about. For Jesus is the

Holy One (Rev. 3:7). He is the the perfect image of the Father, the Holy One. He also is the standard for human wholeness. Paul saw the goal for all of us to be "the stature of the fulness of Christ" (Eph. 4:13). Psychiatrist Frank Lake was deeply convinced of this. Jesus, he wrote, is "the one normal and unspoilt specimen of humanity."[7] Only as we contemplate him and attempt to follow him do we realize how miserably unwhole and needy we are.

But Jesus also represents our true nature and destiny. *Now* we are purifying ourselves, walking in his steps, not just because the Bible says we must, but because *then*, when he appears, "we shall be like him" (1 John 2:6; 3:2-3). It is men and women who are experiencing this transformation whom the early Christians called "holy ones" (saints).

How much there is for him to change! For God's call to holiness does not allow us neatly to compartmentalize our lives and to confine holiness to the "religious department." "As he who calls you is holy," Peter writes (1 Pet. 1:15), "be holy in all your conduct." *In all your conduct!* In our life of prayer and worship? Yes! In our sexual morality as well, for this is an area in which we are vulnerable to the ways and values of our milieu (1 Thess. 4:3-6). Also in other areas where we are just as vulnerable. For example, our diet, savings, work, and recreation, which we haven't generally thought of in terms of holiness. God calls us to holy living. He calls us to live distinctively, unlike the nations and like Jesus. And his call applies especially to our nitty-gritty concerns for economic well-being and physical security. God calls us to *social* holiness.

This is not the place to provide evidence for this claim. The rest of the book will try to do that. But I can mention one or two things which will enable us to see it in broader perspective. Holiness, I have shown, is wholeness. God is satisfied with nothing less than comprehensive, all-inclusive holiness. Since this is so, it only makes sense that God is concerned about the parts of our lives which we habitually protect as "private", as "our business." It is not, by implication, anybody else's business, not even God's. We are secretive about our income and insurance policies, for example, because finances raise within us a primal sense of fear and insecurity. In these areas, especially, we sense the drive to control our lives. In them we flex our muscles, put up a brave front, or cower in our impotence. In no other area are we less inclined to take chances. Power—economic, political, personal—has always been fraught with spiritual significance. But the sad fact is that Christians have rarely been aware of this. We haven't responded to God's call to be different. All too often we have lived just like everyone else.

Provision and Protection

The most important of these power concerns have to do with our needs for *provision* and *protection*. We are concerned about these for good reason. According to psychologist Abraham Maslow, these are our primary human needs ("the most prepotent of all needs").[8] For people who are "extremely and dangerously hungry, no other interests exist but food." When that interest is satisfied, their attention transfers to their next most acute need, that of physical safety. Thereafter, according to Maslow, human concern will shift to other needs—belongingness/love, esteem/prestige, and self-fulfillment.[9]

As Christians we may be uncomfortable with Maslow's ranking of needs. Surely the grace of God is our most important need. But is this borne out by the way we organize our lives? What, for example, do our insurance policies and investments say about our day-to-day security? Is God's grace so central to our existence that we base our arrangements for provision and protection upon it?

However we may answer these questions for ourselves, it is clear that the Bible views provision and protection as problem areas. Indeed, from the Exodus onward, nothing caused God more often to wrestle with his people—and to despair of them—than their approach to these "prepotent needs." God's people were often willing enough to acknowledge his lordship in the temple, but when it came to their economic institutions or their way of defending themselves, they were more inclined to follow "the devices and desires of their own hearts!"

Pattern of Un-Graceful Living

In this book, as we set out to reread the Bible together, we will observe a recurrent pattern that goes something like this:

(1) God recognizes his children's need for *provision* and *protection*—for the physical necessities of food and shelter and for security from physical harm. Lovingly he provides for them with the bounty of his good creation and with safety from those who would molest them. Both Provider and Protector, God shows his grace by acting (at times miraculously) for their provision and protection.

(2) God also prescribes for his people a pattern of holy living. This way of living can be risky. To be faithful to it they must trust in God's concrete grace. But it is the only way to right relationships—among humans, between them and their natural environment, and between them and their God. It is the way to wholeness.

(3) But God's people prefer to avoid the risks. They often choose to adapt their lives—often very gradually—to the pattern of the surrounding nations. This riskless living is unholy living. Leaving grace in the realm of "theology," God's people decide to base their decisions about the "real world" upon calculations of self-interest.

(4) God's people find themselves trapped by their false securities. Unanticipated risks suddenly appear. Somehow they are more insecure than they were before and more afraid. Indeed, they find themselves giving their ultimate loyalty (in terms of time and resources) to their new sources of "security." In both the areas of provision and protection, they have been ensnared by idolatry through an escalation of private wealth (ma-

terialism) and a proliferation of armaments (militarism).[10]

This pattern raises questions of ultimate importance. Is God's grace so real that we can trust him even when our lives and possessions are at stake? Can life really be transformed like this? Is God's power so great that we can risk being faithful to his pattern for holy living even if it means our being powerless? Is it God's plan that the power of his Spirit should come to those who have other forms (e.g, economic and military) of power? If social holiness is possible, what does it mean in practice?

As we face these questions, all of us will at times feel profoundly alone. But they are not meant to be answered by isolated individuals. For ultimately, the transformed life of holiness cannot be a private matter. In the Bible, the "holy one" (saint) is not an individual with a halo. In fact, except for God and Jesus, the term never occurs in the singular.

On the contrary, *holiness is always social*, something that we ultimately must enter into along with others. John Wesley was well aware of this: "The gospel of Christ knows of no religion, but social; no holiness, but social holiness."[11]

Not only are we meant to be in the company of others to grow in holiness, the families, races, and nations that result from our being together are tools designed by God to implement his purposes. God calls us, you will recall, his "holy nation." By our holy lifestyle, which bears the "peaceful fruits of justice" (Heb. 12:11), we now stand in contradiction to the ways of the nations. Our orientation is towards the future. Our life is an anticipation of the holy city.

Response (3): Mission

Awestruck by a vision of God's holiness and empowered for change, we find God impelling us into a third response to holiness—*mission*. The goal of God's project is all-embracing. When the time is ripe God will "unite all things"—things celestial and things terrestrial—in Jesus Christ (Eph. 1:10). No more will there be hurting or destroying in "all my holy mountain, for the earth shall be full of the knowledge of the Lord as the waters cover the sea" (Isa. 11:9). In the holy city *all* things will be made new (Rev. 21:5).

Towards this goal the Holy God is now working, and he calls us to be partners in his project. Already God has given *all* authority to his Son Jesus. And Jesus has commanded us, his friends, to "make disciples of all nations" (Matt. 28:18-19). There is nothing small about this vision. With joyful anticipation we invite others to follow Jesus. And when we do so, we invite them to carry a new passport—that of the holy nation which God is forming. This nation lives in holy nonconformity to the patterns of other nations. Its life is sustained by concrete grace. And its citizens are participants in a drama in which the future shape of the world is at stake.

For following Jesus is coming to be like him (Luke 6:40). And that means joining him in his work. Jesus was the medium of creation. Jesus is the pioneer of the new creation. Jesus indicates where history is going. As the obedient Son, he perfectly demonstrated what life under God's kingship is to be like. And somehow, through our corporate life in him, we will find a life of social holiness. As we journey toward the holy city in which his rule will be unchallenged, he will never let us down.

Part II
The Old Testament Landscape

CHAPTER
4

Protection, Provision ... and Worship

Holiness is dynamic. The Holy One is on the move. The Holy One is Lord of history. Glorious, resplendent, majestic—these convey something of the character of the Holy One. But in order to really know God, we must watch him at work (Exod. 14:13; John 5:17).

History is God's workshop. So we learn to know God by telling, retelling, and retelling again his story. We will watch him at work from the time that God liberated his people in the Exodus until God saved them and reshaped them by the Messiah Jesus. I cannot, of course, tell the whole story. In the Bible there are too many subplots and too many details for that to be possible. In fact, it can be dangerous to get so preoccupied with this incident or that idea that we lose track of where we are in the story. The story, we must remember, has an overall shape. It has ebbs and flows, a climax, and a conclusion.

In what follows, I will concentrate on the people, events and characteristics which I find most significant. I will try to see them in the perspective of a large, unfolding story. Holiness is the lens through which I have chosen to look. And I have chosen to observe events from a peculiar vantage point—an *aerial balloon!*

Like the balloonist, I want to be able to travel high enough to see the overall contours of the countryside. But at times I will need to swoop low enough to examine some features carefully with the aid of a telescope. And I don't want to move so slowly or so fast that things get either stalled or blurred! In looking at things like this, I'm in a good tradition. Like Joshua and Stephen (Josh. 24; Acts 7), I contend that God's story can be told briefly. And when it is, it has point and power.

In the Brickyard

As we begin, our balloon is hovering over the well-irrigated fields of northeastern Egypt. The calendar reads 1300 B.C. However, the story which will preoccupy us is only incidentally that of the Egyptians. Of greater interest to us, because according to the Bible it was central to the purposes of God, is the story of an extended family of immigrants living on the fringes of Egyptian society.

The immigrants had descended from a pair of sturdy nonconformists, Abraham and Sarah. At what they took to be God's call, they had left a cultural center, Ur in Mesopotamia. Living in the improbable lifestyle of nomads, they had come to move about in the uncultured place of Canaan. But the family hadn't stayed in Canaan. To escape famine, their grandson, Israel (originally known as Jacob), had moved to Egypt where his son Joseph had become a senior civil servant much in favor with that country's king, Pharaoh.

So far, so happy. But relations between the Israelites and their Egyptian hosts soon soured. The reasons for this are not hard to understand. The Israelites, after all, were immigrants. Like many immigrants, they were hard workers who soon be-

came rich. Their tendency to have large families led to a population explosion. It seemed that "the land was filled with them"
(Exod. 1:7).

"Whose country is this anyway?" influential Egyptians
began to mutter. Joseph was long dead, and the current
Pharaoh had no ties of sentiment or self-interest to the Israelites. Why not clip the wings of these immigrants before
they become too numerous and too wealthy? They might even
be open to liaison with Egypt's enemies.

So Pharaoh changed the rules. Resorting to racial discrimination, he both punished the Israelites and profited from them.
He forced them to do hard labor, some on "state farms," others
in public building projects. Still others he forced to work in the
hot, repetitive, exhausting task of making bricks. The super-
visors whom he placed over them made them work "with
rigor," establishing impossible quotas for the Israelite workers
to meet and beating them when they fell short. Pharaoh even
tried a measure of population control. In a genocidal decree, he
ordered the Israelite midwives to kill all boy babies who were
born to Israelite mothers. Things were bad in the brickyard.

What should be done? One alternative was civil
disobedience. Midwives such as Shiphrah and Puah, out of
their fear of God, conspired to protect the newly born boys
(Exod. 1:15-22). So also did the Israelite mothers, and some
Egyptians couldn't help sympathizing with them. On one occasion, when an Israelite mother hid her baby boy in a pitch-
covered basket floating in the reeds along a river, an Egyptian
princess discovered the child. But she had no thought of killing
him. With the mother's permission she took the child to court
and raised him as an Egyptian aristocrat.

Anti-Egyptian violence, when the provocation became too
great to bear, was another alternative. The Bible gives us only
one example of this, but it was probably representative of many
other incidents. When the boy in the floating basket, Moses,
came of age, he discovered his Israelite identity. Rejecting the

comforts of the Egyptian court, he "went out to his people and looked on their burdens" (Exod. 2:11). In doing so, Moses, to the best of his ability, was (to use a theological cliché) "identifying with the poor and the oppressed." And he took his identification seriously. When he saw an Egyptian beating one of his fellow Israelites, he felt attacked himself. After making sure that no one was looking, Moses resorted to "justifiable violence." He killed the Egyptian and buried him in the sand.

What motivated Moses to do this? Was it a burst of anger? Was it, possibly, the first blow in a struggle for liberation? After all, courtiers are used to thinking in terms of power and every revolution has got to start somewhere! The Bible does not tell us. But it does tell us that news of his murderous act got out. The Israelites were suspicious of his motives. Pharaoh and his associates were furious at what they took to be an act of treachery. To save his skin, Moses ran away into the arid wilderness to the southeast. There, in the land of Midian, he settled down, married the daughter of the local priest, and worked as a shepherd. Moses' "downward mobility" had landed him in obscurity and apparent irrelevance—far from the court, far even from the people about whose suffering he had cared so much.

Holiness in Action

Why focus our telescope on an amateur revolutionary like Moses? Surely he had earned what his impulsive action deserved: obscurity. But this time of human failure was important to God. He chose it to reveal his holiness. And as we shall see, God's holiness produced a powerful effect—action and change.

God cared even more about the oppression of his people than Moses did. When the Israelites "groaned under their bondage," when they "cried out for help," God heard (Exod. 2:23-25). In fact, the Exodus text reports that he "knew" their condition. He was totally involved; his empathy with them was complete. And, in faithfulness to his covenant with Abraham and his successors, God had determined to act.

But how indirectly he acted! Instead of waving a magic wand over Egypt, God revealed his holiness to a burned out courtier in the desert. Moses was minding his father-in-law's sheep. Suddenly he saw something which he couldn't explain. A bush—a bit of desert scrub—was on fire. That happened now and then. But it kept on burning and didn't burn up. How curious! So Moses proceeded to investigate more closely. Something stopped him in his tracks. Someone called him by name. "Moses, Moses! . . . Do not come any closer. Take off your sandals." In awe Moses obeyed. For the first time in the Bible the Holy One was revealing himself in the language of holiness: "The place where you are standing is holy ground" (Exod. 3:4-5, NIV).

Holy ground. Moses, in amazement, was in the presence of a reality which was unlike anything that he had experienced before. Before him was an ordinary bush. But it burned with an extraordinary fire. In the fire, in fact all around him, there was a "living force."[1] Moses recognized something different from himself, something separate. Moses took off his shoes and covered his face—not only to be obedient, but to show that he recognized this mysterious separateness.

But the Separate One was not out of touch. He addressed himself to Moses, not just in the off-putting heat of a mysterious fire, but in personal terms: "Moses . . . I am the God of your father. . . ." Then God stated his concern. His people were being oppressed by an exploitative system and ruthless rulers. At their cry God was stirred to compassion and action: "I have come down to deliver them." In this incident, the Holy One was revealing himself—directly and personally. But he was doing so for a purpose. God was involved in human history and was determined to change it.

But how? In a long argument, Moses objected to the Holy One's plan. "I will send you to Pharaoh that you may bring forth my people" (Exod. 3:10). Earlier in his life Moses had been attracted to liberating activity, but no longer. It all seemed impractical. After all, Pharaoh and his friends were power politicians. Why should they give up their slave labor force without a fight? And whereas the Israelites were disheartened, disorganized, and weaponless, the Egyptians were a military superpower.

Moses' thinking, to the increasingly irritated Holy One, was an obstacle because it was conventional. He was reckoning without the concrete grace of God. There would be a struggle and eventually a battle, but at no stage would valor and hot bronze be required of any human, not even of Moses. For God himself would be the warrior. "I will stretch out my hand and smite Egypt" (Exod. 3:20) by an escalating series of miracles. Liberation was to be a gift of God. It would be a product of grace, not of works.

God's acts would not cancel the need for human acts. Someone had to lead the people. Someone had to bear witness to the acts and purposes of the Holy One. As leader of the Israelites, Moses would come to Pharaoh armed with a word, not a sword. His political role would be that of a prophet, not a general. "Go to the king of Egypt and say to him" (Exod. 3:18). Should words fail Moses, his brother Aaron could be his mouthpiece. "I will be with your mouth and with his mouth" (Exod. 4:15). What the Holy One was requiring of Moses and the people was the willingness to take a risk. He was calling them to faith, to active trust in his faithfulness and power.

The argument ended. Obediently Moses went back to Egypt, commissioned for confrontation. To the Israelites, Moses announced that God was about to liberate them. This was hard to accept, especially when the Egyptian authorities greeted their strivings toward freedom by imposing even heavier quotas in the brickyard. Yet in their better moments, "the people believed." Realizing that Yahweh had seen their affliction and in anticipation that he was going to do something about it, "they bowed their heads and worshiped" (Exod. 4:31).

To Pharaoh and his courtiers, Moses likewise had a message. It was a demand from the God whom he had met in the burning bush: "Let my people go, that they may worship me in the wilderness" (Exod. 5:1). Understandably enough, Pharaoh was dubious about this proposal. He blamed Moses and Aaron for seducing the Israelites into laxness on the job. And to make sure that the Israelites would have less time for economically unproductive religious activity, he ordered his officials to stop supplying them with the raw materials for brickmaking. When the Israelites failed to do the impossible, Egyptian officials beat them mercilessly, breaking their spirits as they flayed their bodies.

In the face of human hopelessness, God acted. Through his prophets Moses and Aaron, he announced to Pharaoh the sanctions that he would impose upon the Egyptians for their defiant resistance. The result was an escalating series of miracles— "great acts of judgment" (Exod. 7:4), the Bible calls them. Though they were announced by human messengers, they were carried out by "the finger of God" (8:19) without human assistance. Literally, they were "acts of God." Uncomprehendingly the Israelites watched him at work.

Ever since, in their Passover services, the Jewish people have summarized these catastrophes: "frogs, lice, blood, hail, etc." Although at each of these the suffering of the Egyptians was immense, they were unwilling to give in to pressure by freeing their slaves.

But one night a cry of horror rang out throughout Egypt. A final sanction, a virulent plague killed the eldest son of every Egyptian family. Pharaoh had had enough. Grieving, he and his courtiers demanded that the Israelites leave the country immediately. There was no time for packing. "Be gone!"

Risky Living: Protection

So the Israelites left Egypt and headed pell-mell into the wilderness. They were heading into insecurity. In the wilderness there would be no structures—even unfriendly structures—of civilization to sustain them. In terms of *protection* and *provision*, the primary human needs that we have noted in the previous chapter, they were almost powerless. They had few if any weapons,[2] and because of the speed of their departure they had been unable to collect any provisions for the journey (Exod. 12:39). Having been delivered from Egypt by grace and not by works, they would be required to live by grace. To this risky lifestyle only one alternative remained—a return to Egypt where they would have the security of slavery.

In only a few days, the Israelites realized their inability to protect themselves. For Pharaoh had suddenly asked himself how his country, bereft of its slave labor force, was going to carry out its five-year plans. He changed his mind. Quickly he mobilized the mightiest military machine in the world. Spearheading his force were six hundred mobile missile-launching platforms called *chariots*—the most advanced examples of that era's welding together of technology and weaponry. Also in his force were masses of foot soldiers. After a brief pursuit, Pharaoh and his troops caught up with the slow-moving Israelites and boxed them in. Before the Israelites there was the broad expanse of the Red Sea. Surrounding them on every other side were the threatening Egyptian forces.

The Israelites were terrified. In their fear they lost perspective on their recent experiences. God may have freed them from the brickyard by his miraculous interventions, but the present problem—the menacing presence of those chariots—banished the past from their minds. Pathetically they began to fantasize about the securities and charms of slavery.

Moses impatiently swept their hesitations aside. God's message to the people was clear:

> Fear not, stand firm, and see the salvation of the Lord, which he will work for you today; for the Egyptians whom you see today, you shall never see again. *The Lord will fight for you, and you have only to be still.* (Exod. 14:13-14, italics added)

Don't be afraid! Throughout the Bible this will be the keynote of God's call to a more radical approach to provision and protection. And for good reason. Fear is the enemy of radicalism, for it limits the possibilities in any situation to the dictates of prudence and common sense. In this passage as in countless others, God's summons to faith was a summons to unreasonable action, even to "irresponsible" inaction. Here, as elsewhere, "faith meant that Israel should rely on Yahweh's miracle for her defense, rather than upon soldiers and weapons."[3] And a miracle was an act of deliverance that humans could not manipulate. It was a gift—a gift of God's concrete grace.[4]

And so a battle was on. It was a struggle between kings—Pharaoh versus Yahweh; the lord of Egypt, wielder of a rapid deployment force armed with state-of-the art weaponry versus the Lord of hosts (armies), who was apparently unarmed. It was a struggle for sovereignty and for freedom.

In military terms, it was an eccentric battle. Moses, having stretched his hands over the sea, led the Israelites through it on dry ground. Amazing! When the Egyptian forces followed them the dry ground turned to mud. Wheels clogged. Hoofs stuck. As the waters closed in upon them, the Egyptians in panic cried out, "Let us flee from before Israel; for Yahweh fights for them" (Exod. 14:25). It was too late. Moses had once again stretched out his hand, and the sea was returning to its usual shape. Before long a grisly sight appeared: Egyptian corpses washed up along the coast.

Who had won the battle? According to the writer of Exodus, it was Yahweh. It was he who had "routed the Egyptians in the midst of the sea" (14:27). Victory was his "great work" (14:31). Naturally enough, the response of the people was one of relief. But it was more than that. It was fear. It was trust. Most significantly, it was a sense of identity as a nation. As Old Testament scholar Brevard Childs has put it, "Israel left Egypt as fleeing slaves, and *emerged from the sea as a people* who testified to

God's miraculous deliverance."[5] And that response, of telling the story of God's action in the context of thanksgiving and praise, was the response of worship.

Risky Living: Provision

But a new crisis loomed. For the Israelites were now across the Red Sea, in a wilderness far from the gardens and supermarkets of Egypt. Their wineskins were empty, their picnic baskets bare. In this setting, the second of the primary human needs appeared—provision.

"What shall we drink?" (15:24) At the outset, it was thirst which preoccupied the people. They had paused at a pond in the wilderness, at a place called Marah. But its water was brackish. So they *murmured* against Moses.[6] And Moses, in turn, cried out to Yahweh. Mercifully, Yahweh knew what to do. To make the water drinkable, he ordered Moses to cut down a tree and throw it into the pond. For the moment that was sufficient. And shortly thereafter Yahweh led them to a good campsite, Elim, where there were twelve springs (15:27). Yahweh had provided his people with water.

But hunger was a growing concern as well. What do thousands of factory workers and farmers do when they are suddenly forced to be nomads? The Israelites hadn't planned for this. Their departure from Egypt had happened too fast. And by this time their meager provisions had been exhausted.

What should they do? Once again their instinctive response was to *murmur* against Moses. A deceptive form of nostalgia was creeping into their thinking. "If only we were back in Egypt! At least there we had enough bread and fleshpots (fast-food restaurants?). We were slaves, but at least we knew what the rules of bondage were. Freedom is too hard to cope with, too unstructured, too unpredictable. Rather than being killed by hunger in this wilderness, we'd prefer the security of slavery!" (Exod. 16:3, paraphrased).

Moses was distressed at the short memory of the Israelites.

Couldn't the one who had rescued them from Egyptian chariots also feed them in the desert? Couldn't they see that they, by murmuring against their human leader, were in reality declaring their lack of trust in their divine King? Yahweh was less impatient than Moses. After all, he was Provider as well as Protector. Security from hunger was as much a concern of his as security from enemies. To feed his people he drew upon unexpected sources—quails from the sea (Exod. 16:13; Num. 11:31) and "bread from heaven" (Exod. 16:4).

The provision of the bread, called *manna*, had two characteristics—two "manna principles." The first of these was *sufficiency*. Every morning except one, the manna appeared in flat, flakelike form on the ground outside the camp. It was delicious. Depending on how it was prepared, it could become either oil cakes or honey wafers (Num. 11:8; Exod. 16:32). God's material gifts are good! Furthermore, when the Israelites went out to gather the manna, they gathered freely. Miraculously, regardless of the amount that each had gathered, it was always enough and never too much. The people had a sufficient diet, but not an extravagant one.

The second "manna principle" was *equality*. Some Israelites—those with entrepreneurial potential—immediately tried to "improve themselves." The frugal ones schemed to skimp on eating so that, when shortfalls occurred, they would have some left over to sell to people with less foresight. Others—the muscular types—gathered far more than their share. Neither profited from their exertions, for everything that they tried to hoard "bred worms and became foul" (Exod. 16:20). Everyone, therefore, had the same amount, and that was always enough!

On only one day could the Israelites gather more than their normal quota. On the sixth day they were to gather precisely twice as much as usual, for the seventh day was unlike the rest. It was a "day of solemn rest, a holy sabbath to the Lord" (16:23). On that day there was to be no work. None was needed, for there was no manna on the ground, and the extra manna which the people had not eaten on the sixth day was still fresh and delicious. Just as Yahweh showed them his grace by giving them manna, he also graciously gave them rest. And by resting, they indicated that they accepted his grace and recognized the limited role of their own works. Yahweh is faithful. He can provide! At the deepest level, his Sabbath day, specifically designated as a vehicle of holiness, pointed the way to worship.

Worshiping the Holy One

At this stage, the worship of the Israelites (as recorded in Exodus 15—16) was still uncomplicated. The glorious liturgical

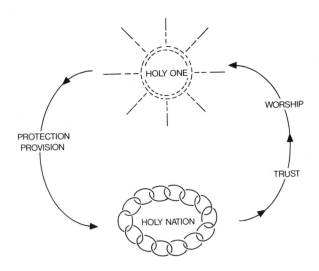

literature of the Psalms, the robing and instruction of the priests and levites, the development of solemn ceremony and appropriate music—all these were to come later. But God had just acted, intervening in hopeless situations to defend them and feed them. As the Israelites responded to these events, there was freshness in their worship, and profundity, too. *Praise* instinctively welled up within them. Their worship was an almost reflexive response to what they had watched God doing. In their relief, they—like modern-day hostages who have been freed from captivity—spontaneously acclaimed the exploits of their liberator. Indeed, the worship service of Moses and the people (recorded in Exod. 15:1-18 and commonly called the "Song of the Sea") is just that—an unrehearsed burst of applause to Yahweh. "I will sing to Yahweh . . . Yahweh is my strength and my song, and he has become my salvation."

The people's praise of Yahweh was not, however, praise in general. It was not extolling him for his attributes or "for who he is" (as the current cliché runs). It was praise of Yahweh for what he had done, for specific deeds which the people had experienced. As important as praise was a second ingredient of their worship, *storytelling*.

Who is Yahweh? "He is the one who . . ." and a story emerges. In Exodus 16:32-35, Yahweh is the one who has fed his hungry and complaining people in a foodless place: a wilderness. So the people, at Yahweh's command, gathered a day's supply of the manna which he had given them, and they stored it in a jar which they placed in a highly significant place: before the ark of the covenant. There, at the heart of their nation's religious life, in the sight of all the people, this jar would be a stimulus to worship. For them, future worship would always be an act of remembering.

Who is Yahweh? In Exodus 15, Yahweh is the one who has "triumphed gloriously; the horse and his rider he has thrown into the sea" (Exod. 15:1, 21). In their worship, the people sang the story. The enemy king Pharaoh had boasted, "I will pursue, I will overtake . . . I will draw my sword, my hand shall destroy them" (15:9). But Yahweh was a mightier king than Pharaoh. He had blown with his wind. Weaponry of the latest design he had cast into the sea. By this action Yahweh had shown "the greatness of his majesty." Yahweh had shown himself to be "majestic in holiness" (15:7, 11). And the worship of Yahweh's holiness was the conscious act, by the whole people, of remembering and telling Yahweh's story.

The worship of the Israelites, however, was not simply focused on the past. A third ingredient—their expression of *trust in Yahweh*—was vital. It was to be their confession that, extending into the present and the future, God would keep on adding new chapters to the story of his actions. In the Exodus 15 song, this future-oriented trust in Yahweh is not yet highly developed, but its roots are unmistakable. Yahweh, they declared, was not only their King during the battle at the sea; he "will reign for ever and ever" (v. 18). And Yahweh has a plan: to plant his people in a place where they can flourish while worshiping him (v. 17).

In Israelite worship, past, present, and future—*all* are intertwined. And this intertwining was of great practical importance to them. It was their means of coping with two temptations which would repeatedly stalk them: pride and despair.

Most of us can readily empathize. Often before a job interview, an operation, or an important decision we have prayed fervently for God's help. Often God has enabled good things to happen that we have felt to be impossible. But at that point, don't we find it attractive to credit ourselves—our good judgment, cleverness, alertness—with our success? The historically rooted worship of the Israelites was an antidote to this prideful tendency. It is not accidental that in the Exodus 15 song, whereas Israel's king, Yahweh, is mentioned ten times, Israel's human leaders Moses and Aaron are not mentioned at all. It was by God's concrete grace that they had been saved. In worship they affirmed their humility before their Savior.

Despair is as lethal a malady as pride. For God not only saves his people by grace; God also calls us—like the Israelites—to a life of vulnerability and risk-taking in which we will continue to be dependent upon him. Often, in periods of crisis, we tend to succumb to "worst-case" assessments of our situation. "The situation's hopeless. Yahweh can't do it again!" So, since we doubt that he can do anything, we have to do our best, even if that means departing from his way.

So it was with the Israelites. When they forgot the story of his actions, when they ignored the one who, "majestic in holiness," could intervene to protect them and provide for them, they had no choice but to trust in themselves. The result was "realism." When they succumbed to false realism, the Israelites departed from the way of holiness. They left the precarious road that Yahweh had mapped for them and chose the broad road of adaptation to the ways of the nations that surrounded them. Storytelling, therefore, was not an incidental part of the worship of God's people. It was their means of nourishing the expectancy and trust which alone enabled them to live as a holy nation.

Exodus: Springboard of Holy History

It is time for us to retract our telescope and, increasing our balloon's speed and altitude, to glide onward in time. But as we do so, we must not forget our wilderness story.

For in the Exodus—in the bush, in the battle, in acts of protection and provision—Yahweh had revealed himself in his holiness. Thereafter, when leading his people, when legislating for them, he repeatedly introduced himself in terms of his liberating action: "I am Yahweh who makes you holy, who brought you out of the land of Egypt to be your God: I am Yahweh" (Lev. 22:32-33). In this way, as in many others, the Exodus serves as a pattern or prototype for the rest of the Old Testament. It is, according to many scholars, the "interpretive center" for the Old Testament writings.[7] The rest of the story unfolds in light of it. Even the coming of Jesus was to be interpreted by the early Christians in light of the Exodus.

After the Exodus, things were never the same again. The Holy One had revealed himself in action. He had shown his holiness through involvement—at times quite dramatic involvement—in history, shattering resistances and liberating an oppressed people. Never could the Israelites justify amassing material or military power by appealing to the Exodus events. For them, the lesson was the opposite: since Yahweh had freed them by his grace, they were called to a life based on trust, not on power. No longer did they have to manipulate events to make them come out right, for history was in the hands of the Holy One. "Stand firm, and see the salvation of Yahweh, which he will work for you" (Exod. 14:13).

Yahweh had freed the Israelites for a special purpose. This was not a classic revolution, in which the oppressed group turned the tables on their oppressors. Yahweh's interest was larger than who should rule in Egypt. Yahweh was interested in nothing less than the completion of his project—the re-creation of the world. But his strategy in working toward this cosmic end was a curious one. Yahweh began small, freeing an obscure band of Israelite slaves to leave their place of oppression and to become a new nation, a nation with a special relationship to God. Henceforth the Israelites would be "the people whom you have redeemed." In a special sense they would be "your people" (Exod. 15:13, 16). Through them he would, in the fullness of time, bless all of creation.

That, however, would be a long road. As he accompanied them on it, Yahweh had to train them in the disciplines of holy living. In many areas of their life (including those of the primary human needs of protection and provision), his people had to learn new patterns of living—patterns different from the ones which they had observed in Egypt. Law and hard experience—these are the means by which God taught them. In the next chapter, we shall turn our attention to them.

CHAPTER

5

Holy Living ... and Whining

Free at last! As God's people slowly moved camp into the Sinai peninsula, they breathed a sigh of relief. No overtime in the brickyard! No quotas! No murdering of their baby boys! Their experience in Egypt seemed to have been a bad dream. And now, thanks to the intervention of a God about whom they knew next to nothing, they were free!

But free for what? Not free to rule Egypt. Yahweh hadn't intervened so they could get back at their oppressors. No, he had loosed the grip of the nation that was grinding them down for another purpose: to enable them to become a new nation, a nation that would be different.[1] Their differentness would be rooted in their experience of holiness—the holiness of the God who had fought for them and fed them. And their differentness would be prescribed for them by another of God's gifts to them—a code for living called the *Law* which would give form to their freedom. Their lifestyle would reflect the holiness of the one who had sprung them loose.

Our balloon has risen. We are now hovering somewhat higher than in chapter 4, so we can get a wider perspective on how this happened. We can see how, over a period of four hundred years, Yahweh served as their King. Not only did Yahweh do such kingly things as fighting for his people and feeding them; Yahweh also made laws for them, punished them, and directed their national life.

When the people were good, they were very good. They responded to Yahweh's rule by thanking him and obeying him. And in their experience something new happened. They developed a national lifestyle which, in the view of Old Testament scholar Martin Noth, had "no parallel at all elsewhere."[2] Despite their four hundred years in Egypt, they weren't living like Egyptians any more. Nor were they living like the people of the various nations that they met as they moved toward Palestine. They lived in a new way. They were a "holy nation."

We will also see, of course, that the people of God weren't always on good behavior. For holiness had its price—obedient dependence. This wasn't easy. All around them were nations who lived by conventional values. They worshiped gods whose primary requirements were religious observances. These gods made no real demands on lifestyles. Obligingly they helped their adherents do what they already wanted to do. How tempting it was, when Yahweh demanded the insecurity of trust, to bow to common-sense deities! God's people were torn between Yahweh's call to be a "holy nation" and the gravitational pull of unholy living which meant losing their national distinctiveness—living "like all the nations," the Bible (Deut. 17:14) calls it.

Later in our story we will find the people of God giving in to this gravitational pull and becoming unholy. But in the period that we are looking at, at the moment—their forty-year sojourn in the wilderness, their conquest of the Promised Land, and their life in the land as a loose confederation of twelve tribes—they managed much of the time to be faithful to Yahweh's way. Let us look at what being a holy nation meant for them and for their life together.

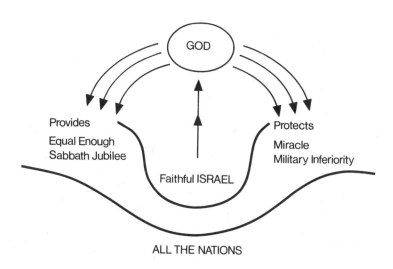

The Law: Framework for Holy Living

Three months after their escape from Egypt, the Israelites came to a mountain in the heart of the wilderness. Once again they encountered holiness. When their representative Moses climbed the mountain to meet the Holy One, the people—at a safe distance—sensed themselves to be in the presence of a power of terrifying otherness. The earth trembled beneath them. The air was charged with electricity (Exod. 19:16-19). Out of the thunder Yahweh spoke. Yahweh's aim was not to give the people an unforgettable religious experience. His concern was rather, just as it had been when he met Moses in the burning bush, to bring about action and change.

For the people of Israel truly to be liberated from Egypt, they needed to be taught how to live in a new way. Yahweh was calling the people to play demanding roles (Exod. 19:6).

For them to be his "kingdom of priests" they needed to live in obedience to their divine King. For them to be his spearhead in history—"a holy nation"—they needed to live according to his holiness. By giving them successive waves of Law, Yahweh was graciously equipping them for these high callings.

The Law was God's primary teaching aid. Without it, the people of God would have been, in the things that really mattered, just like all the other nations. Emphatically, Yahweh stated that "you shall not learn to follow the abominable practices of those nations" (Deut. 18:9). Yahweh's people must be unlike the Canaanites. They must also be different from the Egyptians whose land they had so recently left. For if the Israelites reverted to Egyptian ways and values, they would be rejecting the gracious work of Yahweh on their behalf.

Repeatedly in the Law there are impassioned appeals to *remember* the Exodus. "Yahweh has taken you, and brought you forth out of the iron furnace, out of Egypt, to be a people of his own possession. . . . Take heed to yourselves, lest you forget. . ." (Deut. 4:20, 23). By remembering, they would both understand what Yahweh's concerns were and remind themselves of his faithfulness. They would also have a motive for action. "You were poor. You were strangers. You were oppressed. And I freed you. *Therefore*, you must act toward others as I acted toward you" (Exod. 22:21-23; 23:9 paraphrased). "Imitation of God" is language which was not used until the New Testament. But already in the Old Testament it is implicit in the texts. And its aim is holiness. "You shall be holy, for I Yahweh your God am holy" (Lev. 19:2).

Holiness, in fact, was to pervade their lives. It was to characterize their religious ceremonial and their family patterns. And it was to shape the way that the Israelites dealt with the primary human concerns that we have discussed in earlier chapters—*provision* and *protection*. In the Exodus, Yahweh had demonstrated his concrete grace, providing for his people and protecting them without their assistance. In doing so,

Yahweh demonstrated values that were precious to him. And Yahweh invited them into a relationship with himself—a relationship of trust and vulnerability.

Now, in the Law, Yahweh took his people a step further. He showed them that although the events of the Exodus were unique, the principles involved were repeatable. In fact, they would be the acknowledged basis for Yahweh's prescriptions for his people's lifestyle. Theirs would be a lifestyle of vulnerability. In both the areas of wealth and war the Law limited the people's "works"—their capacity to become strong and self-reliant. Indeed, its provisions institutionalized their dependence on Yahweh. Only by faith—faith in the ongoing concrete grace of the One who had delivered them from Egypt—could the people hope to keep the Law. In this manner, the Law was a miraculous fusion of two things that some people today see as irreconcilable—God's radical grace and a socially radical lifestyle. God's "holy nation" would be a deviant community living by grace.

Provision: Sabbath and Jubilee Years

To illustrate this, let us look at the Law's prescriptions for the area of *provision*. From the earliest passages in the "Covenant Code" (Exod. 20—23), it is clear that something remarkable was afoot. A seventh year (a *sabbath* year) was specified (Exod. 21:1-2; 23:10-13) which was to be holy, in three ways different from other years.

In the first place, the sabbath year was to be a year of recovery for the land. Through lying fallow, the land would be reenergized for six more years of productive harvests. Second, the sabbath year would be a time of *liberty* (release, forgiveness). Those who had been sold into slavery during the previous six years would be set free. Regardless of the ups and downs of their economic fortunes, no Israelite could be a slave for more than six years.

Third, the sabbath year was to be the time for attacking the misery of the poor. According to the earlier Law code (Exod. 23:11), this was to be done by empowering the poor to gather as much as they needed from the fields' spontaneous growth. The later code (Deut. 15:2) added to this by calling for a proclamation of liberty (release, forgiveness), not just of slaves, but also of debts. In the sabbath year "every creditor shall release what he has lent to his neighbor." The wealthier people must be alert that their attitudes not harden against their poor brothers. Even in the sixth year, when the debt forgiveness of the sabbath year was approaching, they must "open their hands" to the poor in granting them credit.

Every fiftieth year there was to be a sabbath of sabbath years—a year of *Jubilee*. In this year, which was specifically designated as "holy" to the people (Lev. 25:10, 12), remarkable things were to happen. It was not simply that in the Jubilee the people were to do the normal sabbath year things such as forgiving debts and leaving the land fallow. They were also to proclaim liberty on a massive scale—a release of the land. And it was immensely important to God that they do this. According to missionary and Old Testament scholar Chris Wright, the Jubilee was "the central core of Old Testament economics."[3]

Here, in brief, is how the system was to work. The Promised Land into which the Israelites came was the "private property," not of any individuals or families, but of God himself. "The land is mine" (Lev. 25:23), said the only Freeholder. As Gordon Wenham, an Evangelical Old Testament scholar, has pointed out, the land "does not really belong to [the Israelites]; they inhabit it thanks solely to the mercy and favor of their God, the great landowner."[4] As a result, the land was not to be sold, but was to be graciously apportioned to the newly arrived Israelite families according to need. The people were to be stewards of the land, not its owners.

In the course of the fifty years, some families, through good fortune or hard work, would prosper. As a result, they might acquire additional lands from less fortunate or less industrious families. But they would have these lands only on a kind of leasehold. At the jubilee there would be a great re-equalization. The leases would expire and the lands would be released— returned to the families who originally held them. And every family, on the basis of equality, would have a fresh start.

The sabbath and Jubilee years were not the only parts of the Law in which God prescribed economic justice for his people. The laws concerning tithing and gleaning were also important (Deut. 14:28-29; 24:19-22; Lev. 19:9-10). Nevertheless, the intermingled theological and economic ideas which lay behind the sabbath and Jubilee laws were remarkable. Let us look at them in greater detail.

The first thing to note is the repeated reference, in both the sabbath and Jubilee laws, to the Exodus. Why release slaves? Why forgive debts? Because "you shall remember that you were a slave in the land of Egypt, and Yahweh your God redeemed you" (Deut. 15:15). The land, like their freedom, was theirs not by right or merit, but as Yahweh's gift to them. The people were warned not to think, "My power and the might of my hand have gotten me this wealth" (Deut. 8:17). Instead, their prosperity was the product of Yahweh's concrete grace.

The people, in turn, were to respond to Yahweh by gracious living and faithful living. Because Yahweh had been gracious, giving them freedom, food, and land, they also were to be gracious. Having themselves been released from bondage, they were to be the instruments by which others were released from the bondages of slavery and poverty.

To do this, they needed to live by faith. The Israelites who remembered the Exodus trusted that the God of the Exodus could do it again. God could intervene by acts of concrete grace to vindicate them when they engaged in acts of financial foolishness. For what else but foolishness could it appear when they refrained from planting or harvesting in a sabbath year, or redistributed property in a Jubilee? The people's instinctive desires to fulfill their primary human need of provision were aroused. "What shall we eat in the seventh year?" (Lev. 25:20) was a reasonable question—if one thought in conventional human terms and forgot the Exodus. But the institutions of Israel, prescribed in the Law, were based on a premise of faith which defied common sense. For Yahweh was still gracious!

We must also keep our eyes fixed on the social sense of this legislation. In it there is not a hint of the so-called "sanctity [holiness] of private property." That is disowned by the Levitical legislation in which Yahweh is freeholder and his people are "strangers and sojourners with me" (Lev. 25:23). Instead, the language of holiness is reserved for the act of reequalization (Lev. 25:10,12). That is where the holiness of God is manifested—in reequalization, when men and women, trusting God, deny their personal economic advantage to create a society in which everyone has enough.

Sufficiency and equality—these "manna principles" undergirded the sabbath and Jubilee years. In the desert, Yahweh had demonstrated his commitment to sufficiency and equality: he wanted everyone to have enough, but no one to have too much. As the Jewish scholar André Neher noted, "All had been rendered equal by the justice-making act of God."[5] It is not surprising, therefore, that the legislative texts recall the manna (Deut. 8:3-4). And they order life for the Israelites so that sufficiency and equality can be maintained. The aim was to eradicate poverty among God's people. "There will be no poor among you ... if only you will obey the voice of Yahweh" (Deut. 15:4-5). Even if that remained an unattainable goal (Deut. 15:11), nevertheless it was one towards which God's people, by being faithful to the law and reliant upon his grace, were to continue to orient their lives.

Protection: Holy War

The principles of holiness and grace, rooted in the Exodus, are equally to be found in the Law's prescriptions for *protec-*

tion. Safety was bound to be a primary concern of the Israelites. They had emerged from Egypt equipped with only the lightest of weaponry. As they moved into the Promised Land, they encountered other nations that had the latest weapons that the oriental arms bazaars could offer. For them security questions were uppermost.

How were they to cope? In the Covenant Code (Exod. 23:20-23), Yahweh gave some hints. "I [will] send an angel before you, to guard you on the way and to bring you to the place which I have prepared. . . . I will be an enemy to your enemies." Yahweh himself would personally intervene against Isrel's enemies: "I [will] blot them out." The means by which he would do this must have sounded somewhat unreliable. "I will send my terror before you, and will throw into confusion all [your enemies]." The "hornets" which he promised to send into battle would have had a familiar ring, evoking memories of the miracles which had preceded the Exodus. And the people, apparently doing nothing, were to accept Yahweh's vindication as a gift of concrete grace.

A fuller statement of the ways in which Yahweh wanted to protect his people occurs in the Deuteronomic Code (Deut. 20), which established the institution of the "holy war". How can war be holy? A necessary evil, some think. Others put it more strongly. General Sherman, whose Union troops put Southern cities to the torch during the American civil war, stated it succinctly: "War is hell."

Yet in the Law, war, like other Israelite practices, was to be "holy." The Hebrew word was *herem*, which means "dedicated." In the *herem*, the defeated enemies and their possessions were to be dedicated to Yahweh. In practice, this meant banned, cursed, and utterly destroyed. As a holy event, a war would begin with an act of "sanctification" (Jer. 6:4; Mic. 3:5). The participants in it would need to ensure that their camps were holy (Deut. 23:14). For the holy war was not "a continuation of political activity by other means." It was an act of religious ritual, a "vast, bloody sacrifice" to the God who graciously protected his people.[6]

As a holy event, the Holy War was bound to be different from ordinary warfare. According to the biblical accounts, it had two major peculiarities. In the first place, it was incredibly destructive. Not uniformly so, of course. The closer the battle came to the heart of Israelite life, the greater the carnage. When a distant city surrendered after siege, for example, the Israelites were to put to the sword only the entire male population. The women, animals, and spoil they could take as "booty" for themselves (Deut. 20:10-15). In the cities of the Promised Land the destruction was to be greater—the Israelites were to "save alive nothing that breathes" (20:16). Nor were the Israelites to save any of the artifacts of civilization. They were to put them to the torch (e.g., Josh. 7:11). Equally total destruction was to be the fate of Israelite cities that had surrendered to idolatry. Their inhabitants—all of them—were to be killed along with all of their animals. Their possessions were to be piled up in the city's central square, whereupon they, along with the rest of the city, were to be set alight, offered "as a whole burnt offering to Yahweh your God" (Deut. 13:15-16). The destruction of the city—its people, its economic resources, and its culture—was to be total.

Why this destructiveness? No modern ideology—Christian or otherwise—would justify such a conflagration. Indeed, the just war theory came into being precisely to prevent even a pale reflection of it from taking place.[7] Nor does this destructiveness make military sense. A defeated populace can be a bother to govern. But certainly every victorious power would be open to seizing the economic resources (the cattle, precious metals, etc.) of the defeated country. What kind of warfare rules out economic profit and penalizes the victors?

It is *holy* war. The overwhelming destructiveness is part and parcel of its distinctiveness. Because of their oppression and idolatry, the surrounding nations were "Yahweh's adversaries."

Their total destruction was an expression of his punishment (Num. 24:8; Lev. 19:25). Even more to the point, the destructiveness was a protection of the victors. Time and again, Yahweh repeated his worry that his people would become "like all the nations" which they were displacing from the Promised Land. Yahweh clearly wanted to ward off their becoming worldly. In ordering the blotting out of the enemies and their culture, the Law was expressing his concern "that they may not teach you to do according to all their abominable practices" (Deut. 20:18). The colossal destructiveness of holy war was thus a means of keeping worldliness from infecting God's people. The holy war was a protection of their holiness.

The second peculiarity of the holy war was its insistence upon weakness. What an unorthodox approach to warfare! Imagine going into battle without attempting at least to match the enemy in manpower and firepower!

This absurd approach to military strategy was, however, very much in the Exodus tradition. According to Deuteronomy 20, the holy war was to begin with the following appeal:

> When you go forth to war against your enemies, and see horses and chariots and an army larger than your own, you shall not be afraid of them. (Deut. 20:1)

Outmanned and outarmed, the Israelites might well have been terrified. Yet they were not to fear, for "Yahweh your God is with you, who brought you up out of the land of Egypt". The priest who, in lieu of a human king, was to lead them into battle, was to remind them that their divine King could do it again. Yahweh will "fight for you . . . to give you the victory" (Deut. 20:4). Of course the Israelite soldiers might have to fight. Indeed, they might have to engage in genocidal violence. But their activities would be secondary to the prior act of Yahweh, whose surprising intervention would be decisive. Yahweh was the victor. As in the Exodus, victory would be the product of Yahweh's concrete grace, not of human works. And Yahweh's people were to respond by obediently trusting him for their national survival.

The holy war legislation of Deuteronomy 20 did not simply recommend this dependence. It made radical dependence unavoidable by establishing the principle of *intentional inferiority* (Deut. 20:5-9). Before the battle, the officers were to address their troops as follows:

> Is there any man here who has just built a house, but has not yet dedicated it? If so, he is to go home. Otherwise, if he is killed in battle, someone else will dedicate his house. (Deut. 20:5, TEV)

So also those who had planted new vineyards or betrothed their intended wives: Let them go home! Even, significantly enough, those who were "fearful and fainthearted" (i.e., those who could not trust Yahweh to protect his people): *Let them go home!* For their fear might be contagious. When going into battle, Israel would thus be behaving in a very strange way. Far from conscripting all available manpower, the Israelite leaders would be ensuring that their army would be *numerically inferior* to their enemies.

The Israelites were also to be *technologically inferior*. In Deuteronomy 20:1 it is assumed that Israel's enemies would not only have larger armies but also ones equipped with horses and chariots. The lethal chariots, especially, were the shock forces of Near Eastern armies of the time. As early engines of mechanized warfare, they gave to the armies that possessed them both mobility and brute strength.

Israel was not to have chariots. In Joshua 11 we find the Israelites encountering the "great host ... with very many horses and chariots," of the central Canaanite king, Jabin. With the enemy in full sight, Yahweh, the God of the Exodus, made a characteristic promise: "I will give over all of them, slain, to Israel." On one condition, however. "You shall hamstring their horses and burn their chariots with fire" (Josh. 11:6).

In this way as well, Israel's behavior was to be strange. If anyone had the conventional military idea of using the captured enemy weaponry in the next battle, he was to forget it. Instead, the Israelites were to treat the chariots like things accursed, like idols. They were to *burn them with fire*.

This dramatic gesture is a fitting symbol of the holiness of Israel's warfare. It simultaneously destroyed pagan weaponry and secured Israel's intentional inferiority. For Israel was not to trust in anything but Yahweh for its protection lest they "vaunt themselves against me, saying, My own hand has delivered me" (Judg. 7:2). Using unorthodox military techniques, Yahweh would intervene personally to help them in their obedient foolishness.

Working It out in Practice

What was the pay-off for obedience to Yahweh? According to the Law, it was blessing. Yahweh would bless his people, providing for them and protecting them. He would bless the fruit of their body. Yahweh's blessing would be upon their barns. And when they were threatened by enemies, Yahweh would defeat them: "They shall come out against you one way, and flee before you seven ways" (Deut. 28:7). By deeds of concrete grace, Yahweh would establish Israel as "a people holy to himself" (Deut. 28:9).

But did it work? Did the Israelites really engage in these practices which required them to rely on Yahweh's provision and protection?

Concerning the laws on provision, it is hard to tell. According to the account in Joshua (5:12), the daily supply of manna never gave out as long as the Israelites were in the desert. It ceased only when they entered into the ample farmland of the Promised Land. Were the sabbath and Jubilee laws put into practice? The biblical account does not say. In view of later practices of leaving the land fallow and forgiving debt, it is likely that the sabbath laws *were* observed from an early date. The Jubilee laws, on the other hand, "never became an integral part of the Hebrew way of life."[8] But they were known, and they had their effect. Witness law-abiding Naboth's reluctance, so infuriating to pagan queen Jezebel, to sell his family's vineyard to king Ahab (1 King 21).[9]

There can be no doubt, on the other hand, that the life of the Israelites was profoundly affected by the laws on protection. This was evident from the start of their campaign to conquer the Promised Land. After capturing the Canaanite city of Jericho, for example, they "burned the city with fire, and all within it" (Josh. 6:24). When one of their number tried to convert a little Canaanite clothing and precious metal into his private property, Yahweh suspended his military help and the Israelite troops were put to flight. "I will be with you no more, unless you destroy the devoted things [*herem*] from among you" (Josh. 7:12). So the people discovered the culprit, stoned him, and burned him and his secret goods with fire (Josh. 7). By these acts of destruction, Israel's distinctiveness—its holiness—was protected.

The biblical story is likewise full of Yahweh's protection of his people in their intentional inferiority. Think of the battles of this period. Who fought the Battle of Jericho? Not, despite the famous spiritual, Joshua! It was Yahweh, who won the victory by architectural catastrophe—the walls fell down! Yahweh's means in other battles equally combined the material and the miraculous: illness, a rumor, thunder, hailstones, a swollen stream.[10] Of course, by this time the human element was now present in the battles. The Israelites were participating as warriors. But their efforts were of secondary importance. After Yahweh, the real victor, had routed the opposition, the Israelites mopped up.

Of many examples of this bizarre type of battle, I shall mention two. The first of these is the battle between the Israelites and their Midianite neighbors (Judg. 6—7). To lead his people,

Yahweh called upon Gideon, a pious winegrower not at all inclined to become a warrior. But once he did so, he was determined to wage war by the book (of the Law). At Yahweh's instruction, Gideon followed the procedure set down in Deuteronomy 20. He sent home the fearful—twenty-two thousand of them. But there were still ten thousand warriors, far too many for Yahweh's purposes. So Gideon—by watching how the men drank water from the stream—pared them down to a mere three hundred. At this point, arrayed against a numerous Midianite force (Judg. 6:5), Israel was inferior enough for Yahweh to demonstrate his point: it was *Yahweh*, not any Israelite heroes, who would protect the people.

The equipment that the Israelites carried into battle was unorthodox. At Yahweh's suggestion, they deployed trumpets, smashable clay pots, bright lights, and lusty voices. When they blew their trumpets, Yahweh himself intervened. He "set every [Midianite] man's sword against his fellow and against all the army" (Judg. 7:22). The Israelites then brought the battle to a conclusion by chasing off their terrified opponents.

The second example is Israel's battle against a Canaanite army led by Sisera (Judg. 4—5). The Canaanites were as technologically advanced as the Midianites were numerous. They were armed with "nine hundred chariots of iron" (Judg. 4:3) and were led by professional soldiers. The Israelites, in contrast, were chariotless and led by an unarmed woman, Deborah. Israel's military leader, an apparently faint-hearted man named Barak, was persuaded to go into battle when Deborah promised him that she would be by his side. She also warned him that Israel's victory would not lead to his own glory, because Yahweh would be the victor. "Yahweh will sell Sisera into the hand of a woman" (Judg. 4:9).

Battle ensued. Sisera deployed all his chariots and all his mighty men. But Yahweh intervened. The river Kishon burst its banks, clogging the chariot wheels, and forcing Sisera and the other charioteers to flee on foot. The Israelite army pursued their hapless enemies. That evening the exhausted Sisera died, the victim, not of Barak or any Israelite hero, but of Jael, a woman who drove a tent peg through his skull. Israel's victory was that of a powerless people, dependent on their Protector.

Whining and Idolatry

The Israelites responded to Yahweh's acts of concrete grace by worshiping him. In bursts of spontaneous praise and in more elaborately composed psalms they celebrated his faithfulness. Yahweh, they proclaimed, was their "sun [provision] and shield [protection]" (Ps. 84:11). "The angel of Yahweh encamps around those who fear him, and delivers them [protection] . . . those who seek Yahweh lack no good thing [provision]." "O taste and see," the psalmist exults in the God of concrete grace, "that Yahweh is good!" (Ps. 34:7-9). He is the victor over the enemy chariots: "Hear, O kings; give ear, O princes . . . I will make melody to Yahweh, the God of Israel" (Judg. 5:3). The worship of the Israelites was a celebration of Yahweh's acts and a retelling of his story. It was also an expression of trust. By providing for his people and protecting them, the God who had brought them out of bondage would keep on doing it again!

Or would he? There was room for doubt. For living in trustful insecurity is always difficult, especially when one is confronting hard reality. Empty barns or a squadron of chariots could spur anyone to a quick rethink. So also could the example of other societies who could have religion without needing to have faith. It is inconvenient to have a God who gives people freedom only insofar as they are living in dependant deviance. Much of the time, the Israelites in trust put up with this inconvenience, and persisted in their patterns of holy living.

But at times the Israelites wavered. They forgot the story of Yahweh's acts. They ceased to expect his new interventions to vindicate their peculiar lifestyle. And they altered their religious practices accordingly by turning to two forms of false worship—whining and idolatry.

At whining (the Old Testament calls it *murmuring*) the Israelites were experts. It was a form of nostalgia. The present is bad. The past was better. How wonderful Egypt had been! "We remember the fish we ate in Egypt for nothing, the cucumbers, the melons, the leeks . . ." (Num. 11:5). And we forget the bondage and the saving acts of Yahweh. We ascribe to the slavery of the past ("you have brought us up out of a land flowing with milk and honey" [Num. 16:13]) the benefits that God has promised for our future. And we turn back, back to the security of slavery. "Let us choose a captain, and go back to Egypt" (Num. 14:4). Anything is better than the riskiness of freedom!

The risks did indeed appear imposing. It was not simply that manna was getting tiresome. A forward party of Israelite spies warned of giants in the Promised Land. "The people who dwell in the land are strong, and the cities are fortified and very large . . . and we seemed to ourselves like grasshoppers" (Num. 13:28,33). Only two of the spies, Caleb and Joshua, dissented from the majority report, which seemed to them to be "rebelling against Yahweh." But the other Israelites responded by pelting the two with stones. Having dismissed the past as irrelevant, they were grasping after a riskless future.

Yahweh was outraged by this attitude. *Putting me to the proof*, he called it. At root, it was a denial of his gracious presence. In the early days in the desert, at a place which was called Massah [proof], the thirsty Israelites had put Yahweh to the proof by asking, "Is Yahweh among us or not?" (Exod. 17:7). Thereafter they often asked the question, especially when they were feeling insecure about their primary human needs of protection and provision. Yahweh eventually had had enough.

> None of the people who have seen my glory and my signs which I wrought in Egypt and in the wilderness, and yet have put me to the proof these ten times and have not hearkened to my voice, shall see the land which I swore to give to their fathers. . . .
> (Num. 14:22-23)

Moses himself would be denied entry into the Promised Land, for even he had despaired of Yahweh's power to provide (Num. 20). The Land would be settled by the next generation of Israelites, led by the two spies who had had faith.

Putting Yahweh to the proof was thus of great, literally make-or-break, significance. For good reason it was a theme that permeated the psalms with which Israel worshiped:

> They put him to the proof again and again,
>   and provoked the Holy One of Israel.
> They did not keep in mind his power,
>   or the day when he redeemed them
>   from the foe. (Ps. 78:41-42)

The reliability of Yahweh in practical matters leading to risk-taking was a spiritual matter. Indeed, it was a matter of *holiness*. As Yahweh reproved Moses, "You broke faith with me in the midst of the people of Israel at the waters of Meribath-kadesh . . . because you did not revere me as holy in the midst of the people of Israel" (Deut. 32:51). To worship the holy God was to remember that God alone—against all appearances—can protect and provide.

Like whining, idolatry was a form of false worship. It did not take the Israelites long to explore this idolatry. Worshiping an imageless God was, for people of that era, something of a strain. Not only was Yahweh invisible; he also was demanding a lifestyle that seemed to flout ancient Near Eastern common sense.

How inviting it seemed, therefore, to worship other gods. Not that the people would forget Yahweh. They would simply accord him an honored place alongside other gods in the divine club. So when Aaron led the Israelites in constructing a golden calf, he proclaimed, "Tomorrow shall be a feast to Yahweh" (Exod. 32:5).

Religious two-timing (syncretism) was attractive, especially since many of the alternative gods seemed to be more responsive to the people's needs. For example, the gods Baal and Astarte, who appear to have been Yahweh's two chief rivals for the allegiance of the Israelites, dealt with eminently practical issues. Although protection and provision were said to be important to both of them, each appears to have engaged in some specialization.

"Powerful Baal" was "the Prince, Lord of Earth." In ancient depictions he brandished a club in his right hand, while in his left hand was a lance which he cast, lightninglike, upon the earth. A male god, Baal was a warrior. Astarte, on the other hand, was a goddess. On amulets, which expectant women kept for protection in childbirth, she could be seen with cascading locks of hair swirling around her breasts. She was the goddess of human reproductivity—and of the productivity of the soil.[11]

The physical depiction of these gods—*idols*—was offensive to Yahweh. But more seriously, he was offended because the people had made these gods in their own image, according to their own convenience. The gods were demanding, but only of correct ceremony. They did not require, as Yahweh did, a deviantly dependent lifestyle. One could worship Baal and live like everybody else did. One could worship Astarte and be self-reliant. The gods, unlike Yahweh, helped those who helped themselves.

Here is how the Assyrian king Shalmaneser III reported his exploits.

> [Twelve kings] rose up against me for a decisive battle. I fought with them with the support of the mighty forces of Ashur [god of Assyria], which Ashur, my lord, has given to me, and the strong weapons which Nergal [god of the nether world], my leader, has presented to me, and I did inflict a defeat upon them. . . . I slew 14,000 of their soldiers. . . . [12]

Shalmaneser, to be sure, believed that the gods were involved in the battle. But they were helping him, who was the main protagonist and who was fighting like all the other nations—by the most advanced military techniques that were available.

Set this self-congratulatory account aside and explore again the biblical accounts of Israel's battles. One enters a different world—a world of holiness. For the Israelites confessed that Yahweh was so inventive, so concretely gracious, that he could defeat their enemies without their help! He could provide for his people and protect them when they entered into the risk of a lifestyle which rejected military and economic strength. Yahweh's concrete grace was sufficient. It was among a powerless people that he could manifest his power. How strange to Shalmaneser, how unlike the nations ancient and modern, this confession of faith is! And, as we shall see in the next chapter, how hard to maintain!

CHAPTER
6

Losing Holiness: The Monarchy

Suddenly we've lost altitude! As we look out of our balloon, we can see more detail but less territory. It's important to be closer to the ground at this point, for we are going to be examining a watershed. At this particular moment—about 1020 B.C.—the people of God made a choice. As they themselves put it, they decided to become "like all the nations" (1 Sam. 8:20).

It was a momentous decision. As we have noted in earlier chapters, the people of God were to be a nation, but a nation that was different. Their calling was to be a "holy nation" unlike "the nations whom you go in to dispossess" (Exod. 19:6; Deut. 12:29). In fact, in Hebrew the word for *nations* has negative overtones much like those of the English word "heathen." Throughout the Law, Yahweh repeatedly warned his people— his nation—not to be like the nations. The nations were Yahweh's adversaries (Num. 24:8). They lived by their own conventional values of strength and self-reliance, not by his

Law. But the Israelites were to be different. If they would be faithful and dependent upon him, Yahweh would set them "high above all nations that he has made." The result would be holiness. "You shall be a people holy to Yahweh your God" (Deut. 26:19).

Oh, it was tempting to be like the nations! Yahweh recognized this fact, warning them: "Take heed that you be not ensnared to follow them [the nations]" (Deut. 12:30). Yahweh knew that copying the ways of the nations would disfigure his people's worship and lifestyle. It would blunt their effectiveness as his instrument in history. And it would change their nature. By becoming like the nations, his people would no longer be like him. They would have lost their holiness.

Fear and security, protection and power—these were the crunch points at which the people's nonconformity finally broke down. These were the concerns which were behind the people's demand for a king. Once they had their wish, Israel's life would never again be the same. Let us watch as the changes happen.

Living with Yahweh as King: the Judges

For two centuries after their conquest of the Promised Land, the Israelites had a countercultural form of government. In a world in which every nation great and small had its king, the Israelites were apparently kingless. Their tribal confederation had no central government. The leaders of each tribe would try cases and adjudicate disputes. All served under the overarching lordship of Yahweh, their divine King, the Lord of armies, who ever since the Exodus had protected his people.

Towards the outside world, Israel, with no standing army, was vulnerable. As long as the Israelites were obedient to Yahweh, they lived in *shalom* (Lev. 26:6). When they aped the practices of surrounding nations, however, they got into trouble. Foreign rule and economic oppression were the bitter results of their infidelity.

Even then, however, their King, Yahweh, remained committed to them. Suddenly, in surprising ways, Yahweh sent his Spirit upon unsuspecting Israelites, both male and female. Without regard to family tradition, economic privilege or military prowess, God made them his representatives. Despite their lack of a conventional power base, these ordinary people (Othniel, Gideon, Jepthah, to name a few) became his instruments. Empowered by Yahweh's Spirit, they judged his people and restored their freedom. Voluntarily the Israelites gave viceregal authority to the judges (as these Spirit-appointed leaders were called). But they recognized Yahweh as their real King. And Yahweh responded by protecting his people by thunderbolts, rumors, and other deeds of countercultural warfare.

In chapters 6 and 7 of 1 Samuel, we read an excellent account of Yahweh's kingly rule. In about 1030 B.C., shortly before the decisive watershed, the Israelites fell prey to the cultural and religious enticements of their neighbours, the Philistines. As a result, they soon found themselves dominated politically and militarily as well. Not only were they the slaves of the Philistines; they also suffered the gnawing sense of the absence of Yahweh (1 Sam. 4:9; 7:2).

Religious revival was a necessary response to this crisis. So Yahweh raised up a judge, Samuel. Inspired by him, the people disposed of their Baals and Astartes. They reaffirmed the Law. And they confessed, "We have sinned against Yahweh" (1 Sam. 7:3-6). The covenant relationship restored, Samuel could judge the people in the name of Yahweh their King. The Philistines correctly found this to be a challenge to their political authority, so they massed to attack the Israelites. At the news of this, the Israelites were terrified. In panic they appealed to Samuel, who sprang into action. What did he do? Did he lead an anti-Philistine counterattack? No, he took a sucking lamb and sacrificed it to Yahweh. In this posture of dependence and worship, Samuel "cried to Yahweh for Israel, and Yahweh answered him." While Samuel was still at worship, while the Israelites were still immobilized in their terror, Yahweh acted. He "thundered with a mighty voice" and the Philistines fled in disarray, pursued by the suddenly energized Israelites (1 Sam. 7:7-11).

What a great victory! How should they celebrate it? By erecting a war memorial, of course! Samuel took a boulder and placed it in a prominent location. Nothing unusual so far. But there was something strange, something countercultural about this war memorial. Samuel named the stone "Ebenezer" (stone of help), indicating that he and the people had been helpless. But their King, Yahweh, had come to their aid when his people had turned to him. Samuel was at pains to remind the people of Yahweh's faithfulness throughout their history: "To this point . . . Yahweh has helped us" (1 Sam. 7:12 NEB). There was nothing plaintive about it, unlike many modern renditions of the hymn "O God Our Help in Ages Past." For Israel was not recalling its victims. Nor was it glorying in its exploits. Israel was remembering the concrete grace of its King Yahweh, who had helped them when they were helpless. In erecting this memorial, Samuel was thus helping the people to participate in the grand tradition of Israelite worship—*remembering* the mighty deeds of Yahweh. *The people must not forget!* For only through worship, which is remembering, could they respond in faithful vulnerability to their next crisis of insecurity.

To see how unlike the nations, how *holy* the approach of Samuel and the Israelites was, let us turn once again to the inscriptions of the Assyrian king, Shalmaneser III. For Shalmaneser also erected a war memorial:

> At that time, I extolled for posterity the heroic achievements of [Assyrian gods] Ashur and Shamash by fashioning a sculptured stela with myself as king depicted on it. I wrote thereupon my heroic behavior, my deeds in combat, and erected it beside the source of the Saluara river.[1]

Shalmaneser's monument duly mentions the gods, but the real victor is never in doubt. How different were the Israelites, who credited the victory to the gracious intervention of their invisible King!

Rejecting Yahweh: The Ways of a King

Being different was frightening. Often responsible leaders of the Israelite tribes must have been plagued by uncertainty. How would they cope with their next crisis of insecurity? The history of Yahweh's actions as recounted in their psalms and depicted on their monuments was inspiring. But the geopolitical facts were intimidating. Their enemies had the latest model of chariots and they didn't even have an ordinary central government!

In 1020, late in Samuel's life, such thoughts were certainly in the minds of the elders of Israel. There was a crisis of succession. Despite the fact that the judgeship had never been hereditary, Samuel had named his sons to be judges in his place. But the sons were not up to the task. They were financially corrupt and they "perverted justice" (1 Sam. 8:2). It would have been only right if the elders, in their concern for the welfare of the people, had exposed the dubious dealings of the sons and queried Samuel's act in appointing them. After all, up to that time the judges had always been raised up by Yahweh's Spirit!

But instead, the elders chose another approach. In a body they came to Samuel and said, "Behold, you are old and your sons do not walk in your ways; now appoint for us a king to govern us like all the nations" (1 Sam. 8:5). As they made clear, they were concerned for both the domestic justice and the external security of the nation (1 Sam. 8:20). Their concerns were those of responsible people. Their suggestion was, by the standards of every other country of their day, a common sense one. And the idea was not a new one. A century before, after the victory over the Midianites, the people had urged Gideon to become Israel's hereditary monarch (Judg. 7:22).

A form of kingship may even have been in Yahweh's plan for his people (Gen. 49:10). (Certainly a passage from the Law would seem to indicate as much [Deut. 17:14-20]). The king which Yahweh envisaged, however, was a countercultural king—a king not at all "like the nations." For one thing, the king was to be an Israelite who was immersed in the Law. "He shall read in it all the days of his life," that he may learn to fear Yahweh and obey his statutes. Furthermore, since the king would inevitably be tempted to be unfaithful to Yahweh and his way, the Law established some safeguards. It prohibited the king from multiplying in three areas: from multiplying horses, thereby building up a technologically sophisticated standing army; from multiplying wives, no doubt to conclude alliances with neighboring kingdoms; and from multiplying silver and gold. If the king obeyed these regulations, his heart would "not be lifted up above his brethren." Under these conditions the Israelites would be allowed to have a monarchy. It would be an egalitarian, antimilitaristic monarchy quite unlike that of the other nations.

Despite the proposal's apparent common sense and the Deuteronomic Law, Samuel was dismayed by the elders' request. In prayer he brought his distress before Yahweh. Although grieving himself, Yahweh attempted to comfort Samuel. The people were not rejecting Samuel. Their rejection was deeper, more radical than that. "They have rejected me," Yahweh stated, "from being king over them" (1 Sam. 8:7).

In rejecting Yahweh as their King, the Israelite elders were choosing between two themes in their national history. There was the theme of Yahweh's grace, rooted in the Exodus, repeated in countless acts of protection and provision, celebrated in their worship. There was also the theme of whining and faithless complaint, of putting Yahweh to the proof by doubting his capacity to care for them, of repudiating the Exodus which delivered them from slavery into the insecurity of freedom, even of idolatry, of "forsaking me and serving other gods" (1 Sam. 8:8).[2] By choosing a human king "like all the nations," the Israelite elders were basing their national life on the latter of these themes. They were choosing to forget the concrete grace of God. And by so doing, by spurning their countercultural form of government for an ordinary Near Eastern kingship, their nation would lose its holiness.

The elders could not know all the implications of their choice. So Yahweh instructed Samuel to try to communicate these to them. "Show them the ways of the king who shall reign over them" (1 Sam. 8:9). So, in a remarkable speech (1 Sam. 8:11-18), Samuel gave the elders an introductory lecture in Near Eastern political science. Samuel knew what was going on in the neighboring nations. According to Old Testament scholar Millard Lind, "Each aspect of Samuel's criticism can be documented as a characteristic of Canaanite kingship from the texts [of the nearby Ugaritic kingdom]."[3] But Samuel did not limit himself to commenting on politics and society. He also talked about religion. As he proceeded with passionate intensity, he could not help pointing out the impact which the Israelites' choice of a human king would have upon their relationship with Yahweh.

According to Samuel, the "ways of the king" could be summarized in one phrase: "He will take." Four times Samuel repeated this prediction of monarchical graspingness: he will take your sons, he will take your daughters, he will take the best of your fields, and he will take your servants and your cattle. How different, Samuel implied, have been the ways of Yahweh who, as their gracious King, had dealt with his people by giving, giving, and giving still more.

Kingship would bring fundamental changes to Israel's whole society. Its approaches to the primary human concerns of protection and provision would be "normalized." Samuel started with the *militarization* of society which kingship would entail. The king, by taking the people's sons, would be introducing military conscription (and, incidentally, undercutting the Law's requirement that Israel be militarily inferior to her foes). The conscripted sons would serve in the king's *chariots*. Israel's commitment to technological inferiority, which had exempted her from the arms races of her day, would thereby disappear. "Commanders of thousands and commanders of fifties" would appear, introducing a military command structure into a nation that had up to now relied upon spontaneous leadership in a crisis. And of course there could be no chariots or "implements of war" without another innovation, an arms industry. Kingship would take Israel a long way from the dependance upon Yahweh's concrete grace of the holy war.

Kingship would bring to Israel *materialism* as well as militarism. By taking the people's sons, daughters, and servants, the king would be introducing something common to the ancient Near East, but previously unknown to the Israelites—*forced labor*. He would also be seizing the best of their lands—fields, vineyards, and olive orchards. He would be taking a tithe of their flocks and harvests.

The implications of these changes were staggering. Kingship would alter the entire structure of Israelite society. For the lands and harvests which the king requisitioned from his subjects would not just go to himself personally or to the "state"; they would go as his gifts to a new class of courtiers—"his officers and his servants." The people's sons would plough *his* lands; their daughters would bake and make perfume in *his* court. The very words "his lands" indicated the way that things were going. A concept of human ownership, borrowed from the "nations," was being introduced which would make it impossible to be obedient to the Law which required the reequalization of landholding in Jubilee. Not only would the rich become richer at the expense of the poor; the gulf between them would become permanent, negating the goal of the sabbath year that "there will be no poor among you" (Deut. 15:4). The "manna principles" which we have observed in previous

chapters would thus be flouted. Equality would shrivel. Sufficiency would be known only by a few, primarily by those who
already had more than they needed.
What did all this add up to? Samuel put it succinctly. To
express his utter revulsion at what was going to happen, he
reached for the most potent, history-laden word in Israel's vocabulary: slavery. As a result of your choice of a king and your
accommodation to the ways of the nations in matters of protection and provision, Samuel declared, "you will be his slaves"
(1 Sam. 8:17). Israel will in effect be *back in Egypt*. Samuel's
conclusion harks back to the Exodus experience. In your bondage "you will cry out," as your foreparents did in Egypt. But
there will be an all-important difference. When you cry out,
"Yahweh will not answer you" (1 Sam. 8:18, cf. Exod. 2:23-25).
The result of human kingship will not only be a loss of holiness;
it will not only be a return to slavery; it will be the silence of
God.
The elders were unmoved by Samuel's speech.

> No! but we will have a king over us, that we also may be like all
> the nations, and that our king may govern us and go out before
> us and fight our battles. (1 Sam. 8:19-20)

They were tired of holy living, tired of the riskiness of dependance upon Yahweh, tired of being defended by miracle. No
matter what Samuel's stone monument might say, being saved
by thunder seemed cowardly and unpredictable. Let's try hot
bronze instead! When faced by his people's determination to
be like everyone else, Yahweh submitted to their will. In a kind
of abdication, Yahweh ordered Samuel, "Make them a king"
(1 Sam. 8:22).[4]
Samuel complied and anointed Saul to be the first Israelite
monarch. But Samuel had not yet expressed his final verdict on
kingship. On two occasions he summoned the people to mass
meetings to rage at them for their rejection of the God of the
Exodus. On the second of these, Yahweh sent an unseasonable

thunderstorm to add his terrifying "Amen" to Samuel's words (1 Sam. 10:17-19; 12:6-18). When the people penitently blurted out that "we have added to all our sins this evil, to ask for ourselves a king," however, Samuel relented. Yahweh would not reject his people because they had spurned his best way for them. But they must not "turn aside after vain things which cannot profit or save." If they do, "you shall be swept away, both you and your king" (1 Sam. 12:19-25).

The Unhallowing of the Nation

So the Israelites had their king. Changes came slowly in the early years. At the start of his reign, Saul was only a part-time king and continued to work in the fields as a farmer (1 Sam. 11:5). When he went into battle, he took along the old judge, Samuel (1 Sam. 11:7). The victory which ensued he credited to Yahweh: "Today Yahweh has wrought deliverance in Israel" (1 Sam. 11:13). In his early battles, the destructive, genocidal aspect of the holy war was still present. In fact, Saul is recorded as having outraged Yahweh by his refusal, after having slaughtered the Amalekite people, to kill their king as well (1 Sam. 15:18-19). Even the energizing of the Spirit, which had equipped the judges to do the impossible, was evident in Saul's early years as king (1 Sam. 10:6-10; 11:6).[5] And there is no better statement of the protecting power of Yahweh than that which the almost unarmed teenager David shouted to the Philistine hero Goliath:

> You come to me with a sword and with a spear and with a javelin; but I come to you in the name of Yahweh of armies. . . . This day Yahweh will deliver you into my hand . . . that all the earth may know that there is a God in Israel, and that all this assembly may know that Yahweh saves not with sword and spear; for the battle is Yahweh's and he will give you into our hand. (1 Sam. 17:45-47)

Soon, however, change became more rapid. "Saul has slain his thousands, and David his ten thousands" (1 Sam. 18:7).

This popular song is an indication of what was to follow. Henceforth victory would be credited not to the Lord of armies, but to the lord of the Army. The kings and heroes, the people were convinced, were their benefactors. So they flattered them and retold the stories of their victorious deeds. With the coming of kingship, the curious combination of dependence and destruction that made holy war so unique disappeared. Israel's warfare was secularized, profaned. The formerly holy nation now fought like the Philistines.

There was more to this profanation of warfare than who got the credit for the victory. There was also the question of how to decide whether or how to fight. In the days of the judges and early in the history of the kings, no war was begun without *consulting Yahweh* by casting lots. At times, Yahweh's counsel could be quite specific. At other times, he would only give a word permitting or prohibiting the battle.[6] But by the latter half of David's reign, military decisions had come to be made in a more conventional way. Counselors, schooled in Near Eastern statecraft, superceded the casting of lots. The best-known of these "Kissingers" was Ahithophel, whose counsel "was as if one consulted the oracle of God" (2 Sam. 16:23). Their advice could be sensible (2 Sam. 17:14), but it represented a turning away from Yahweh towards the ways of the nations.

Israel's armed forces, too, adapted to the ways of the surrounding nations. In the days of the judges, the Israelites had had no standing army. When a holy war was declared, the judge would summon men from the tribes who might, according to the procedure prescribed in Deuteronomy 20, be deemed suitable for battle. From the early days of the monarchy, however, the kings felt the need for troops who would be constantly available. Saul recruited mercenaries (1 Sam. 14:52). So did David—from the Philistines as well as from his own people (1 Sam. 22:2).[7] These professional soldiers formed a special corps, immediately loyal to the king. "By this policy," comments Roland de Vaux, "David was copying an institution of the Canaanite and Philistine principalities."[8]

In such a process of adjustment to the patterns of other neighboring societies, it was impossible to resist the lure of the chariot. As the heirs of the judges, of course, Saul and David at first had only foot soldiers. But in his expansionary warfare, David was constantly encountering chariots.[9] With admirable fidelity to the holy war traditions of Israel, David never used them in battle. We can see him wavering, however. After defeating the Aramean king Rehob, David captured seventeen hundred horsemen, whereupon David, like Joshua before him, "hamstrung all the chariot horses." At that point there entered the thin wedge of accommodation: "but he left enough for a hundred chariots" (2 Sam. 8:4; cf. Josh. 11:9). And soon the chariots were being used, not by David, to be sure, but by his sons Absalom and Adonijah in their rebellions against him (2 Sam. 15:1; 1 Kings 1:5). Israel's full adoption of chariotry would come under David's son and successor, Solomon (1 Kings 10:26). Under the monarchy, Israel—keeping step with the military prudence of her neighbors—was departing from her earlier commitment to technological inferiority.

The same happened to Israel's commitment to numerical inferiority. Most of David's battles were fought by his palace guard of mercenaries, a small force of elite troops.[10] But for certain campaigns, vastly larger forces were required. The traditional holy war methods of summoning them seemed far too haphazard. How many troops might David mobilize if he were to be really systematic about it? To find out, David decided to conduct a census.

Not everybody thought this was a good idea. For reasons that are not totally clear, his commander-in-chief Joab opposed it strenuously from the outset. Was it, as Yigael Yadin speculates, that Joab, a standing army man, opposed anything that would increase the role of the amateur "monthly militiamen"?[11] Or was it, as the account in 1 Chronicles seems to indicate, that Joab was afraid that an attempt to count the nation's potential military manpower would "bring guilt upon Israel" (1 Chron. 21:3)? If it was the latter, Joab was probably thinking back to the Law of the holy war, in which Yahweh had required the numerical inferiority of Israel. At any rate, there can be no doubt as to Yahweh's reaction to the census. He sent a plague which decimated David's newly numbered troops. Only when the king humbly confessed, "I have sinned greatly in what I have done," did Yahweh end the scourge (2 Sam. 24:10).

Under David's successor, Solomon, Israel's accommodation to the patterns of her neighbors reached its climax. No longer was there hesitation about chariot warfare. By the end of his reign, Israel's forces included fourteen hundred chariots manned by twelve thousand horsemen. Some of these Solomon kept in Jerusalem for his own protection. The remainder he garrisoned in massive, specially constructed "chariot cities" (1 Kings 9:15; 10:26). Furthermore, he proceded to erect military fortifications at potentially vulnerable spots across the kingdom.[12]

Indeed, it was as a builder that Solomon made his special mark. In addition to the chariot cities and forts, Solomon commissioned the building of "the house of Yahweh and his own house" (1 Kings 9:15). Never had the people seen such religious or civic opulence. While work on these public projects proceeded, Israel (and Lebanon, where much of the timber came from) were centers of industry and artistry. There was, of course, a price to be paid for this public magnificence: forced labor. Already in David's reign there had been a conscription of Ammonites for work on the royal projects (2 Sam. 12:31). Solomon extended this to cover "all Israel," raising a total of 180,000 forced laborers (1 Kings 5:13-16).[13] As Samuel had predicted, Israelites once again were slaves.

But what magnificence! Foreign monarchs found it as unbelievable as did the Israelite people. The Queen of Sheba came to Jerusalem to see whether reality could possibly live up to reputation. She was overwhelmed.

> And when the queen of Sheba had seen the wisdom of Solomon, the house that he had built, the food of his table, the seating of his officials, and the attendance of his servants, and their clothing, his cupbearers, and their clothing, and his burnt offerings which he offered at the house of the Lord, there was no more spirit in her. (2 Chron. 9:3-4)

How fortunate a land was Israel, with a king like Solomon whom God had established to "execute justice and righteousness" (2 Chron. 9:8). Having entered the competitive world of Near Eastern monarchies, in an amazingly short time of only three generations, Israel had become a winner.

But at what price? The queen was too overawed by the clothing and ceremonial of the court to note one of the biggest costs—an unjust society. The burdens of royal magnificence rested upon the mass of the people. This injustice had political consequences. Shortly after Solomon's death, the inhabitants of the northern part of his kingdom rejected his son Rehoboam, stoned to death the civil servant who was "taskmaster over the forced labor," and established a second kingdom centered in Samaria (1 Kings 12, esp. v. 18).

Injustice is also the theme of the archaeological evidence. According to Roland de Vaux,

> In the early days of the settlement, all the Israelites enjoyed more or less the same standard of living. . . . Excavations in Israelite towns bear witness to this equality in standards of living. . . . At Tirsah . . . the houses of the tenth century B.C. are all of the same size and arrangement. Each represents the dwelling of a family which lived in the same way as its neighbors. The contrast is striking when we pass to the eighth century houses on the same site: the right houses are bigger and better built and in a different quarter from that where the poor houses are huddled together.[14]

In two centuries, a transition had occurred from a society of equals in Samuel's time to a society divided between the rich and the very poor. This development, which De Vaux has called a "social revolution," was rooted in monarchy and the extravagant inequality which the king and his courtiers fostered.[15] It also was a rejection of the Law, in which Yahweh had communicated his vision of life for a "holy nation" and established certain mechanisms to achieve it. And the people suffered.

A second cost of the magnificence of Solomon was religious. Emerging from the very heart of Israel's life there was confusion about where her religious loyalties actually lay. Solomon was a man of undoubted piety and wisdom. The temple which he commissioned was a wonder of the world. But Solomon's entry into the world of Near Eastern statecraft was bound to affect his faith. The alliances by which he secured Israel's interests abroad brought him wives—seven hundred of them! And seven hundred wives brought a rabble of gods. The palace in Jerusalem was full of them. Solomon found some of them to his liking. It was not that Solomon rejected Yahweh. The worship in the temple continued, with Solomon as its most prominent adherent. But Solomon found a place for the new gods, too. "His heart was not *wholly* true to Yahweh" (1 Kings 11:1-4).

Why should Solomon be wholly true to Yahweh? For all his wisdom, Solomon could not see that Yahweh had anything tangible to give him. Solomon had his own sources of provision and protection! There was no room in his life for dependence, for the holiness with which Yahweh shows his acts of grace in the world. Let Yahweh remain in his domesticated passivity within the temple's walls. And let there be recognition of other gods as well. For their action is as predictable as the seasons. They promise security without risk, and their stories and rituals do nothing to challenge conventional, common sense ideas about how to live in the world. Glorious worship in Yahweh's temple plus a Baal-Astarte lifestyle—this was the religion that made sense of Solomon's own experience.

Yahweh would have none of it. Through his prophet Ahijah, he predicted that Solomon's kingdom would be torn in two (1 Kings 11:30-39). For Solomon's glory was built upon unreality. The people of the northern part of his realm, infuriated by the way he had exploited them with forced labor, so threatened his son Rehoboam that he had to get into his chariot and flee (1 Kings 12:18). Internationally, the nation's position was equally shaky. King Solomon may well have "excelled all the kings of the earth in riches and in wisdom" (2 Chron. 9:22). But this competitive relationship was fraught with difficulties for the future. For in time, other nations, with larger populations and more solid economic foundations, would send their armies to test Israel's strength. When confronted by Assyrian and Babylonian might, how would the divided legacy of Solomon fare?

There remained hope, however, for the people of God. The Spirit of God, which had empowered the judges to rescue the people in their predicaments, was about to become active once again. Under the early kings, he had largely been silent. Somehow, amidst the emphasis upon hereditary privilege and human strength, the Spirit had been superfluous. But among a handful of prophets he was about to express himself anew.[16] Among these people—powerless folk whose only strength was in Yahweh—the Spirit would again find room to move. And what a fire he would ignite! "As for me," a powerless person would proclaim, "I am filled with power, with the Spirit of Yahweh, and with justice and might. . . . Hear this, you . . . rulers of the house of Israel" (Mic. 3:8-9). To these powerless persons we must now turn our attention.

CHAPTER
7

Towards Catastrophe

Our balloon is floating high again. In the last chapter we had to fly low. The watershed required close examination. After all, it had in less than a century altered the direction of Israelite life. Now, however, we once again need a larger perspective. For although it doesn't take long to decide to change directions, it takes much longer to see what effect the new route is having on the travelers. So in this chapter and the next our peripheral vision will have to be vast. We'll be looking across almost an entire millennium.

It was an eventful millennium. Immediately after Solomon died in 922 B.C., his realm split in two. The larger of the two kingdoms that resulted, Israel, centered in Samaria. To the south, the much smaller kingdom of Judah had Jerusalem as its capital. Generally speaking, the kings of both kingdoms continued in the steps of David and Solomon, "normalizing" Jewish social and political life into patterns similar to those of other minor monarchies of the time. At times, this "normalization" appeared to bear fruit. Both kingdoms knew periods of security and their citizens—the top people among them, at any rate—were prosperous.

But such security was short-lived. The Israelite kingdoms could not remain isolated. For this was an age of vast, expansionist empires. Egypt, to Israel's south and west, was still a powerful force. And to the north and east appeared a succession of empires: Assyria, Babylonia, Persia—all of whom had the economic basis for military might. Caught in between were the two Israelite kingdoms, whose misfortune it was to occupy strategically valuable territory without the economic means to defend it.

The results, for the Israelites, were disastrous. In 722, after a period of escalating threat, the Assyrian forces overran the northern kingdom. For one hundred and thirty-five years thereafter, the southern kingdom of Judah clung to a semblance of Jewish national sovereignty. But in 587, its capital of Jerusalem, the city of David, fell to the Babylonian forces of king Nebuchadnezzar. These defeats were not mere humiliations for the Jewish people; they were national catastrophes. For the victorious powers deported them. In the north, the Assyrians installed a more pliable people in their lands.

Some of these Jewish people found exile to be a permanent lifestyle. From Assyria and Babylonia they dispersed throughout the ancient Near East. Others of them were eventually allowed to return to their Palestinian homeland. Never again, however, did they know true national independence. This proud people, which at the start of the millennium was spreading its wings under King David, was by its end cowering under the imperial eagle of Rome.

What was the meaning of this millennium? Where was Yahweh? Why did he allow these events to take place? These were not questions that first occurred to the Jewish people in the postmortems following the fall of Jerusalem. As the catastrophes approached, they had been arguing about them and searching for answers. Songwriters shouted their perplexity.

> Now you [Yahweh] have rejected and humbled us;
> you no longer go out with our armies.
> You made us retreat before the enemy,
> and our adversaries have plundered us.
> You gave us up to be devoured like sheep
> and have scattered us among the nations. (Ps. 44:9-11, NIV)

Israel, Yahweh's "holy nation" was being crushed by the nations. Why? Was Yahweh taking a nap?

> Awake, O Lord! Why do you sleep?
> Rouse yourself! Do not reject us forever.
> Why do you hide your face
> and forget our misery and oppression? (Ps. 44:23-24, NIV)

Or was something else wrong? Brusquely the psalmwriter brushed aside the possibility that the Israelites might have departed from Yahweh's way (Ps. 44:18). Yet the mystery of the humiliation of the "holy nation" remained.

In the midst of this uncertainty, occasional individuals arose who seemed to understand what Yahweh was doing and why he was doing it. These were people who listened, who filtered out the noise of fads and phobias so that they could stand "in the council of Yahweh to perceive and to hear his word" (Jer. 23:18). From this vantage point, things began to be clearer. The people's present predicament became comprehensible in light of their past experience. The future also became less obscure. Yahweh—despite superficial appearances—was directing events toward a destination that he had planned. These sensitive individuals were known as prophets.

Prophets: Establishment and Dissident

Alas, the prophets did not agree among themselves. There was, it appears, a consensus among the majority of them. The bands of prophets who had wandered the countryside at the time of king Saul (1 Sam. 10:5) had found a secure base in the royal courts. There the prophets had proliferated. Some of them, such as Nathan in David's reign, had maintained a critical distance. It was no supple courtier who looked the king in the eye and pronounced, "You are the man" (2 Sam. 12:7). Within a century, however, the prophets had become a part of the royal establishment. When King Ahab inquired of Yahweh about the likelihood of success in a military venture, there were four hundred prophets who assured him—falsely, it turned out—of Yahweh's blessing (1 Kings 22:6). The counter-cultural prophet Amos discovered that there were limits to what one could prophesy in Bethel. "Go, flee away," a priest hissed at him, "[and] never again prophesy at Bethel, for it is the king's sanctuary" (Amos 7:12-13). What was welcome in such places was the kind of optimistic message that the prophet Hananiah was spreading about Jerusalem only a decade before the city capitulated to Nebuchadnezzar. "Thus says Yahweh of armies, the God of Israel: I have broken the yoke of the king of Babylon" (Jer. 28:2). Like the other establishment prophets, Hananiah was a purveyor of good news to order, a proclaimer of sham "shalom."

There was also, however, a tradition of dissident prophets. The tradition was bound to be discontinuous, for it depended not on human succession, but on the action of Yahweh's Spirit. But to individuals without strength or connection, with no in-stitutional power base, Yahweh could reveal himself with an ar-resting immediacy that transformed their lives and gave them a message. As Ezekiel, exiled in Babylon, was praying, "the Spirit entered into me and set me upon my feet; and I heard him speaking to me. . . . 'Son of man, I send you to the people of Is-rael, to a nation of rebels' " (Ezek. 2:2-3). As Isaiah was worshiping on safer terrain, the temple in Jerusalem, the Holy One revealed his majesty, touched Isaiah's lips, and gave him a message about waste cities and a desolate land (Isa. 6). To be a prophet, Hosea was intensely conscious, was to be a "man of the spirit" (Hos. 9:7).

What were these men and women of the Spirit to say? They could never know in advance. They were to be alert observers of their own times. Over and over, they are referred to as *watchers*.[1] Habakkuk affirmed this role when he said, "I will take my stand to watch, and station myself on the tower" (Hab. 2:1). Out of their sentinel-like vigilance, at the inspiration of Yahweh, would come a message to the people. "I have made you a watchman for the house of Israel," Yahweh informed Ezekiel. "Whenever you hear a word from my mouth, you shall give them warning from me" (Ezek. 3:17).

The warnings of these dissident prophets were generally bad news. People didn't like their messages and told them so. The people of Jeremiah's hometown were infuriated by his words: "Do not prophesy in the name of Yahweh, or you will die by our hand" (Jer. 11:21). Ahab said of Micaiah. "I hate him, for he never prophesies good concerning me." And he put him in prison on rations of bread and water (1 Kings 22:8, 27).

The dissident prophets were simply not saying what they were supposed to say. They were not giving a religious gloss to governmental policy. They were not promising the people *shalom*. From the perspective of the establishment, they were traitors encouraging the nation's enemies and "weakening the hands of the soldiers" (Jer. 37:13; 38:4).

It was natural that the two prophetic traditions—establishment and dissident—should clash. Their views of the world were different. Yahweh, according to the Old Testament accounts, was not neutral in this conflict. He was on the side of the dissidents. "Prophesy," Yahweh urged Ezekiel, "against the prophets of Israel" (Ezek. 13:2).

The Establishment Prophets

What was Yahweh's case against the establishment prophets? In part, it was that they were failing in the fundamental task of the prophet—listening to Yahweh (Jer. 23:18) and speaking his word. They used the right religious formulas—"Hear the word of Yahweh"—but they themselves had not heard it. Since prophecy was their job and their public duties required them to say something, they prophesied "out of their own minds" (Ezek. 13:2). They were spiritually insensitive. Having "heard nothing," they had no choice but to "follow their own spirit" (Ezek. 13:3). How different was Amos! "The Lord Yahweh has spoken; who can but prophesy?" (Amos 3:8).

Yahweh's second grievance against the establishment prophets was a product of the first. Because they had not listened to Yahweh, they, claiming the authority of his name, were taking his name in vain. "They have spoken falsehood and divined a lie" (Ezek. 13:6). In the mouth of the prophets there was a "lying spirit" (1 Kings 22:22). In their utterances there was a "lying vision, worthless divination, and the deceit of their own minds" (Jer. 14:14).

The consequences were destructive, and they drove Yahweh to grief and outrage. For the heart of his case against the establishment prophets was not that they were spiritually deaf or that their messages were authoritative-sounding lies. It was rather that their messages, by keeping the people from realizing the desperateness of their situation, were preventing them from repenting. And the people, in their lack of knowledge of Yahweh and his ways, were going to suffer.

Assured "Shalom"

The establishment prophets' message was one of *shalom*. This radiant word expressed superbly Yahweh's all-embracing concern for human welfare. In it, everything that made for wholeness was intertwined: health, right relationships, justice, physical safety, good harvests, prosperity, the presence of Yahweh. And shalom, the establishment prophets told the people, was what Yahweh had in store for them.

There may be oppression at home, and the buildup of

Assyrian and Babylonian military might may appear inexorable. But the future will be prosperous and safe. Yahweh has said, "You shall not see the sword, nor shall you have famine, but I will give you assured *shalom* in this place" (Jer. 14:13). Assured shalom, guaranteed by the prophets. How encouraging it is to hear what you want to hear from a supposedly unimpeachable source.

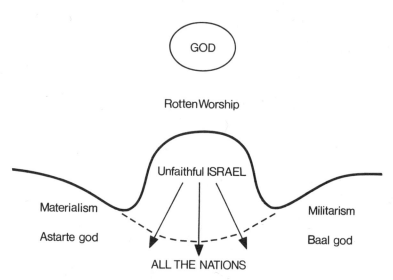

Why will there be *shalom?* Because Yahweh is in his holy temple. "This," they chanted, "is the temple of Yahweh, the temple of Yahweh, the temple of Yahweh" (Jer. 7:4). And his people are worshiping him according to the prescribed pattern. Sacrifices are taking place. Fasts are being observed. "Is not Yahweh in the midst of us? No evil shall come upon us" (Mic. 3:11). There is no need to change course. Everything will be all right.

It was this blessing of human rebellion that outraged Yahweh. Top people of the religious establishment were reassuring "those who despise the word of Yahweh, 'It shall be *shalom* with you' " (Jer. 23:17). The prophets were too complacent to understand what was going on. They didn't realize how close their nation was to annihilation. They didn't recognize that it had lost holiness (Jer. 2:3). They couldn't see that its institutions and folkways had deviated from "the ancient paths ... the good way" (Jer. 6:16). In their earthladen, compromised confusion, they were not able to comprehend that their decisions had made the Exodus and the Law irrelevant. There was no room in their lives for concrete grace. Indeed, they had consigned trust in Yahweh for provision and protection to the department of religious mythology. The common sense of the nations ruled, and the establishment prophets crooned "*shalom, shalom.*" This, said Yahweh, was healing "the wound of my people lightly" (Jer. 6:14). The prophets were like a builder who treated a crumbling wall by *whitewashing* it (Ezek. 13:11)!

Yahweh's Accusation (1): Unjust Living

Many of the people could sense the rottenness. They knew that their nation was in worse trouble than the establishment prophets were willing to admit. "We hoped for *shalom*, but no good has come, for a time of healing but there was only terror" (Jer. 8:15, NIV). The dissident prophets were similarly scathing, and their analysis was much deeper. Although they prophesied at different times and at different places (in the two Israelite kingdoms), they nevertheless developed analyses of this *shalom*-less condition which were remarkably similar. And they did not stop with analysis. Unless the people repented, Yahweh's judgment, they knew, would break out upon the people in disasters of unparalleled severity. In passionate outpourings, which scholars have called "judgment speeches," the dissident prophets stated Yahweh's accusations against his people, pleaded with them to repent, and warned of doom if they didn't.[2]

As stated by the dissident prophets, Yahweh's accusation

against his people commonly had three parts. The first of these was that his people were *living unjustly.* We have already observed how seriously Yahweh took his people's basic human need of provision. Yahweh's design, which he had stated in the Law, was for a just society, a society in which the manna principles of sufficiency and equality could be realized. It would be a society in which there would be protection for the weak and "there will be no poor" (Deut. 15:4).

But when Yahweh surveyed the people, what did he see? "He looked for justice, but behold, bloodshed; for righteousness, but behold, a cry!" (Isa. 5:7). Once again, as in Egypt, God's people were in bondage, crying out under oppression. But this time they were crying out against their own Israelite leaders, who in theory worshiped the same God.

The leaders—the successors of those who had chosen a king "like all the nations" (1 Sam. 8:20)—were exploiting the poor people. Although it was their calling to promote justice, they were instead issuing "iniquitous decrees" and writing oppressive laws (Isa. 10:1). In their lawcourts they were failing to "judge . . . with justice the cause of the fatherless, to make it prosper" (Jer. 5:28). Indeed, they were turning "aside the needy from justice" and robbing "the poor of my people of their right" (Isa. 10:2).

As the poor people got poorer, they—the top people—were getting richer. Despite the Jubilee-vision of a nation of equal small landholders, the rich were joining house to house, and adding field to field, until there was no more room (Isa. 5:8). In housing, the same was happening. Rich people were acquiring more than one house—summer houses as well as winter houses (Amos 3:15). And the scale of their houses was expanding. The most recent designs provided for upper stories with spacious rooms (Jer. 22:13).

By doing these things, the Israelites were not acting in keeping with some unchangeable economic law. They were breaking the Law. They were departing from their own traditions, from Manna, Sabbath, and Jubilee, and behaving like the neighboring nations who had no salvation history.

Yahweh was outraged by what his people were doing. Yahweh knew that the wealth of the rich was the product of the poverty of the poor. "The spoil of the poor," Yahweh reminded the Israelite ruling class, "is in your houses. What do you mean by crushing my people, by grinding the face of the poor?" (Isa. 3:14-15).[3] If only the powerful would trust him enough to live justly—to forgive debts, to free slaves, to restore the means of economic opportunity to everyone—they would be collaborating with him, for "the Holy God shows himself holy in justice" (Isa. 5:16).

Yahweh's Accusation (2): Militarism

Yahweh's second accusation against his people was that they were *militaristic*. No less than at the time of the Exodus, Yahweh was concerned for his people's basic human need of protection. His design, which he had stated in the Law, was for a people who would trust in him alone for their security. He, rather than a numerous or technologically sophisticated armed force, would be a sure protection for them.

But the Israelites' choice of a king to "go out before us and fight our battles" had changed all that (1 Sam. 8:20). Fortifications, chariots, a large infantry—all of these prerequisites for ancient warfare they quickly adopted.[4] But that was not enough to ensure their security. Since they were only small kingdoms, Israel and Judah sensed the need to form alliances with other countries. Sometimes they banded together with other minor monarchies. At other times they looked to the great neighboring empires for protection.

Although this seemed the height of sense to the establishment prophets, it did not please the Spirit-driven dissidents. They sensed that there was a relationship between the graspingness which led to domestic injustice and the interkingdom rivalries which led to war.

No person spares his brother. They snatch on the right but are still hungry, and they devour on the left, but are not satisfied; each devours his neighbor's flesh. Manasseh Ephraim, and Ephraim Manasseh, and together they are against Judah. (Isa. 9:19-21)

Furthermore, the military hardware and alliances changed the nature of the people's faith. Chariots were tangible. Their military capabilities were obvious. It was far easier to trust in them than in an invisible God. Furthermore, the Egyptians, Assyrians, or some neighboring principality could supply horsemen in a crisis. How many chariots did Yahweh have?[5] So the Israelites shifted the basis of their trust from Yahweh, "their helper," to their own artifacts and arrangements.

Only the dissident prophets seemed to be aware of what had happened. And they didn't like it. Vehemently they proclaimed Yahweh's denunciation of the Israelites for trusting in alliances. "Woe to the rebellious children . . . who carry out a plan, but not mine; and who make an alliance, but not of my spirit, who . . . take refuge in the protection of Pharaoh" (Isa. 30:1-2).[6] Equally forceful were the prophets' condemnations of the Israelites for adopting the latest in weaponry and fortifications. "Woe to those who . . . rely on horses, who trust in chariots because they are many and in horsemen because they are very strong, but do not look to the Holy One of Israel" (Isa. 31:1); "I will cut off your horses from among you and will destroy your chariots; and I will . . . throw down all your strongholds" (Mic. 5:10-11).[7]

Yahweh's Accusation (3): Rotten Worship

Yahweh's third accusation—that the people's *worship was rotten*—was related to the two previous complaints. His complaint was that the Israelites were worshiping him cheaply. Prophet after prophet repeated this charge. According to some of them, Yahweh was ready to take a permanent leave of absence from his people's religious observances. "I take no delight in your solemn assemblies. . . . Take away from me the noise of your songs," he raged through Amos. "But let justice roll down like waters" (Amos 5:21-24). Other prophets, such as Isaiah, were convinced that Yahweh was receptive to his people's "churchgoing activities"—but only if they did justice. "They seek me daily, and delight to know my ways, as if they were a nation that did justice and did not forsake the ordinance of their God" (Isa. 58:2). They performed the right ceremonies (that was commendable). But while they were fasting and purifying themselves, they were doing contradictory things as well: oppressing their workers, quarreling, and fighting (58:3-4). That was intolerable. And then they wondered why Yahweh paid no attention to their divine services.

What was wrong? Not that the Israelites were fasting, but that their fasting had no social significance. It was religious activity without obedience. Yahweh wanted his people to do a real fast: "to loose the bonds of wickedness, to undo the thongs of the yoke, to let the oppressed go free . . . to share your bread with the hungry, and bring the homeless poor into your house" (58:6-7). He wanted the Israelites to *proclaim liberty* to the poor. He wanted them to engage in an act of release and forgiveness, an act of Sabbath and Jubilee, an act of reequalization. If his people worshiped him in the world, trusting him enough to obey his commands even when obedience would threaten their security, he would take care of them. "Then you shall call, and Yahweh will answer" (58:9).

In other situations, Yahweh's complaint was that his people were worshiping idols. He grieved that the Israelites had turned from him, the living God, to bow before images which they had carved and sculpted. He was outraged that idol worship, as practiced by the neighboring nations, involved revolting sexual practices and even ritual burnings of their own children (Jer. 7:31). But the core of his complaint had to do with trust.

To people then as now, trust is central to worship. We worship what we trust—what we, in our everyday lives, rely upon for our basic human needs. "The workman," Habakkuk observed, "trusts in his own creation" (Hab. 2:18). Humans turn to their artifacts and say, "Deliver me, for you are my god!" (Isa. 44:17). The gods of the neighboring nations seemed to be successful. As King Ahaz of Judah explained, "Because the gods of the kings of Syria helped them [in battle], I will sacrifice to them that they may help me" (2 Chron. 28:23).

Not least of the idols' attractive qualities—to Israelites who had forgotten the salvation story, that is—was that they were undemanding. One could worship Baal and acquire the latest in chariots and battering rams. One could worship Astarte and amass wealth without thought of reequalization in favor of the poor. For Baal and Astarte were lawless. Yahweh, in contrast, had given his people a life-giving Law which required them to trust in him enough to live differently from everybody else. So to the easygoing Yahweh worship centered in temple sacrifices, the Israelites found it convenient to add the gods of the nations. In a time when their personal and national welfare was threatened, it was good to have some common sense deities about.

This interrelated trustlessness in Yahweh was the heart of the dissident prophets' accusation of the Israelite people.

> Their land is filled with silver and gold,
> and there is no end to their treasures;
> their land is filled with horses,
> and there is no end to their chariots.
> Their land is filled with idols;
> they bow down to the work of their hands. (Isa. 2:7-8) [8]

Yahweh's "Strange Work"

Tragedy was inevitable. For this misdirected trust—in silver, chariots, and false worship—would have its consequences, which Isaiah and the other prophets called "the day of

Yahweh" (Isa. 2:12). It would be a terrible day, a day of "darkness, and not light" on which "the songs of the temple shall become wailings" (Amos 5:18; 8:3). It would be a day of defeat and national dismemberment. It was not, the prophets were convinced, that Yahweh would act capriciously or arbitrarily. There was moral sense in his universe. His people's trustless actions would lead to appropriate consequences. As Sir Herbert Butterfield observed, the prophets seem to have regarded Yahweh's judgment as "embedded in the very constitution of things."[9]

Thus, those who sowed the wind would "reap the whirlwind" (Hos. 8:7). The evil which Yahweh would bring upon the Israelites was "the fruit of their devices" (Jer. 6:19). Hosea (10:13-14) stated it boldly: "Because you have trusted in your chariots and in the multitude of your warriors, therefore the tumult of war shall arise among your people, and all your fortresses shall be destroyed." Then as now, cause leads to effect. Trust in chariots (i.e., lack of trust in Yahweh for protection) produces war and destruction. "Trust in oppression" (resulting from a lack of trust in Yahweh for provision) produces a society so weak in its structure that it can't resist the crash when it comes (Isa. 30:12-13).

To bring about this crash which would judge his people, Yahweh resorted to the bluntest instrument imaginable. The Israelite mind, even that of the prophets, reeled at the thought. Yahweh's primary means of attaining his purposes, the Israelites had always assumed, was his "holy nation," Israel. But now, through the prophets, Yahweh was pressing into his service the *nations*. Assyria was "the rod of [Yahweh's] anger," his staff, his ax (Isa. 10:5, 15); the Babylonian king Nebuchadnezzar was Yahweh's "servant" (Jer. 25:9).[10] The Persians were Yahweh's "hammer and weapon of war" (Jer. 51:20). To the prophets this appeared to be a reversal of Yahweh's social strategy, and they struggled with it. Habakkuk was amazed that Yahweh would use the "bitter and hasty" Chaldeans to judge the "more righteous" Israelites (Hab. 1:6, 13). Isaiah, on the other hand, bowed before the mystery of Yahweh's action—"strange is his deed . . . alien is his work" (Isa. 28:21).

What was Yahweh's strange work? Not his justice as opposed to his love, as theologians have often assumed. It was more upsetting, more threatening than that—something which (now as then) jars the underpinnings of militaristic nationalism. It was Yahweh's recruiting of pagan nations to judge his own nation. It was Yahweh's holy warring on the side of the pagans (Isa. 29:3). It was awe-inspiring—Yahweh presiding over the destruction of his own holy city, Jerusalem.

Yahweh would not, the true prophets insisted, leave the pagans unpunished for their atrocities against Israel. In these wars there was no guiltless side. Both were in the wrong, and Yahweh would judge the pagan nations for their pride and violence just as he had used them to judge his own nation's rebellion (Isa. 10:12f.; Jer. 25:12f.). But the prophets did not gloat over the eventual collapse of their nation's enemies. They were preoccupied with what Yahweh, using these nations, would do in the immediate future. Against his people's wall, which the establishment prophets had so carefully whitewashed, Yahweh would hurl "hailstones in wrath" (Ezek. 13:13). These hailstones were significant. Up to this time, they had been a means of Yahweh's holy war against Israel's enemies. Now, however, they were a symbol of Yahweh's "strange work"—his holy war against his own unholy nation, Israel (Josh. 10:11; Job 38:23; Is 30:30). The reversal appeared complete.

The Politics of Repentance[11]

But it didn't have to be like that! The dissident prophets were not gleeful in predicting catastrophe. They were realists, noting the direction in which history was moving and expressing Yahweh's condemnation of it, unless. . . . Unless his people would return to Yahweh and to their ancient paths. Unless they

would turn from their uncritical copying of the nations to a
trusting response to Yahweh's call to holiness. "Seek good, and
not evil," Amos pleaded with the people, "that you may live;
and so Yahweh, the God of armies, will be with you. . . . Hate
evil, and love good, and establish justice" (Amos 5:14-15). The
heart of the prophets' message was thus an appeal to turn
around.

The hour, they sensed, was late. Judgment was looming. But
it was not too late. There was not much time, but there was
enough time. Even as late as the 590s, just before the
Babylonian obliteration of Jerusalem, Ezekiel and Jeremiah
were urging the people to turn around. "I have no pleasure in
the death of anyone, says the Lord Yahweh; so turn, and live"
(Ezek. 18:32). Turning would have social consequences. "If
you truly amend your ways and your doings, if you truly execute justice one with another, if you do not oppress the alien,
the fatherless or the widow, or shed innocent blood in this
place, and if you do not go after other gods to your own hurt,
then I will let you dwell in this place" (Jer. 7:5-7).

For the people, the way forward would be the way back.
They would rediscover the "ancient paths" (Jer. 6:16). They
would find living reality in the tradition of the Exodus and in
obedience to the Law (Jer. 7:22-28). As Micah pointed out,
they would find a future in *remembering*. And in this future
they would "know the saving acts of Yahweh" (Mic. 6:4-5).
Their only way into the future was that of trust, of dependence,
of social holiness. In their faithful powerlessness, they would
rediscover the power of Yahweh.

It was possible. Despite the common sense of the nations, it
could be practical politics. When people return to their roots,
who can tell what might happen? Hence the excitement when,
around 620 B.C., under king Josiah, the books of the Law were
rediscovered. When he heard them read, Josiah repented.
Humbly he turned to a woman, the prophet Huldah, to inquire
of Yahweh. And out of his repentance came change. Religious

festivals which reminded the people of Yahweh's saving acts were reactivated. Idols and the chariots of the sun were burned with fire (2 Kings 22-23). Josiah may even have reinstituted the practice of *proclaiming liberty* (forgiveness and release) associated with the Sabbath and Jubilee years, for that is what "doing right in the sight of Yahweh" could mean (2 Kings 22:2; Jer. 35:15).[12] Whether or not he actually proclaimed liberty to the slaves and debtors, we know that, at the very least, he performed acts of justice and righteousness. And this was spiritually significant. By championing the cause of the poor and needy, Josiah knew Yahweh (Jer. 22:15-16).

It was similarly possible to base Israelite foreign policy upon trust in Yahweh. The prophets, by denouncing the nation's reliance upon alliances and weaponry for its security, were calling for an alternative foreign policy. For example, when King Ahaz of Judah learned that the military forces of several nations were mobilizing against his kingdom, "his heart and the heart of his people shook as the trees of the forest shake before the wind." What should he do? Modernize his forces? Turn to the Assyrians for help? Isaiah's answer came right out of Israel's Exodus experience: "Take heed, be quiet, do not fear, and do not let your heart be faint. . . . If you will not believe, surely you shall not be established" (Isa. 7:1-9). If the people would trust in him instead of in their own preparations, Yahweh would protect them. Some years later Yahweh gave the same message to king Hezekiah. The nation's security could not be in the speed of their warhorses or their alliance with Egypt; it would be in an alternative politic of powerlessness. "In returning and rest you shall be saved; in quietness and in trust shall be your strength" (Isa. 30, esp. v. 15).

"Be Still"

Yahweh did defend his people, but on one precondition. Whenever the Israelites—even in the period of the kings— expressed their practical trust in Yahweh by adopting a military policy unlike that of the other nations, he came to their aid. Repeatedly the miraculous themes of the holy war reappeared. There are several examples of this.[13] Let us look at one.

In approximately 860 B.C., King Jehoshaphat of Judah received some terrifying military intelligence: a large army drawn from nations to the southeast of Judah was invading his realm. In the face of this crisis, Jehoshaphat did something extraordinary. Instead of mobilizing all available forces and scurrying to find allies, he proclaimed a nationwide fast. At his summons, the people assembled to seek help from Yahweh (2 Chron. 20:1-4).

When all the people—men, women, and children—had gathered, Jehoshaphat led them in prayer. He reminded Yahweh of his universal kingship and of his saving acts in the Exodus and the invasion of the Promised Land. He then stated the nation's vulnerability: "We are powerless against this great multitude that is coming against us. We do not know what to do, but our eyes are on you" (20:5-12).

In their powerlessness, Yahweh showed his power. As they were worshiping, his Spirit came upon Jahaziel, who encouraged the king and the people in phrases straight out of the Exodus story. "Fear not, and be not dismayed at this great multitude; for the battle is not yours but God's. . . . You will not need to fight in this battle; take your position, stand still, and see the victory of Yahweh on your behalf." In response to this, the king, followed by all the people, prostrated themselves before Yahweh and then rose to praise him "with a very loud voice" (20:14-19).

Just as eccentric as this preparation for battle was the battle itself. In words virtually identical to those of Isaiah to Ahaz (Isa. 7:9), Jehoshaphat appealed to his people's trust: "Believe in Yahweh your God, and you will be established" (20:20). An advance force of singers and worshipers then started off for the battlefield, praising Yahweh "in holy array." At a safe distance there followed the regular army. While the people were worshiping, Yahweh was performing an act of concrete grace: he set the invading armies against each other, who slaughtered each other instead of the Israelites. The Israelites, in their powerlessness, were victors without drawing a sword (20:21-24).

It was events like this which lay behind Israel's hymns, the psalms. Many of them (such as Psalms 78 and 136) retell the story of Yahweh's liberating acts, his acts of protection and provision. Singing a story, they realized, was one of the most effective ways of remembering it. But in other psalms they celebrated the character of the one whom they worshiped. In Psalm 46, for example, they recognized that Yahweh was their source of security, their "refuge and strength, a very present help in trouble." For that reason they did not need to fear, no matter how many nations were raging (46:1-2, 6). For Yahweh was at work. He was busy destroying things—wars, bows, and spears—and he was burning the dreaded chariots with fire (46:8-9).

At this point in the psalm, Yahweh addressed his people and gave them the proper response to his holiness (46:10):

Revised Standard Version	*Good News Bible*
Be still,	Stop fighting . . .
and know that I am God.	and know that I am God,
I am exalted among the nations,	supreme among the nations,
I am exalted in the earth!	supreme over the world.

The former translation represents a conventional Christian understanding of how to respond to God's holiness. Practice has shown that it is a good response. Through silence, believers in all ages have encountered the Holy One. But it is an incomplete response, for it is a private, "religious" response. The meaning of the original Hebrew word *(raphah)* was much broader than silence. Far from being a private matter, the theology behind *raphah* propelled religion into public life, into the midst of human concerns for security. The psalmist was, after all, writing about a faithful response to Yahweh of armies, who twice is asserted to be "with us . . . our refuge" (46:7, 11). We are safe because of the protection which he provides, because of the disarmament which he brings about. It is not surprising, therefore, that the full meaning of the Hebrew word is not "be quiet" but "stop fighting"—even better, "*lay down your arms.*"[14] The appropriate response to Yahweh's holiness is a social response, an act of unmilitarized trust.

Enjoying Its Sabbaths

Increasingly, however, the Israelites of both kingdoms found it impossible to muster trust of this kind. The language of worship seemed distant from their everyday experiences of economic and military cut-and-thrust. In similar fashion, to their common sense ears the prophets' call to trust seemed slightly batty. It was easier, and more reasonable, to do things like the other nations did them.

To the very last, Yahweh persisted in holding out alternatives to his people. When the Babylonian forces were massing for the final assault on Jerusalem, Yahweh sent Jeremiah to make a final appeal to the feckless king Zedekiah. Zedekiah, amazingly enough, responded by repenting dramatically. With all of the people of Jerusalem he made an agreement: he and the other Israelite top people would issue a *proclamation of liberty* (forgiveness and release). Effective immediately, in keeping with the Law of the Sabbath year, all slaveholders would free their Hebrew slaves. A great act of liberation ensued. Slaves went free—until Zedekiah and his friends had second thoughts. Without slaves their lifestyle would be less luxurious. So Zedekiah revoked his act of repentance, reenslaving the newly freed men and women (Jer. 34:8-11).

At this point, Yahweh was driven to action. Over a century earlier, the Assyrians had crushed the northern kingdom of Israel. But the southern kingdom of Judah centered in Jerusalem had continued to give political expression to Jewish nationhood. No longer! Through Jeremiah Yahweh explained his decision. Five hundred years earlier, when he had liberated his people from Egypt, Yahweh had made an agreement with the Israelites: at regular intervals, in Sabbath and Jubilee years, they should reequalize their society by freeing their slaves. The people had seldom honored this agreement. And then, after Zedekiah and his cronies had "[done] what was right in my eyes" by *proclaiming liberty*, they "profaned my name" by resubjecting the slaves (Jer. 34:13-16). Yahweh announced his sentence:

> You have not obeyed me by proclaiming liberty, every one to his brother and to his neighbor; behold, I proclaim to you liberty to the sword, to pestilence, and to famine (Jer. 34:17).

The shattering result, in 587 B.C., was the destruction of Jerusalem. The Babylonian army demolished the walls of the city, burned the royal palace, and reduced the temple to rubble. At the command of the Babylonian king Nebuchadrezzar, Zedekiah's sons were killed "before his eyes." This was the last thing he was to see. Babylonian soldiers gouged out his eyes and led him, in a miserable caravan of Israelite captives, to exile in Babylon (Jer. 39:6-9; 2 Kings 25:9).

The Babylonians, however, did not deport all of the people. Unwittingly carrying out what Yahweh had intended all along, they "left in the land of Judah some of the poor people who owned nothing, and gave them vineyards and fields" (Jer. 39:10). From the pagan nations, and not from their own rulers, the Israelite poor experienced Jubilee. The historian who wrote Chronicles put it poignantly (2 Chron. 36:21; cf. Lev. 26:34): By deporting the majority of the Israelites, the Babylonians had enabled the land to "enjoy its sabbaths."

CHAPTER
8

Hope for the Nation

Jerusalem, the beautiful city of David, a smoking ruin; the Israelite people deported to Babylon: it is hard for us to imagine how deeply these catastrophes shook the Israelites. As a nation, they could look back to liberation from slavery in a foreign country, to the conquest of the land which they believed had been promised to them, to political and cultural power under kings such as David and Solomon. And now they had come full circle. Their power was gone. Once again, in a foreign land, they were exiles. Poets led them in their grieving:

> By the waters of Babylon,
>   there we sat down and wept,
>   when we remembered Zion . . .
> How shall we sing Yahweh's song
>   in a foreign land? (Ps. 137:1, 4)

Where indeed was Yahweh in all this? How could the God of Israel allow his people to suffer and his own name to be mocked? What was the way forward for the "holy nation"? For generations, as disaster had approached Israel and Judah, these questions had preoccupied the dissident prophets. And now—with the nation deported and dispersed—they became questions for the entire Israelite people. Disasters had shaken their sense of national identity. Only if they could find a way into a common future could they know what it meant to be Israelites, members of Yahweh's holy nation.

Not surprisingly, the Jewish pundits and prophets came up with a variety of strategies for their national future. Of these, let us consider four.

Territorial Nationhood

The first and most popular of these was probably that of the *territorial nation*. By his gracious acts, Yahweh had given to the Israelites a land. Recent disasters had distanced them from it. But it only seemed right that, after a period of purging in exile, they should return to the place that was rightfully theirs.

The prophet called Isaiah gave his blessing to this strategy of restoration to the land. Yahweh's method of bringing this about, he was convinced, would be characteristic: as so often in the past, Yahweh would make use of "the nations." In this case, he would employ the Persians, the Babylonians' successor to the status of the world's superpower. Yahweh would call their king Cyrus "his anointed" and give to him an exalted mission: "I will make straight all his ways; he shall build my city and set my exiles free" (Isa. 45:1, 13). Ezekiel had a similar vision. Yahweh's people, in their unholiness, had profaned his name among the nations. But at the right time, to "vindicate [his] holiness before their eyes," Yahweh would purify his people and bring them home (Ezek. 36:22-25).

But it was a long road to national restoration. Indeed, the nation as it had first been constituted could never be restored. For one thing, many of the exiles from Israel and Judah were simply irretrievable; from Assyria, Babylonia and Egypt they had been scattered in all directions. Some of these became submerged in the populace of their new countries; others, even in dispersion, tried to retain their Jewish faith and identity. But, as prophet after prophet reminded the people, it was only a "remnant" that Yahweh would restore to the land (Isa. 11:16; Jer. 23:3).

Furthermore, the returned remnant would not be politically independent. As the scribe Ezra bewailed, "We are slaves in the land you gave our forefathers so they could eat its fruit. . . . Because of our sins, its abundant harvest goes to the kings you have placed over us" (Neh. 9:36-37, NIV). Zealous Jewish revolutionaries such as Judas Maccabaeus, in the assurance that "no one who trusts in Heaven shall ever lack strength" (1 Macc. 2:61, NEB), did their violent best. But with the exception of brief periods, it was foreigners—Egyptians (Ptolemies), Syrians (Seleucids), and Romans—who ruled the Jews who had returned to Palestine.

Scattered Nationhood

A second strategy for the Israelites' national future was that of the *scattered nation*. Out of the realities of their experience, new thoughts about nationhood began to emerge. Could a nation, Jeremiah pondered, be a nation without land? Were there forces—a common faith, a common history, a sense of peoplehood—which were more potent and durable in nation-building than territory? At least as a temporary strategy, Jeremiah seems to have thought so. He therefore urged the Israelites in exile to get ready for a long stay—seventy years—and to make the best of it.

> Build houses and live in them; plant gardens and eat their produce. . . . Seek the shalom of the city where I have sent you into exile, and pray to Yahweh on its behalf, for in its shalom you will find your shalom. (Jer. 29:5-7)

This was a strategy for a creative minority. Even while living far from their homeland, even when their numbers were small, the Jewish people could continue to keep their sense of national identity. For they knew one thing very deeply: they were citizens of a transnational nation, a nation that could be found in many lands. As members of that scattered nation, they would be in a minority everwhere. Therefore they would lack the political power that members of each nation's majority had. But, despite their small numbers, they could use their resources, skills, and vision to make a difference. By seeking the shalom of the nations in which they had been exiled they would discover a welcome by-product—their own shalom.

This strategy was so novel that few of the prophets seem to have joined Jeremiah in considering it. The outstanding exception is the writer of the book of Daniel, for whom this was a major theme. Daniel knew what it was like to be a citizen of Yahweh's nation in Nebuchadnezzar's land. From his own experience and that of other Jewish aliens, he had learned that conflicts of loyalty leading to lions' dens and burning fiery furnaces were almost inevitable. But he also knew that it was worth the trouble. Yahweh's people could make contributions to the pagan nations that no one else could make. And when they got in trouble, surprising things could happen to them if they trusted Yahweh (Dan. 3:27; 6:23).

To the Jewish people, the strategies for Israel's future that we have been considering so far—those of the territorial nation and the scattered nation—would not have seemed farfetched. The former of these represented the professed desire of all Jewish people, whether or not they actually returned to Palestine. The latter, in contrast, required a leap of spiritual imagination. But it was a way of giving meaning to what they were actually experiencing.

A New Internationalism

At times, however, Yahweh inspired prophets to set forth strategies for the nation's future which went far beyond anything that their saner contemporaries could have imagined. These visions could be mind-blowing in their imaginative power. They could help the people see the world—and the role of their nation in it—in a new way. They could deepen their faith in Yahweh. And above all, in a time of pain and perplexity they could give the people hope.

A striking example of this is a third strategy for Israel's future—participation, along with men and women from every nation, in a *new internationalism.* What a thought! Yahweh, through the history which the Old Testament records, had been working on his project—the blessing of "all the families of the earth" (Gen. 12:3). His route toward this goal had been characteristic. He had called real people, Abraham and Sarah, to respond in risky faith; and out of their response he had formed the Israelite nation which had been very conscious of being alone, unlike other nations. Now, however, according to several prophets, Yahweh was planning to take another giant step toward his goal. Yahweh was going to burst the boundaries of nation and race.

How was Yahweh going to accomplish this? By reasserting his kingship. During the period of the Israelite monarchies his royal role had been eclipsed.[1] But Yahweh was now once again about to assert himself as king. "As I live, says the Lord Yahweh, surely with a mighty hand and an outstretched arm, and with wrath poured out, I will be king over you" (Ezek. 20:33). And not only King over Israel. Yahweh will be "king over all the earth" (Zech 14:9); he will be "King of the nations" (Jer. 10:7). He is not merely the savior of his own nation; there is no nation whose savior he will not one day be!

> Turn to me and be saved,
>   all the ends of the earth!
> For I am God, and there is no other.
> By myself I have sworn. . . .
>   To me every knee shall bow,
>   every tongue shall swear. (Isa. 45:22-23)

Every knee, from every nation. Two prophets, Isaiah and Micah, had a vision of how things will look when Yahweh establishes his kingship over all the nations (Isa. 2:2-4; Mic. 4:1-4). From every direction people are streaming toward Yahweh's mountain. "All the nations" are coming, exuberant in their eagerness to study his Law and to walk in his paths. As Yahweh carries out his royal task of judging the nations, the nations are discovering that his Law opens new possibilities for them. No longer are they doing war studies; they are in their factories and arsenals, converting military machinery into tools that foster life. "They shall beat their swords into plowshares, and their tanks into tractors."

This was a vision for "the latter days," but it was also an invitation which had immediate relevance. "Come," Isaiah invited the people, "let us walk in the light of Yahweh" (Isa. 2:5). Because Yahweh is their common King, all nations will find their unity.

The Man

This strategy for Israel's future was shattering in its scope. But how could it come about? How would Yahweh reassert his kingship? By means of a fourth strategy which takes us, as it took the Israelites, into the realm of wonder and mystery, indeed of holiness. Yahweh would send *a Man*. This person would represent the nation of Israel as it was meant to be. He would be a King, not "like all the nations" after the manner of Saul and his successors, but like Yahweh himself. By his life and his suffering, he would show the nation what it meant to be holy. Indeed, by his faithfulness he would enable God's people to be holy.[2]

Some prophets were sure that the Man would be a king. Not only do they give him royal titles—"your king" (Zech. 9:9) and "Prince" (Isa. 9:6); he will also descend from the Israelite royal line, the house of David (Isa. 9:7; 11:10). And like all kings he will be anointed. Messiah (*mashiah*) means "anointed one."

But there would be something strange about the Man, something which would invite people to think again about the real meaning of kingship. The most characteristic title that is used for him is not king but *servant* (Isa. 42:1; 49:3; 52:13; Ezek. 37:24). Furthermore, his anointing would be peculiar: it would be, not by the customary oil, but by nothing less than "the Spirit of Yahweh God" (Isa. 42:1; 61:1). And in neither his servanthood nor his anointing would he remain alone. He would be the first among a nation of men and women, all of whom would be anointed by the same Spirit (Ezek. 36:26; Joel 2:28).

This servant people, following in the steps of the Servant, would point the way for all of humanity. "I will give you," said Yahweh, "as a light to the nations" (Isa. 49:6). And this light would not only shine. In its brightness new ways of dealing with old problems would become clear. When they had called for a human king, the Israelite people had chosen to live "like all the nations." They did so in the ways they sought security, especially in their basic human needs of provision and protection. Now that would change. Through sending a new King who would be different from the old kings, Yahweh would enable his people to turn their backs on the ways of the nations. Indeed, through the riskiness of faithfulness which the Messiah would pioneer, Yahweh would give to his people new alternatives which would be good news for all nations.

Messianic Provision and Protection

When the Servant-King would come, there would thus be change in the area of *provision*. There can be no question of his commitment to justice: the Servant will persist until "he has established justice in the earth" (Isa. 42:4). The poor and the meek he will judge with justice (Isa. 11:4; 9:7).

This justice will not be theoretical; it will be a new expression of an old program. The Anointed One (Messiah) will do nothing less than proclaim Jubilee! He will bring good news to the poor, "proclaim liberty to the captives," and "proclaim the year of Yahweh's favor" (Isa. 61:1-2). According to Jewish writings in the centuries just before Jesus, Isaiah had the Jubilee in mind.[3] And in view of the words that he used in this text, and in light of the story that we have told so far, this is not surprising.

Why should Yahweh, in doing something new, not bring out the original intent of something old? Would not the Messiah be a prophet like Moses (Deut. 18:18)? Would he not bring Israel's earliest traditions to fulfilment by bringing a new Exodus and by genuinely observing the Law? If a human king, in a restored Israel, would proclaim a "year of liberty" so that "none of my people shall be dispossessed of his property" (Ezek. 46:17-18), how much more would the Messiah proclaim liberty in a definitive way! When the people of God put to work the "manna principles" of sufficiency and equality, everyone will see "that they are a people whom Yahweh has blessed" (Isa. 61:9).

When the Servant-King would come, there would also be change in the area of *protection*. As "Prince of Shalom" (Isa. 9:6) he will have a peacemaking agenda of breathtaking scope. Nothing less than the reconciliation of all warring parts of creation—wolves and lambs, sucking children and snakes—will be the goal of his kingdom (Isa. 11:6-8). Where his holiness is manifested there will be fullness, fullness of the knowledge of Yahweh. And there will be no hurting or destroying (Isa. 11:9).

This shalom-making will not be theoretical; it will be pursued by new acts of faithfulness similar to those that we have observed throughout the Old Testament. Thus the Servant-King, like Joshua but unlike David, will smash the latest in military machinery.[4]

> Rejoice greatly, O daughter of Zion!
> Shout aloud, O daughter of Jerusalem!
> Lo, your king comes to you;

> triumphant and victorious is he,
> humble and riding on an ass,
> on a colt the foal of an ass.
> I will cut off the chariot from Ephraim
> and the war horse from Jerusalem;
> and the battle bow shall be cut off,
> and he shall command shalom to the nations.
>
> (Zech 9:9-10)

In the Messiah's kingdom, there will be victory by new means—by humility, persistence, and faithfulness (Isa. 42:3-4).

Shalom through Suffering

And by *suffering*. So far, in stating the approaches to justice and peace, to protection and provision, that the Messiah would bring, the prophets were conservative; they were reaffirming the best in Israel's traditions. In predicting the Servant-Messiah's suffering as a means of establishing justice, however, one prophet, Isaiah, was being radical. There were, of course, hints of this before. Throughout the Old Testament there are repeated references to God's suffering with his people, and to his taking the initiative, unmerited by his people, to bring them life and peace. The story of both Testaments is one of grace.

Now, however, we encounter the Just One, Yahweh's Servant, who would make many people to be accounted righteous by bearing, in himself, their sins (Isa. 53:11). We meet the One who would be battered for their wrong-turnings. We realize that it would be upon him, the Servant-King, that Yahweh would impose the "punishment that gave us shalom" (53:5). In the Person who would bring about shalom, who would introduce Jubilee and ban chariots, there would be not success but suffering. And somehow suffering—as no amount of chariots and battle bows—would change the world.

This idea was almost unthinkable. For good reason it would "startle many nations." Kings especially, experts in conventional ways of managing events, would be dumbfounded; they "shall shut their mouths because of him" (Isa. 52:15). But for those who had listened to Yahweh, new possibilities—for both the Messiah-King and the nation who would recognize his sovereignty by living in his way—would become clear. They would know that it is "not by might, nor by power, but by my Spirit, says Yahweh of armies" (Zech 4:6). This Spirit-anointed Man, Servant, and King, will have the biggest chapter all to himself.

Part III

The New Testament Landscape

CHAPTER
9

Holy Solutions
for an Unholy Mess

Whew! We've survived the long haul of the previous chapters. Our balloon's airworthiness has been tested. And, despite momentary doubts, we're still on course, with our trusty telescope at the ready.

This is fortunate, for we are now beginning the most important part of our journey. After the lofty arc which took us across Old Testament kings and prophets, we are now going to see how reliable our balloon is at a low altitude. For we are going to be looking not across a milennium but at the events of three years. And, despite our low altitude, we shall have to use our telescope and focus it sharply. For our primary interest will be in one man, a man who was obscure and, by all ordinary indicators, unsuccessful. His brief life ended in rejection and apparent failure. But, mysteriously, miraculously, this man—Jesus from the village of Nazareth in the Roman province of Galilee—is the key who enables us to understand the whole story that we've been telling. In him, according to missionary theologian Lesslie Newbigin, "the whole meaning of the story is disclosed."[1]

But what is that meaning? Christians, both learned and simple, love to tell the story of Jesus; but they have often differed in their understanding of him. My treatment in this chapter and the next will not settle these disputes. But I do insist on one thing. Our interpretation of Jesus depends upon more than our general knowledge of the Bible and our spiritual perceptiveness; it also depends upon our understanding of the times in which he lived. We may well believe that "Jesus Christ is the answer," but we won't understand his answers unless we know more about the questions that were being put to him. History is important after all!

To see why this is so, let us take a good look at Jesus' country and his contemporaries. To do so will take a pinch of patience, but it will be time well spent. For some background will help us to hear Jesus better as he spoke to his own situation—and to ours—with the authority of God.[2]

Palestine in Crisis

When Jesus was born, probably about 5 B.C., Palestine had been under the rule of foreigners for over five hundred years. The Assyrians and Babylonians, you will recall, had deported a large proportion of the Jewish people. And when the exiles were allowed to resettle the land of their ancestors, they never again had true political independence. The scribe Ezra who was instrumental in this resettlement was deeply conscious of this. "Behold," he wailed, "we are slaves this day; in the land that you gave to our fathers to enjoy its fruit and its good gifts, behold, we are slaves" (Neh. 9:36). The Israelites, Ezra realized, were back in the brickyard. As the years went by, the national identity of their oppressors varied; army after army trampled the land and empire after empire asserted its dominance. The Jewish people bewailed their bondage and longed to govern themselves.

As Jesus grew up, Palestine was governed by the superpower of the moment, Rome. (Part of it, Galilee, was ruled on the Romans' behalf by client kings, the Herods.) For most of us, the Roman Empire has a good reputation for effective justice and enlightened administration. This was not at all the way that most of Jesus' Jewish contemporaries perceived it. Indeed, in three vital areas of their national life they had bitter grievances against Roman rule.

The most important of these was religion. Sometimes intentionally, sometimes uncomprehendingly, Roman governors committed outrages against Jewish law and custom. The provincial governor Pilate, for example, had the audacity to import graven images—of Caesar no less—into the Holy City of Jerusalem.[3] To the Jewish people, provocations such as this were attacks upon the very heart of their national life; and they responded—sometimes nonviolently, sometimes very violently—with acts of anti-Roman defiance.

The second area of national grievance against Roman rule was that of economics. To the customary Jewish tithes and temple taxes, which by themselves demanded 20 percent of the income of most citizens, the Romans added their own taxes— customs, tolls, and tribute—which doubled the people's tax burden. Only in the best of years could the Jewish small farmers pay 40 percent of their earnings and have enough left over for essential purchases. So they faced unpalatable choices—either to cut corners on their religious taxes, thereby becoming "sinners" in the eyes of observant Jews; or to borrow money, thereby running the risk of losing their lands and becoming "hirelings."[4] Under Roman rule, tax and debt and landlessness were interlinked. No wonder the people were angry. At the very outset of the Jewish Revolution in A.D. 66 , pent-up hostility at the economics of Roman rule burst out. The revolutionaries marched to the Jerusalem Record Office and put it to the torch, destroying the bonds which recorded their indebtedness.[5]

The third area of Jewish grievance had to do with government itself. Roman rule was foreign rule; it was a perpetual
reminder to the Jews that they were being governed, ultimately, in the interests of others. Furthermore, they had
theological objections to Roman government. Yahweh was Israel's rightful King. Never, he had commanded them, were
they to appoint a foreigner to rule over them (Deut. 17:15).
And now they were serving Caesar as represented by third-rate
colonial administrators!

The indignity of all this, and the theological offense, were
compounded by the Romans' habitual brutality. The New
Testament writers give us glimpses of the pain of the Jewish
people. Luke, for example, records that Pilate, in an attempt to
deter revolutionary activity, mingled the blood of Galileans
with their sacrifices (Luke 13:1); we can easily imagine how
much this action, which combined cruelty and desecration, in-
flamed Jewish religious passions. The first-century Jewish historian Josephus gives us a fuller account of a similar episode.
First of all, Pilate, who had a strong practical streak, seized
something apparently useless (the sacred treasure of *corban*) to
pay for something obviously useful—a fifty-mile long aque-
duct. When the citizens of Jerusalem howled their protests, Pilate ordered his troops, in mufti, with clubs under their cloaks,
to mingle with the crowd.

> He now gave the signal from the tribunal and the Jews were
> cudgelled, so that many died from the blows, and many as they
> fled were trampled to death by their friends. The fate of those
> who perished horrified the crowd into silence.[6]

All of these aspects of Roman rule threatened the future of
the Jewish nation. There was also something less visible and
more seductive at work. Roman rule represented more than
politico-military imperialism; it also represented *cultural* imperialism, the imperialism of the dominant, pagan Hellenistic

world-culture (as powerful then as the world-culture today which is represented by Coca-Cola and *Dallas*). To some Jews, tired of the law-laden rigors of Jewish life, the values of Greco-Roman civilization seemed liberating (1 Macc. 1:11-15). And, even for those Jews who found Hellenism offensive, it all seemed so irresistible!

Observant Jews were aware of the dangers of this adaptation. They knew that the spiritual resources of the people were at a low ebb. For centuries they had not had a prophet (Ps. 74:9; 1 Macc. 4:46); they were experiencing a famine—a famine of Spirit, of "hearing the words of Yahweh" (Amos 8:11). What, in their situation, could they do to protect their nation's Jewish identity? How could they prevent it from being engulfed by the alluring ways of the nations? How could they keep from becoming like everybody else?

Part of the answer lay in defining precisely who everybody else was. Around 460 B.C. the scribe Ezra made an important contribution to this definition: he extended the Law prohibiting intermarriage with seven Canaanite nations (Deut. 7:1-4) to include all non-Jews (Ezra 9:2). The Jews called these non-Jews the *nations* (Gentiles), and they had a low estimate of them. The citizens of the "nations of the world," they were convinced, were idolatrous, immoral, and untrustworthy. Intermarriage with them would contaminate the Jews.

The Jewish people even viewed their cousins the Samaritans, descendants of the kingdom of Israel who shared a great deal of common history and faith with the other Israelites, as Gentiles (Luke 17:18). The Samaritans responded to Jewish disdain by erecting an alternative temple on Mount Gerazim and, on occasion, by symbolic acts of violence. In A.D. 8, for example, a group of Samaritan commandos entered the Jews' temple in Jerusalem to scatter human bones, thereby ritually desecrating it. To this the Jews responded with "implacable hatred."[7]

And they built walls. Between themselves and the other *nations* (including the Samaritans) the Jewish leaders attempted

to construct an "impenetrable barrier."[8] A Gentile woman
suckling a Jewish baby? Never, save in the presence of a Jewish
person. Otherwise the Gentile nurse might poison the child![9]
This wall-building, the Jewish leaders felt, was necessary for
the survival of their nation. Only if they were distinct from the
nations could they be a *holy nation*, retaining their national
identity and honoring God by their whole compass of life. It
was through *holiness* that the Jews hoped to survive as a nation.

Strategies for a Holy Nation: the Establishment

But how should they go about promoting the holiness of the
nation? The Jewish leaders never completely agreed. In fact,
during Jesus' lifetime there were two major approaches.

The first of these was that of the religious establishment in
Jerusalem. Priestly aristocrats such as Annas and Caiaphas
belonged to this; so also did other members of the Sadducees, a
conservative religious party. The Sadducees' observances were
guided solely by the written books of the Law. Unlike the
Pharisees, they were not willing to accept the more recent,
unwritten interpretations of the rabbis. Furthermore, again unlike the Pharisees, the Sadducees had no time for relatively
recent theological concepts such as the resurrection of the
body.

In the crisis facing their nation, the members of the establishment adopted a characteristic approach. They were
responsible realists. Through the council called the Sanhedrin
they, on behalf of the Jewish nation, exercised as much civil
power as the Romans allowed them. To be sure, where
necessary, as in matters of law and order and of taxation, they
cooperated with the Romans. But they did so for good reasons.
They cared about the Jewish nation and wanted to preserve as
much independence for it as possible; even more important,
they were determined to protect the religious core of Jewish
life, the worship in the temple in Jerusalem.

What was the alternative to making the best possible arrangement with the Romans? The Romans, after all, were the world's superpower. And if the Jews proved offensive, the occupation forces would "come and destroy both our holy place and our nation" (John 11:48). The holiness of the nation, the members of the establishment were convinced, could best be maintained by observant worship in the Temple. And that required realism and compromise.

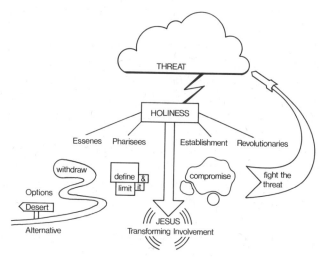

Strategies for a Holy Nation:
Renewal Movements

To the other approach, that of the Jewish renewal movements, the establishment's position seemed flabby and unprincipled. Holiness, after all, meant separation—separation from everything impure. Unholiness was contagious. Collaboration with the Gentile occupation forces was ritually defiling; and the troops were a major importer of the cultural influences that were threatening Israel's way of life. Moreover, according to the Law Israel was to be a nation holy in *all* aspects of her life. It wasn't enough to have one place—the Temple—that specialized in holiness.

The renewal movements could agree on some things. They could agree that the establishment was selling out to the enemy. They could also agree that national holiness must be the focus of the Jewish people's response to the crisis posed by Roman occupation. They could even agree that this holiness could only be obtained by building walls, isolating themselves from all things impure, and protecting themselves against the seductive pollution of the nations. But they could not agree about how, in practice, to pursue this goal of national holiness.

One renewal movement, the *revolutionaries*, had a forthright approach. They were convinced that there could never be true national holiness until one essential thing happened—the occupying forces of the nations must be driven out! John the Baptist's father, the priest Zechariah, may or may not have been sympathetic with the revolutionaries; but in his famous song he expressed an understanding with which they would agree. The Jewish nation could only serve God "without fear, in holiness and justice" when it was "delivered from the hand of our enemies" (Luke 1:73-74).

In the century and a half since the revolt of Judas Maccabaeus,[10] groups who were "zealous for the law and who strove to maintain the covenant" (1 Macc. 2:27, NEB) frequently gave paramilitary expression to this strategy. These "Zealots" do not seem to have been an organized political movement until the outbreak of the Jewish War in A.D. 66. But throughout Jesus' lifetime they represented a tendency which had constant popular support, and which on occasion could lead to insurrections which the Romans had to take seriously. At about the time of Jesus' birth, for example, a large-scale Jewish rebellion forced the Romans to use drastic means to restore "law and order"; they burned the town of Sepphoris, only four miles from Nazareth, and crucified two thousand alleged rebels.[11] In the succeeding years, even when this movement was lying dormant, its strategy for holiness retained its appeal to many. Individuals and small bands of pious rebels could easily act upon it.[12] And in the national crisis of A.D. 60s, there were thousands of people, Essenes and Pharisees among them, who flocked to the anti-Roman revolutionary cause.

A second renewal movement, the *Essenes*, had a strategy for national holiness which was equally clear-cut—total separation from the world. No one, they felt, who was rubbing shoulders with Gentiles and sinners could achieve the holiness which the Law required. So they—the "people of perfect holiness"— withdrew from the hurly-burly of daily Palestinian life and constructed an ideal community at Qumran, a remote spot by the Dead Sea.[13] There they, unlike the apostate Jews who remained behind, shared their possessions and strenuously attempted to keep the whole Law—oral as well as written. By living as a holy remnant, the Essenes had the interest of the entire Jewish nation at heart. They were aiming to remain faithful until God would act against the nations who were polluting his land. Then, when he acted, they would renounce their usual nonviolence and join his angels in the battle for holiness.

Better known than either the Revolutionaries or the Essenes was a third renewal movement, the *Pharisees*. In matters of doctrine and practice, the Pharisees had much in common with the members of the other movements. Holiness was central to their goal for the Jewish nation as well; for good reason they chose the name Pharisee, which in the local vernacular of Aramaic meant the "separated ones."[14] But they advocated a unique strategy for achieving this goal—separation *within* society.

How could they achieve holiness without withdrawing from society altogether? They advocated two methods. The first of these was a strict *observance of the Law*, not only the written Law of the Pentateuch, to which the Sadducees limited themselves, but also the orally transmitted interpretations by the rabbis. These oral interpretations, "the tradition of the elders" (Matt. 15:2), intensified the written Law in two ways. They required meticulous tithing; not only must one pay a tithe upon everything that one earned or harvested, but also upon everything that one bought and ate, in case earlier handlers had failed to tithe properly. In addition, the oral interpretations required strict ritual purity. Contact with anything unclean was prohibited. Indeed, the Pharisaic movement expected its members, most of whom were laymen, to observe the same requirements of holiness—ritual hand-washings and all the rest—as the priests in the Temple.

To this requirement of Law-observance the Pharisees added a second requirement—*selective association*. Of course, the Pharisee must avoid contact with "the nations of the world," the "godless Gentiles"; in the quest for holiness there could be no room for the outsider. But ritual impurity could also result from contact with less observant Jewish insiders as well, whom the Pharisees called "sinners." And of these, people "who do not know the Law [and] are accursed" (John 7:49), there was a growing number.

There were many reasons why these "sinners"—probably the large majority of the population of first-century Palestine—failed to keep the Law. But a major reason was economic. As we have already seen, the taxes—religious as well as Roman—which first-century Jews were required to pay were crushing. Only the better-off could afford to pay them both, and many poorer people stayed solvent only by defaulting on the religious taxes, which were optional. Furthermore, paying tithes upon purchases as well as income could be burdensome, especially for people who, struggling to make ends meet, were in danger of losing their land. As the first century progressed, therefore, more and more Jewish people were, by the Pharisees' standards, manifest Law-breakers. And the Pharisees responded by disparaging them, avoiding them, and most decidedly by never eating with them.

These three renewal movements thus had much in common. In their prescriptions for the national crisis of their time, all of them—revolutionaries, Essenes, and Pharisees alike—advocated a more intense observance of the Law. And this involved holiness as the key to national renewal. Furthermore, all of the movements viewed holiness defensively. The holiness of things, of people, even of God, must be protected from defilement by contact with everything that was unclean.

This sounds like a purely religious matter, but like most aspects of religion in first-century Palestine it had economic and political implications. Economically, we have noted that holiness was expensive; one could maintain one's holiness only by paying taxes and tithes and by engaging in acts of purification that could be financially draining. Only the better off could afford this; and some of the poorer Jews, in their attempt to sustain a holy lifestyle, lost their lands. The result of the cost of holiness was an increasing internal division within Jewish society, between a shrinking number of observant Jews and a growing number of marginal people whom their wealthier counterparts called "sinners."

Holiness also had political consequences. All of the Jewish renewal movements agreed that the Gentiles who ruled Palestine were an offense to God's holy sovereignty over the land. Their very presence was a transgression of the separateness which holiness required. As a category, the Gentiles were outsiders, without hope. "No Gentile," one rabbi declared, "will have a part in the world to come."[15] The pious and powerful Jews viewed the Gentiles as fundamentally different from themselves; they excluded and dehumanized them. The next step was to be prepared to kill them—in good conscience. When in A.D. 66 (about thirty years after Jesus' crucifixion) the Jewish War against the Romans broke out, there were many causes. But not least among them was the Jewish renewal movements' quest for holiness.[16]

CHAPTER
10

Jesus,
the Holy One

Get out the telescopes! For some time now we have been hovering low over first-century Palestine, but we must now focus our sights even more precisely. As we do so, we shall see an outburst of holiness. This came in a surprising form. And no one was more surprised than a Galilean peasant named Mary, who heard this from God's messenger Gabriel about a child which she would bear:

> The Holy Spirit will come upon you,
> and the power of the most High
>   will overshadow you;
> therefore the child to be born
>   will be called holy,
>   the Son of God. (Luke 1:35)

During his short career, Mary's son—Jesus—was rarely to be called holy. It was only the forces of the spiritual opposition who recognized him for who he was, "the Holy One of God"

(Mark 1:24).[1] Furthermore, Jesus himself apparently had little to say about holiness; according to the New Testament accounts, Jesus rarely used the word. Nevertheless, when we look at Jesus' teachings more closely, we shall see that much of the time he was talking about holiness, indeed *social* holiness. Echoing the Holiness Code of Leviticus but with a new accent that spoke into the crisis of his time, Jesus said, "Be merciful, even as your Father is merciful" (Luke 6:36).

Furthermore, there was something about Jesus himself which was holy. Living force, separateness, God-likeness, dynamism—his contemporaries saw all of these qualities of holiness in Jesus. And their response to him was that of men and women in every age to holiness—both fascination and repulsion, deep attraction and dread. Representative of this response is that of his follower Peter. Kneeling at Jesus' feet amidst a deck-full of miraculously caught fish, Peter blurted out, "Depart from me, for I am a sinful man, O Lord" (Luke 5:8).

Jesus didn't depart from Peter. By remaining faithful to him and his other followers, Jesus was schooling them, not only in faithfulness, but in holiness. By listening to him, watching him, imitating him, they were learning to be like him. "Every one," Jesus said, "when he is fully taught will be like his teacher" (Luke 6:40). Their attempts to follow him were often inept. But in them something important was happening. As Jesus' followers imitated Jesus and allowed him to shape their common life so that it looked like him, these men and women were extending the person and work of the Holy One. In fact, they were the first citizens of a new nation—a nation of Jesus-people drawn from "every nation, from all tribes and peoples and tongues" (Rev. 7:9). Through them God would work to liberate the entire human race and restore his creation.

Encountering the Holy One

These momentous developments began very simply. In about A.D. 30, Jesus left his job in his hometown of Nazareth and came to the Jordan River, where his cousin John was preaching.

According to the Gospel writer Luke, God's Holy Spirit had been exceptionally active of late, more active in fact than for hundreds of years since the end of the age of the prophets (Luke 1:15, 35, 42, 67; 2:27). John was the most prominent of these Spirit-visited men and women. When people came to him who really wanted to change their allegiances and lifestyles, John baptized them in the river. But he also pointed them toward the future. Soon, he promised, a mightier one would come who would baptize with something purer and more powerful than water—"the Holy Spirit" (Luke 3:16).

Jesus approached his cousin, asking to be baptized. We don't know very much about his baptism; the Gospel writers' accounts of it are brief. But they give enough detail to indicate that, through his experience at this event, something deeply energizing happened to Jesus. Luke records that "the Holy Spirit descended upon him in bodily form, as a dove" (Luke 3:22).

Jesus, in short, encountered the Holy One. And he did not simply experience a living force. He knew the presence of a person who, as Father, addressed him as Son and deepened their parent-child relationship of trust and caring. Because of this relationship, the words which followed, commissioning him to be a justice-bringing Servant-King, would sustain Jesus: "You are my beloved Son; with you I am well pleased."[2] Thereafter, through temptation and conflict, God's fatherly care would never fail Jesus.

Founding a Fourth Renewal Movement

Empowered by God's Holy Spirit, Jesus began to appear in public in his home province of Galilee. When he spoke to people, others gathered round, for there was something authoritative about his teaching and compelling about his person. Furthermore, when ill and possessed people were brought to

him, Jesus touched them and healed them. In compassion Jesus
reached out to the people. For good reason, crowds began to
follow him wherever he went.

One can understand why his contemporaries were attracted
to Jesus. Even today, communicated by the written word, he
looks at us and addresses us individually, challenging us to use
our imaginations and to enter new depths that we previously
had hardly known were there. His personality, teaching, and
action in an amazing way cover the breadth of human concern.
No writer can do justice to him, which is probably the reason
why so many of us go on writing about him! To say anything
worthwhile about Jesus, one must therefore be disciplined; and
in talking about him as the Holy One I shall be deliberately
restricting my scope. Nevertheless, we will not be able to appreciate how concerned Jesus was about holiness unless we
begin with some basics.

We must start where Jesus did when he first toured Galilee.
The Gospel writer Mark summarized Jesus' message in one
sentence:

> The time is fulfilled, and the kingdom of God
> is at hand; repent, and believe in the good
> news. (Mark 1:15)

It is hard for us to appreciate how arresting this message
sounded to Jesus' contemporaries, for the vocabulary tends to
strike us as either old-fashioned or piously irrelevant. But Jesus'
hearers knew that he wasn't simply speaking about what
people did when they were in church (synagogue); he was,
they immediately realized, talking in bold terms about the
whole of life and the direction of history.

First of all, Jesus was announcing an event. "The time is
fulfilled." NOW! The time of preparation is over; the age of in-
completeness has been superseded. Something is happening
which, while built on what God had done earlier, takes it to its

destination. What is the event which brings everything to a climax? It is the *arrival of God's kingdom*. Week in and week out in their synagogues, the people had dutifully listened to rabbis reading from scrolls the words of the prophets about the future. Yahweh will reassert his kingship and power. Yahweh will overcome all opposition. Yahweh will root out all injustice and heal all unwholeness. And now, as Jesus addresses the people, the scrolls leap to life. God is going on the offensive, initiating a renewal movement of cosmic proportions. Is it true? Are the power and authority of God's future breaking into the present, our present?

If so, then Jesus' hearers could respond to the second part of his message—his pronouncement, directed to each one of them, of a *demand*. Repent! Change your mind. Change your heart. Change your lifestyle! God's kingly offensive will be upsetting firmly entrenched ways of doing things and exploring new ground. If you want to participate in what God is doing, you must be committed to ongoing change. You must also be willing to face risk. As God turns the world upside down, things won't be easy; political, economic, and religious structures will not submit to his authority without a struggle. So if you repent you must also believe. You must respond to God's initiative by living at the edge of the possible—by active trust in his concrete grace.

Jesus did more than announce the imminence of God's kingdom. By his every action he himself brought it into the experience of his contemporaries. Where there was illness and demon-possession he confronted it. Where there were people whom the other renewal movements had marginalized—tax-collectors, the poor, "sinners"—he gave them the token of genuine acceptance: table fellowship. And quickly he began to build a movement, a community of people (some on the road with him, some in their homes) who were willing to take risks for the kingdom which he was bringing.

Holiness on the Offensive

Why did men and women join his renewal movement? Why did they respond to him in risky ways? Why did Peter and Andrew, when Jesus said "Follow me!" leave all their sources of security—their nets, boat, father, and servants (Mark 1:16-20)? Why, similarly, did the tax-collector Levi give up his thriving business for the dicey prospects of discipleship (Mark 2:13-14)? Why did so many women, including Joanna, the wife of Herod's steward, join his entourage and support him with their resources (Luke 8:3)? There were many reasons, no doubt. But none was more important than this: in Jesus they encountered the holiness of God.

All of us, whether we recognize it or not, have a deep longing for a living experience of ultimate reality; and when we experience God's presence personally we can discover reserves of energy and commitment that we did not know we possessed. So it was with the men and women who were drawn to Jesus. In him they came face to face with all four of the characteristics of holiness which we noted as early as chapter 2. Jesus' being was filled with a living force, not only when he was transfigured before their eyes (Luke 9:29) but in everyday circumstances. In the fullness of his humanity, which radiated loving energy, Jesus was somehow separate, different from anyone they had met before. When Jesus looked at people, he took them seriously, so seriously that he penetrated their facades and exposed their inner beings; he really saw them. And they, in turn, saw in him no less than the Father (John 14:9). In this encounter, Jesus was demonstrating godlikeness, challenging and deepening their intuitions of what God is like. And out of him flowed a dynamic power through which holiness flooded into the world in order to change it.

True holiness, Jesus was showing them, far from needing to be protected with sanitary wrapping, was a life-giving force that bursts through all human limits. It was not in danger of being infected by the ways of the nations; it was itself contagious.

When holiness encountered impurity, impurity was put on the defensive. When the woman who had been ritually unclean because of her flow of blood touched Jesus, she knew that according to the rules of the other Jewish renewal movements she would be making him unclean, unholy. Instead, to her surprise and joy, holiness flowed in the other direction! Wholeness, life, acceptance were Jesus' gifts to her, for his holiness was a force for change (Luke 8:42-48).

For good reason, members of the other renewal movements found Jesus' approach hard to understand. Their chief concern was defensive; it was protection of the separateness of holiness. And Jesus, this man of immense spiritual power, kept challenging their rules. As a result, many of them must have experienced deep inner conflict; we know that a number of Pharisees did (Mark 12:34; John 19:39). And yet the majority of them rallied round their traditional convictions. Confrontation was inevitable. Pharisees criticized Jesus' disciples (and by implication Jesus himself) for breaking the rules of purity: they had eaten without washing their hands properly (Mark 7:5). And Jesus attracted their ire by sitting at table with unholy people— "sinners," collaborators, the poor. Does he not know, they asked as a woman washed his feet with her tears, "what sort of woman this is who is touching [that is, polluting] him, for she is a sinner" (Luke 7:39)?

Jesus took the Pharisees' concern for holiness seriously. But he tried to deepen their understanding. It was easy enough, Jesus told them, to honor God with lips and limits; but it was quite another matter to honor God with one's heart. Swallowing something ritually unclean didn't defile a person; it was "from within, out of the heart" (the motivational core) of a person that came all kinds of corrosive filth that defile the world (Mark 7:1-23). By everthing that he did and said, Jesus was attempting to free people from filth *for* love. By his own actions, and by parables such as that of the waiting father,[3] he invited people to experience God's love for them, his wayward children (Luke 15:11-32). If only they could admit their sin and sickness, God would embrace them with healing forgiveness. And out of his love for them could come a response on their part: love for God "with all their heart" which would express itself in love to others, whether they were Pharisees or enemies (Mark 12:30-31).

The Weightier Matters of the Law

Jesus was also concerned to broaden the dimensions of the Pharisees' concern for holiness. It was all right, Jesus granted them, to pay tithes on the most minor foods that one consumed, even herbs such as mint and dill and cummin. But the really important areas of struggle for holiness were elsewhere: "the weightier matters of the law, justice and mercy and faith."

Jesus was convinced that the religious people of his day, by elaborate acts of piety coupled with an unjust lifestyle, were being spectacularly unholy. As he humorously put it, it was as if they were "straining out a gnat and swallowing a camel!" Ceremonial holiness was not that hard for rich people to achieve; it was injustice, extortion, and greed that were the real challenge. And these things, done in the name of holiness, were tearing Palestinian society apart (Matt. 23:23-26).

Jesus thus not only rooted holiness in the heart; he brought it into every area of life. Even into the areas of primary human need—provision and protection. We should not be surprised by this. For we have seen how, in the Exodus, Law and the prophets, God repeatedly showed his determination to form a nation who would respond to these everyday concerns in a holy way. As the one who came to fulfill the Old Testament and bring God's kingdom, Jesus was bound to reassert God's determination in ways that responded to the cries of the people in his day.

The people of first-century Palestine had good reason to worry about provision and protection. For them these were not "issues" to be discussed. They were questions of survival: how can we keep our heads above water in an age of bad harvests and crippling taxes? How should we respond to the enemy who is oppressing us and occupying God's land? If holiness has to do with "justice and mercy and faith," how does it address itself to questions such as these?

Jesus' Agenda

As Luke tells the story, it is clear that Jesus, from the very start of his first speaking tour in Galilee, was dealing with matters of provision and protection. In the synagogue of his hometown of Nazareth, he read an Old Testament text (Isa. 61:1-2) which served as an agenda for his public life:

> The Spirit of the Lord is upon me,
>   because he has anointed me
>   to preach good news to the poor.
> He has sent me to proclaim release
>   to the captives
>   and recovering of sight to the blind,
>   to set at liberty those who are oppressed,
>   to proclaim the acceptable year
>   of the Lord. (Luke 4:18-19)

By choosing this text from Isaiah 61, Jesus was emphasizing that the "acceptable year of the Lord," the Jubilee, which had been important to the Law and the prophets, was central to his vision as well. In a society in which the pious separated themselves from the "sinners" by an economic barrier, God's kingdom would bring "release" and "liberty" to poor people.[4] It would also bring good news to the outsider and enemy. Jesus scandalized his hearers by stopping his reading just when it came to the good part—"and the day of vengeance of our God" (Isa. 61:2b).[5] What right did he have to amputate the prophetic Word? And what gall did it take to point out that God, by making use of a Sidonian widow and healing a Syrian

leper, had bypassed "many . . . in Israel" (Luke 4:25-27)?
Jesus' hearers were furious, for the Gentiles were unclean; they
were cruel oppressors.

We do not generally view as successful a sermon which ends
in an attempt to assassinate the preacher! But in his Nazareth
sermon Jesus, by proclaiming Jubilee and announcing God's
overture to the outsiders, had stated themes of great importance to his fellow Jews. They were themes to which he
would be returning frequently throughout his public life. And,
as we shall see, they were themes that had everything to do
with holiness as Jesus conceived it. Let us watch him as he
developed them both.

Jesus and Jubilee Economics

Wealth was one of Jesus' favorite topics. He was deeply suspicious of it. This was partly because of what it did in society,
creating separate castes of rich and poor. People like Bigger
Barns, Esq., accumulated an unneeded surplus (Luke 12:16-
20); others, like Lazarus, were oppressed because the rich were
blind to their suffering and deaf to the prophets (Luke 16:19-
31). Jesus was repelled by this situation. His heart went out to
poor people, and he had good news for them.

But Jesus was also concerned for rich people. He knew that
their wealth was an alternative god, which they couldn't serve
at the same time as Yahweh (Luke 16:13). Wealth made a grab
at their heart (12:34); when they tried to respond to Jesus' good
news it choked them (8:14). It created a source of security
which, for the faithless, was more attractive than a reequalization of resources which required one to trust in the Father's
knowing care. Small wonder the rich young man, who had kept
all the rules and whom Jesus loved, walked sadly away from
Jesus rather than give to the poor (Mark 10:17-22). For people
like him, people with vested interests in the way things were,
God's kingdom would be bad news. "How terrible for you who
are rich now; you have had your easy life" (Luke 6:24, TEV)!

For poor people, however, there was good news. There was also good news for those who were willing to respond to Jesus' invitation to new life. For God was on the offensive, and things were going to change. Jesus cautioned his disciples that they should be careful how they went about this change; they should never, for example, "do their justice" (not, most translations to the contrary, "practice their piety")[6] ostentatiously to gain the approval of others. But he assumed that they would be doing justice by giving to the poor (Matt. 6:1-2). Life in God's kingdom would be marked by spontaneous sharing and generosity.

There would also, however, be structures for reequalizing wealth. It is not surprising that the Jubilee was important to Jesus. As we have seen, it had been an integral part of the Old Testament Law; and repeatedly the prophets had tried to get God's people to practice it. For someone who came to fulfil the Law and the prophets, a reactivation of the Jubilee would be natural.

But Jesus was not an antiquarian or a legalist; he was flexible in applying the Jubilee. For circumstances had changed since Leviticus 25 had been written; vast urban wealth and extensive Gentile landholding would make a strict application of Jubilee impracticable. Furthermore, the Romans would almost certainly have nothing of it!

So Jesus began by creating a form of the Jubilee that was appropriate to the social and political conditions of his own day. To all, as in his Nazareth sermon, Jesus announced the possibility of reequalization. Of his disciples, those who had responded to the Father's love by stepping out into insecurity and faith, Jesus expected reequalization. Among them, the spirit of the Law would live. In their love for each other they would find ways to help rich people to stop being rich and poor people to stop being poor. Once again the "manna principles" of sufficiency and equality would demonstrate how valid they were.

So Jesus' disciples would lend without expecting in return, thereby helping the poor (Luke 6:34; Lev. 25:36-37; Deut. 15:7-10). In their awareness of the Father's forgiveness of their debts, they would forgive the debts of others (Matt. 6:12; 18:32). They would sell their goods and give to poor people (Luke 12:33). And to their surprise, they would find that they were not only giving but receiving abundantly (Mark 10:30).

Holiness and Provision

But what do these kingdom economics have to do with holiness? A great deal. For in them Jesus was sketching the outlines of an approach to the primary human need of provision in which all four of the themes of holiness come together.

First of all, Jubilee economics will be possible for Jesus' disciples because they have encountered God as a living force—as the forgiving one, as the all-knowing and caring Father. Without this encounter, nothing truly new is possible; with it, everything is possible! Just before he urged them to sell their possessions and redistribute their wealth, Jesus told his disciples, "Do not be afraid, little flock, for your Father is pleased to give you the Kingdom" (Luke 12:32, TEV). Knowledge of the merciful Father banishes the fear that leads to defensiveness and self-protection, and is a precondition of everything that Jesus asks his disciples to do.

Because the disciples know the Father and are known by him, a second of the holiness themes is possible for them—they can take the risk of being different! Their quality of life requires them to take seriously the goal of the Pharisees—separation—but in a much more fundamental way than the Pharisees had ever considered. For the disciples' lifestyle, unlike that of the Pharisees, is to be truly set apart from the ways of the nations. Jesus took this holiness theme, so familiar to the other Jewish renewal movements, into unfamiliar territory. He was not prescribing ritual purity; he was prescribing a radically trusting approach to life. "Do not be anxious," Jesus told his disciples. Don't worry about possessions, clothing, or food! That's what the Gentiles (and, by implication, the Pharisees) do. Jesus' followers are to be different from them. They will give priority to "God's kingdom and his justice", and God, who knows all their needs, through his concrete grace will take care of them (Matt. 6:25-33).

Not only will God take care of Jesus' disciples; he will also reshape them into his own image. As people who have experienced God's forgiveness of their debts, they will forgive the debts of others. They will begin to treat others as God has treated them. And as they do so, they will begin to express a third of the holiness themes—*godlikeness.* In the Law God has commanded his people, "You shall be holy, for I Yahweh your God am holy" (Lev. 19:2). According to Jesus, that command is still valid; his disciples are to continue to demonstrate the life of God to the world. But they are to do so in a specific way. They, in the sphere of economics, are to "be merciful, even as your Father is merciful" (Luke 6:36).

And finally, as they respond to Jesus' message of Jubilee they will experience the fourth characteristic of holiness, its *dynamism.* God is at work; he is on the offensive to change the world. And, when people encounter his persistent mercy in Jesus, surprising things can happen. This was the experience of a leading tax collector named Zacchaeus. This man was rich, corrupt, and quite unsuitable for the company of a Law-observing Jew. So Jesus invited himself to Zacchaeus's house! Sensing God's acceptance in Jesus, Zacchaeus repented. "Taking the message of Jesus quite literally,"[7] he redistributed his goods. Not only did he repay fourfold everything that he had extracted by fraud; he joyfully gave half of his goods to poor people. It was to Zacchaeus's house, and not that of the rich young rule-keeper, that salvation had come. The tax-collector who practiced Jubilee was the "son of Abraham" (Luke 19:1-10; cf 18:18-23).

Zacchaeus represents the dynamic power of God's holiness to

make unjust lives just. Like all the men and women who followed Jesus, his values had changed, for he had a new form of security. It does not appear, however, that he left *all*— possessions, home, and settled existence—to follow Jesus. He, like others who remained at home (Mary, Martha, and Lazarus, Joseph of Arimathea; the ex-demoniac of Gadara), began to live in a new way where he was.

Others, however, heard Jesus call them to leave home and all the security it represented, to walk with him toward Jerusalem. A group of women, for example, put their resources at the disposal of Jesus and the other disciples as they traveled together (Luke 8:2-3). And Peter on one occasion vehemently reminded Jesus that he and the other itinerant disciples had left "everything" behind. Jesus honored Peter for this. But he reminded him that in God's kingdom, unlike many societies, everyone would be a receiver as well as a giver. A society of justice and sufficiency was coming into being in which those who gave away houses and lands and families would receive back "a hundredfold now" (Mark 10:30). Now! God's kingdom was breaking in, bringing relationships of "justice and mercy and faith" which pointed the way to holiness for all humanity.

The Jesus movement had a distinctive approach to the economics of holiness. God's parental love and mercy were invading all of life—even economics. Far from excluding poor people as the other renewal movements did, Jesus gave them the resources they needed to live and a special place in his affections. Furthermore, to rich people he gave the opportunity to change. And to all, he gave structures for a distinctive lifestyle of social holiness. It would be unlike the nations but like God—and a force for change toward the holy city.

Redefining the Holy Nation

Jesus' attitude to physical security was as distinctive as his teaching on wealth. As we have noted earlier, the Palestine of Jesus' day was a violent society marked by high barriers between the "ins" and the "outs." The other Jewish renewal movements specialized in the business of categorizing people. Either one was a member of God's nation or a member of "the nations" (Gentiles). And whereas the former category was select, the latter category was almost as broad as humanity itself. In this classification, even the Samaritans were counted as Gentiles (Luke 17:18). All of them were God's enemies. On his day of judgment he would have pity upon his people. But he would "rouse his wrath, pour out his fury, destroy the adversary, wipe out the enemy" (Ecclus. 36:7, NEB). The members of the three renewal movements lived in constant anticipation of that day.

From the very start of his public life, however, Jesus set his renewal movement moving in a different direction. It was not that Jesus was flattering in his assessment of the nations. He knew full well that "the kings of the nations exercise lordship over them" and built statues of themselves, calling themselves "benefactors" (Luke 22:25). He knew that the Gentiles hated their enemies, prayed emptily and worried about possessions (Matt. 5:47; 6:7, 32). "It shall not be so among you," Jesus warned his followers (Matt. 20:26). He wanted to start a renewal movement, not simply a pious repetition of what the Gentiles were already doing.

Yet in his understanding of God's purposes, Jesus clearly had a special place for these outsiders. One indication of this was his famous statement, "Render to Caesar the things that are Caesar's, and to God the things that are God's." With these words, Jesus ordered his disciples to view Caesar's local minions—the Roman occupation forces—very differently from the way the other renewal movements viewed them (Mark 12:17). Caesar's place was not equal to that of God's, of course, nor was it independent of it; Caesar's authority was derived from God, and extended over only a petty part of the divine dominion. But Jesus was convinced that the Romans had a role to play—a role of judgment—similar to that which the Assyrians and the Babylonians had played in earlier Jewish history. Like Jeremiah, Jesus knew that the *nations* were not simply there to be hated and evicted. God could use them.[8]

From his Nazareth sermon onward, Jesus also continued to draw illustrations of faith and faithfulness from the enemy Gentiles. It was the faith of an occupying soldier which drew from Jesus the barrier-shattering statement that "*many* will come from east and west and sit at table with Abraham, Isaac, and Jacob in the kingdom of God" (Matt. 8:11). And, to the chagrin of a lawyer who was grilling Jesus, it was the enemy Samaritan who illustrated for Jesus what it meant to be a neighbor (Luke 10:29-37).

In Jesus' scheme of things, unlike that of the other renewal movements, the outsider was important. This was in keeping with the way that Jesus was taking the Law seriously and intensifying it. Love, Jesus concurred with the Old Testament writers, was the all-encompassing principle of the Law (Matt. 22:40; Lev. 19:18). But whereas the Levitical Law commanded love of neighbor (that is, fellow Israelite), Jesus catapaulted the love principle across national barriers to culminate in love for the enemy. It is the enemy Samaritan who demonstrates what neighbor love is; and it is the national enemy, the Romans, whose inclusion displays the Father's love and shapes the love of the Jesus' followers (Luke 10:29; Matt. 5:43-48).[9]

Jesus, in short, was not only intensifying the Law; he was redefining the Jewish understanding of nationhood. He stood at the decisive transition point in holy history and claimed God's promise to Abraham for his own day. No longer did "all the families of the earth" need to wait to claim their blessing (Gen. 12:3). To them, the *nations*, Jesus was opening the possibility of being part of *God's holy nation*. The new covenant would not be for insiders; it would be for "many" (Matt. 26:28).

Through this decisive breakthrough, Jesus ended the era of the holy war. No longer would it be an appropriate means of protecting the purity of God's nation. God's nation, Jesus was implying, is a missionary body; its members are being drawn from the citizens of all nations. The outsider can no longer be seen as someone fundamentally different from oneself who may be sacrificed for the purity of the nation. For the outsider is a potential insider, a potential brother or sister. To protect the holiness of God's expanding, missionary nation, the old methods would no longer do.[10]

Holiness and Protection

The holiness of God's nation would now come to be preserved, not by killing national enemies but by loving them. We have already seen that Jesus had claimed, in the area of provision/economics, that holiness is a social reality. His approach to the area of protection was similar. Indeed, in a compact but powerful passage in the Sermon on the Mount (Matt. 5:43-48), the four holiness themes dovetail beautifully.[11]

Why did Jesus dare to command his followers to love their enemies? Because they had experienced the first theme of holiness—God's *living force*. At the time of his baptism, Jesus in the Spirit had encountered Yahweh—the eternal one, the Almighty, in whose presence one takes off one's sandals—as Father. His great security of person and purpose had been rooted in that parent-child intimacy. In Jesus, the disciples have met the Father as well. They have been moved by his acceptance and mercy. He, they have discovered, is infinitely generous: "He makes his sun rise on the evil and on the good" (Matt. 5:45). The Father who gives good gifts to his children, who lavishes on them persistent parental care, and who longs to know them intimately will empower them to do something that goes against all their reflexes—to love their enemies.

Doing something that seems unnatural leads to the second theme of holiness—*separateness*. For the Jewish renewal groups this was the heart of the matter; nothing was more important to them than being different, especially from the tax-collectors and the nations (Gentiles). Both were, by definition, unholy.

Jesus accepted this concern for separateness, but he deepened it. Both the tax-collectors and the nations, he pointed out, acted lovingly towards their own kind, but *only* toward their own kind (Matt. 5:46-47). But in expressing their love the Jewish renewal groups were no different. They were no less selective. This selectivity, Jesus was convinced, was unholiness. The problem with the Pharisees was that in this all-important area they were just like the nations—just like their oppressors, the unholy Romans. Evicting them at the edge of the sword wouldn't make Palestine a holier place; in Jewish hearts the values of the nations would still reign supreme. Jesus' followers would be holy only if they were genuinely different—different both from the national enemy (the Romans) and from their enemy's most committed enemies (the other Jewish renewal groups).

But holiness is not only being different; it is also, in the third place, being *like God*. The Father, Jesus knew, is an enemy lover; the outsider is within—not without—the bounds of his compassionate caring. Be like the Father, Jesus invited his followers. Be his sons and daughters, sharing his family likeness! You will be his children if you are peacemakers (Matt. 5:9); you will also be his children if you love your enemies (5:45). To be peacemaking enemy lovers is not optional for Jesus' followers; it is essential for them because of the character of the Father whose children they are discovering themselves to be. In the New Testament counterpart to the Old Testament command: "Be holy as I am holy," Jesus issued a new holiness command which at the same time was a love command: 'You, therefore, must be perfect, as your heavenly Father is perfect" (5:48). Perfect, mature, complete, undiscriminating in goodness even to the extent of loving the enemy—in this way God's children are to resemble their Father.

They are to do so for a reason, which takes us to the fourth theme of holiness, its *dynamism*. God's kingdom's stance, we have noted, was offensive, not defensive; and God's holiness similarly is on the move, in the world, for change. God's project is a missionary project—the inviting of men and women from every nation into his holy nation. Jesus' disciples were to pray for their enemies (5:44). May they cease to be unjust! May they be incorporated into your people! For Jesus, people as improbable as an enemy Roman soldier were signs of God's project at work. Faith, Jesus knew, was not limited by national labels. And the time would come when *many* would come from east and west to banquet with the Jewish patriarchs (Matt. 8:11-12). Don't kill the Romans, Jesus was implying. For if you do, you may be slaying a person of faith. And furthermore, you will be impeding God's design, in which Romans and Jews will become fellow citizens in one nation.

Jesus' Prophetic Warning

By calling his followers to be "children of peace" (Luke 10:6) Jesus was challenging some of the most deeply held assumptions of his age. Fears about personal insecurity were bound to arise, for protection is one of the primary human needs. If I am loving (nonviolent), what will happen to me and my loved ones?

To this basic concern for protection, Jesus responded as he had in his teaching about provision—by telling his followers not to be afraid. "I tell you, my friends, do not fear those who kill the body, and after that have no more that they can do" (Luke 12:4). Why? Because you have a Father! God knows his children intimately; no detail of their lives, not even the number of their hairs, is too petty for him. Lovingly he holds them in his hand; and, in the age to come, he promises them eternal life. Such love banishes fear and enables Jesus' disciples faithfully, imprudently to follow him into risky territory.

Personal safety was important. But the most immediate

concern of Jesus' hearers was with their oppressed, occupied nation. This was not simply a matter of taste in governments; it was a matter of deep religious conviction. The Roman occupation of the Promised Land, many Jews were convinced, was an insult to Yahweh. To liberate God's land, they would be willing to use any means that seemed likely to work. And ultimately, military violence seemed the only real possibility. For the Roman legionaries were hard men who kept the peace by overwhelming force, and the situation in Palestine would not change until they were given a taste of their own medicine! In contrast to the commonsense logic of this position, Jesus' approach of nonviolent enemy loving must have seemed the essence of unrealism.

Jesus accepted this challenge and met it head-on. The "realistic" people, he was convinced, had got it wrong. The anti-Roman tendency of the Jewish renewal movements would lead, not to the shalom of the nation, but to its destruction. Repeatedly Jesus warned his hearers of the consequences if they refused to respond to God's kingdom by repenting— changing their ideas and their actions. "Unless you repent," Jesus told them, "you will . . . perish" (Luke 13:3,5).

Jesus sounds just like Jeremiah! Six hundred years later, God was once again offering his people a choice. It was a choice between two approaches to the national crisis: a commonsense approach leading to war, and an eccentric approach which Jesus called "the things that make for shalom" (Luke 19:42). The former of these was not what God wanted; war with Rome was not his preferred means of bringing his project to fruition. Instead, God desired that his people arrest the slide to war by repenting and in faith choosing Jesus' eccentric approach, the kingdom approach of shalom making and enemy loving. The way of holiness, God's way, meant adopting a separate, different approach to the biggest political question of Jesus' day. The people could, of course, choose not to repent. This choice would have inevitable consequences. As in Jeremiah's day, God would not protect the people from the logic of their choices. In judgment, he would permit the violence of the nations to suppress his own people's violence. In Jesus' terse words, "All who take the sword will perish by the sword" (Matt. 26:52).

"Weep for yourselves and for your children," Jesus warned the women of Jerusalem (Luke 23:28). For, through military means, God's judgment is coming. Jerusalem—the city of shalom—will be surrounded by armies (21:20). These armies will use state-of-the-art siege equipment. And when the defenders' resistance has been worn down, their besiegers will "dash you to the ground, you and your children within you, and they will not leave one stone upon another in you" (19:43-44). At this prospect, Jesus, like Jeremiah, wept (19:41; Jer. 9:1).

The School of Holiness

Jesus did not, however, despair. For even if the nation of Israel rejected his holy way, Jesus was preparing clusters of men and women who would respond differently. It sounds grandiose to call this a "fourth renewal movement." During Jesus' ministry, its .inner core must have been numerically tiny. Its comprehension of what Jesus was saying and doing, and even its faithfulness, were also suspect. At critical moments its members were inclined to behave in quite unholy ways or to turn tail and run! Nevertheless, among this group of Teacher and students something important for the completion of God's project was going on.

The Teacher's assignment was both simple and intensely demanding. His students were to do nothing less than to imitate the Holy One. By listening to him, watching him, adjusting their reflexes to his, they were learning to be like him. "Every one," Jesus said, "when he is fully taught will be like his teacher" (Luke 6:40). In his "school of holiness," Jesus was preparing his students to be holy as he was holy. By being extensions of his own person and way, they were to be expressions of

God's intention for all of humanity.

Jesus' students would be a community of doers. They were to obey as well as to imitate. In the past, the Israelites, as God's more or less holy nation, had defined itself by physical descent. Its members were "children of Abraham." Jesus, however, was calling into being a people whose membership would be rooted in their obedience. If they love Jesus, they will keep his commandments (John 14:21). They will be members of his family if they "hear the word of God and do it" (Luke 8:21). They will be children of Abraham, not if their genes are right, but if they *do* what he did in faithfully going out into risk. (John 8:39).

Jesus' followers were sure to get into trouble. People, institutions, and spiritual forces which were committed to unholiness would denigrate and exclude them. The cost could be horrendous. Jesus offered to his followers a paradoxical promise. On the one hand, as we have seen, he assured them of the Father's knowing love, of his provision and protection. On the other hand, he promised them conflict and suffering.

Jesus sent out his followers as "lambs in the midst of wolves" (Luke 10:3). He offered them a tradition, the tradition of the prophets, who through their commitment to the word and way of Yahweh collided with kings and priests and, for their pains, were reviled and persecuted and defamed. For his followers, this tradition was to be not optional nor a cause for complaint; it was to be a source of blessing and rejoicing (Matt. 5:10-12). Above all, Jesus called his followers to "deny themselves and take up their crosses and follow me" (Mark 8:34). For them, God's provision and protection thus did not mean the assurance of a happy old age in a Hebron retirement home; it meant that God would supply everything necessary as they followed their Teacher into conflict.

Cleansing the Holy Place

And into conflict Jesus went. Sensing that his ministry was approaching its climax, Jesus "set his face" to go to the holy city, Jerusalem (Luke 9:51). When he eventually entered the city, a crowd of admirers spread palm branches on his path, thereby proclaiming him as potential liberator from "a formidable enemy" (1 Macc. 13:51, NEB). Shouting his praises, they acclaimed him as King: "Blessed is the kingdom of our father David that is coming!" (Mark 11:7-10). Jesus did not deny their acclamation, but following Zechariah's prophecy (9:9-10) he chose a means of transport—a colt, not a charger—that would force people to rethink the meaning of kingship. In God's plan, it is Jesus, not Herod or Caesar or David, who has spoken the final word about how to be King.

Once in the Holy City, Jesus made straight for the "holy place." He had an unerring sense for the proper setting to exercise his peculiar politics, the temple. What he found there cut him to the quick; it was a denial of holiness as he had been teaching it. He found, in the first place, economic injustice. Jesus does not seem to have objected to the buying and selling in the temple. People had to have properly purified animals for their sacrifices. And since Roman coins, which had idolatrous images on them, were obviously unsuitable for temple transactions, a special temple currency needed to be obtained at the temple *bureau de change*. But under the guise of protecting the temple's "holy" separateness, the temple businessmen were fleecing the poor. Despite the elaborate gestures at purity, this was just like the business world outside; and it was utterly unlike the God, in whose name it was done, who demonstrates his holiness by providing for the weak. Placing himself in the prophetic tradition, the outraged Jesus quoted from Jeremiah: the temple authorities had made the holy place "a den of robbers" (Jer. 7:11; Mark 11:17).

Jesus' second objection had to do with the location of all the buying and selling—the court of the nations (Gentiles). Of course, the transactions had to take place somewhere; but when the animals' cages and sellers' tables sprawled out, the precious space reserved for the outsider was diminished. God's holy purpose, Jesus was convinced, was to include the out-sider—the enemies were to be loved, the nations were to be brought in. But here, in Israel's holy place, in the interests of holiness, the outsiders were being squeezed out. Quoting from Isaiah, the infuriated Jesus proclaimed, "My house shall be called a house of prayer for all the nations" (Isa. 56:7; Mark 11:17).

But Jesus did more than quote the prophets. He took the offensive! This unholy place, in whose "holy" ceremonies Jewish people of all parties were trusting for their security, must be made holy. So Jesus, brandishing a whip of cords, evicted the animal vendors and money-changers.[13] Coins clanked on the ground; animals squawked and lowed (John 2:14-15). God, Jesus knew, wanted more than ritual holiness. He wanted *social holiness*. Just like Jeremiah, Jesus knew that liturgical observances would not protect the nation; it would do no good to chant "this is the temple of the Lord, the temple of the Lord, the temple of the Lord." Only if the temple was a place where people could "truly execute justice one with another" would it be a place of holiness (Jer. 7:4-5).

Jesus in the Least Holy Place

That did it. The top people had had enough. For some time, the religious establishment had been severely irritated by Jesus. Now their patience snapped. They were afraid of Jesus; the strange authority of his holiness, which attracted some, was repellent to them. And now, after the uproar in the temple, they had a perfect excuse to destroy Jesus (Mark 11:18). So they began to negotiate with members of other Jewish groups with whom they were usually at loggerheads.

Playing on the guilty outrage of otherwise antagonistic groups, the leaders of the establishment formed an alliance to silence Jesus once and for all. Among the Pharisees, they found people whose pretensions to holiness had been so searchingly exposed by Jesus that they were ready to join—even with the establishment—to get rid of him (Matt. 23). So also were members of the revolutionary underground, who had given up their hope that Jesus would be a king who would evict the Romans. Even the common people, with whose predicament Jesus had had such sympathy, turned against him. When Pilate offered to release to them one person—Barabbas, who had been imprisoned "for a rising that had taken place in the city, and for murder," or Jesus—the people chose the liberator whom they could understand (Luke 23:19, NEB).

So Jesus was taken to the place of ultimate defilement—the Place of the Skull—to be executed. Nailing people to trees until they died of bleeding and exposure was the most cruel form of capital punishment known to the ancient world. For Jewish people it also was a sign of the absolute opposite of holiness. As the Old Testament Law decreed, "a hanged man is accursed by God" (Deut. 21:23). Mournful followers, mostly women, surrounded the Holy One as he slowly died. Other bystanders mocked him. "He trusts in God; let God deliver him now," unleashing the angelic forces of holy war (Matt. 27:43). Jesus refused. Somehow, amidst his exhaustion and delirium, he focused his attention on his enemies: "Father, forgive them, for they do not know what they are doing" (Luke 23:34, NIV). And then, the victim of injustice and exclusion, he died.

The New Exodus

At that very moment, when the Holy One "yielded up his spirit" in the least holy place, momentous if invisible things were happening. As Christians—Jews and Gentiles alike—later came to realize, the punishment which had killed Jesus was life-giving for them. Because he had borne their sins, they had been accounted just. His blood had been poured out for "many"—for all people (Isa. 53:5, 11; Matt. 26:27-28; John 11:32).

Visible and terrifying things were happening as well. An earthquake rocked the holy city. In the heart of its religious life, the temple, there was a monumental ripping sound as the vast curtain—which enclosed the "holy of holies"—was split from ceiling to floor (Matt. 27:51). And at the Place of the Skull an outsider—the commander of the Roman execution squad, no less—made the statement which was the culmination of Jesus' story: "Truly this man was the Son of God!" (Mark 15:39, NIV).

Almost the culmination, that is. For strange things continued to happen. Two days later, Jesus, in bodily form, began to appear to his disciples, first of all to the women. Soon he appeared to the men as well. As two of his followers walked to the nearby village of Emmaus, Jesus joined them on the road (Luke 24:13-35). They were, they admitted, bitterly disappointed, because the "prophet mighty in deed and word" had not, as they had hoped, liberated Israel. Jesus listened patiently to their story. And then, "beginning with Moses and all the prophets," he began to give them new glasses with which to read the Old Testament.

Why did he begin with Moses? It was no accident that Jesus started there. For the Exodus, in which Moses played such a central role, was the foundational event of Israel's history. The Exodus, in fact, gave the Israelites their sense of national identity. And thereafter the Jewish people kept looking back to the Exodus. In dark times it served them both as a reference standard for their departure from God's way and as a source of hope. And in the future the Jewish people were sure that God would do it again. As one scholar has commented, they were convinced that "all of God's redemptive acts [would] follow the pattern of the Exodus."[14]

The new Exodus: an earthshaking conclusion! But as Jesus' followers met with him during his resurrection appearances, it all fell into place for them. They heard him interpreting the Hebrew Scriptures and broadening their comprehension of the kingdom of God. They realized that they were experiencing, through Jesus' life, death, and resurrection, nothing less than

liberation—the promised *new Exodus*. That, the Gospel writer
Luke was informed, is what Jesus discussed with Moses and
Elijah on the mount of his transfiguring: nothing less than the
Exodus (departure) "which he was to accomplish at Jerusalem"
(Luke 9:31).

Between the new Exodus and the old there were crucial differences. In the new Exodus, like the old, there were miracles;
but in the new Exodus these were not to torture but to heal, not
to coerce but to invite. Even more important, both Exoduses
came to a climax with the deaths of eldest sons. But whereas in
the old Exodus these were deaths of sons of countless Egyptian
fathers, in the new Exodus there was only one death—the only
Son of the Father who loved the world so much.

In other ways, however, the new Exodus was like the old.
Once again God had acted to spring oppressed people free
from hard labor in a brickyard. Once again this was *his* work of
concrete grace. In the resurrection, just as in the battle at the
Red Sea, there was no human participation. Once again God's
action not only freed oppressed people, but freed them to be a
people, to become a nation. Out of Jesus' Exodus, a new Israel,
a transnational holy nation, was coming into existence.

It would take Jesus' followers a long time really to understand what God had done for the world in Jesus. The explora-
tion of their newfound freedom—the "glorious liberty of the
children of God"—would not happen quickly. They would also
face imposing challenges, challenges which would tax their
judgement and their discernment, as they tried to construct a
pattern of common life that would really resemble Jesus, the
Holy One.

How could they do it? Here was the biggest assignment their
Teacher had ever given them. In his farewell words to them
before ascending to the Father's presence, Jesus made a
promise to them. They were to have a new immersion in holiness. Until they had received this they should wait: "Stay in the
city, until you are clothed with power from on high" (Luke

24:49). And when that power was unleashed, who could foretell what breakthroughs would occur when social holiness was unleashed on the world?

CHAPTER
11

Holy Ones:
Breakthroughs

Hold tight! After flying low, which we've had to do to take a close look at Jesus of Nazareth, we may find it takes our breath when our balloon soars high again. But we've got to increase our altitude, because once again we need a broader perspective. The holiness which we saw in Jesus' life was not something just for him. God wanted others to experience it too. And when they did so, remarkable things happened. People changed their ideas, jettisoned their old securities. Some of them began to travel, carrying good news, not just for Jews, but for everyone in the Roman Empire. To watch these things happen, we've therefore got to fly high—high enough to overlook Rome as well as Jerusalem.

What were these people saying as they scattered out across the empire? They were saying things which, to dispassionate observers at the time, were incredible, even scandalous. They were saying that Jesus of Nazareth, so recently crucified as a criminal, was living. They had seen him, touched him, been touched by him (1 John 1:1). After forty days of physical contact with him, they had watched him ascend into the clouds. But he had not departed into irrelevance. This crucified man was "Lord and Messiah" (Acts 2:36), both God and the king that Israel had been waiting for. Far from diminishing his authority, his ascension increased it by making it universal. Jesus was Lord, Lord of all, to whom everyone owed obedience (Phil. 2:11).

But Jesus was not a distant Lord. As he prepared to leave his followers, he had given them a promise. He would not leave them orphans; he would come back to them. Through the same Holy Spirit who had descended upon him at his baptism, he would equip them with the power of holiness, reminding them of his teaching, and enabling them to follow him into conflict (John 14:18, 27; 15:26).

Jesus kept his promise. Through the Spirit his followers experienced the living force of God's holiness. They knew that the Holy Spirit was remaking them. They were different now; in fact, they were convinced that they were coming to resemble Jesus. "Being changed into his likeness from one degree of glory to another" is how one of them put it (2 Cor. 3:18). Others noticed the difference as well. This nondescript bunch exuded the character of Jesus (Acts 4:13).

No longer were they uncertain about who Jesus was. He, they declared, was God's Holy One (Acts 3:14; Rev. 3:7). And they, in turn, were confident in their own status. Repeatedly using the same Greek word for themselves that they used for him, they boldly called themselves "holy ones." If Jesus was "the Saint," they were "the saints."[1] They knew that their "saintliness" was closely linked to his. For they realized that there could be no holiness that was not in keeping with Jesus. His teaching, his character—these were the standards for holy living.

Jesus' followers not only knew who they were; they also had a strong sense of group identity. In view of their diverse social origins, this is remarkable. But just as Jesus had managed to find common ground for incompatibles to stand on, so also the communities of his followers gave dignity to outsider as well as insider, to weak as well as strong. Under Jesus' all-embracing lordship, there was room for non-Jews as well as Jews, women as well as men, slaves as well as free—even for the proverbially wild "Scythians" (Col. 3:11).

And whatever their individual origin, in the Messiah Jesus they sensed that they together had inherited a momentous calling. They were to be nothing less than God's "holy nation" (1 Pet. 2:9). In them God was keeping a promise which he had made many centuries earlier through Isaiah; he was forming a new, transnational nation that would be "a light for the nations" (Isa. 49:6; Acts 13:47; 26:23).

Life for this new "holy nation" would not be easy. The Exodus which they had experienced through Jesus' death had brought them freedom and forgiveness. That was exhilarating. But it had also brought them into the wilderness of change. All kinds of questions must have popped into their minds. If they were not to live like the other nations, how then were they to live? What did it mean, in the society of Ephesus or Rome, to be holy as Jesus was holy?

As they tried to answer these questions, the Holy Spirit led them. Sometimes he did so by calling to mind a teaching of Jesus, or a passage in the Hebrew Scriptures, that spoke directly to their situation. At other times he acted immediately, miraculously, achieving breakthroughs which newly demonstrated the relevance of Jesus' holiness. By this stage of our story, we will not be surprised to learn that several of these breakthroughs have to do with the primary human needs of provision and protection.

Nor will we be be surprised that these breakthroughs, and the Jesus movement that was empowered by them, led to conflict. Unappreciative people whose oppression was being exposed accused them of turning "the world upside down"

(Acts 17:6). The "holy ones" themselves were aware that they, although "mere nothings," had been empowered by God "to overthrow the existing order" (1 Cor. 1:28, NEB). They knew that God's kingdom was on the offensive; it was a force for change toward the holy city. And as the kingdom came, Jesus' followers would have to live in new ways, trusting actively in God's concrete grace. It was exciting business, and intensely risky. Let us lower our balloon as the breakthroughs take place and then fire the burners to soar up for an overview.

Jubilee on Pentecost

It was fifty days after the Jewish Passover. During the first forty of these Jesus had appeared regularly to his followers, teaching them about God's kingdom (Acts 1:3). But now, ten days after his ascension, his followers were gathered together to celebrate the Jewish Feast of Weeks.

"Suddenly a sound came from heaven like the rush of a mighty wind," and the Spirit's first breakthrough was underway (Acts 2:2). Firelike tongues rested on their heads, and, as Jesus had promised, they were enveloped in the Holy Spirit (1:5; 2:3). As they experienced the living force of holiness something expansive, propulsive was happening. The holiness which they were experiencing would not let them stay in the seclusion of their meeting room—it was a force for witness in the streets outside. In the encounters which followed, the Spirit of holiness made the Scriptures come to life and gave to Jesus' followers words which touched their hearers' hearts. And people responded. They repented of their part—whether as bystanders or cheerleaders—in Jesus' crucifixion. In their eagerness to "save themselves from this crooked generation," they opened their lives to radical change (2:40).

What was the first effect of the living force of holiness? It was a change in Jesus' followers' approach to provision and wealth. Their life was not only characterized by temple worship and table fellowship, by prayer and witness; it was also characterized by economic *koinonia*—"making things common" (2:42). It wasn't that all their private resources were communalized; it wasn't that their finances were completely managed by an apostolic central committee. But the Jerusalem church was evolving a form of economic life which was radical and new, and which gave social expression to holiness. How did it work?

In the first place, from Pentecost onward the Jerusalem Christians challenged the privateness of property: "No one said that any of the things which he possessed was his own" (4:32). Individual believers retained lands and possessions. But they no longer said, "They're mine!" and insisted on exclusive control of them. Instead they put "their" possessions at the disposal of the entire church. Even after Ananias had given some property to the church, he, like every other believer, could use it. As Peter reminded him, "After it was sold, was it not at your disposal?" (5:4). The hold of economic security upon the believers' hearts was hard to break. But the sudden deaths of Ananias and Sapphira reminded the sobered believers just how determined God was to break it.

Second, the Jerusalem Christians set out to end inequality. When the economic need of some believers became apparent, others of them who had more than they needed sold their possessions and properties and brought the proceeds to the apostles (2:45; 4:34). Out of a common fund distributions were made to needy members. When administering this fund became too time-consuming, the apostles assigned the task to seven others (6:3). Voluntarily, without compulsion but powerfully, a process of reequalization of resources was taking place among the Christians. The result was striking—"there was not a needy person among them" (4:34).[2] Social holiness was good news for poor people.

What was happening here was risky; in its holiness it was quite unlike sensible first-century economic behavior. But it was not an approach so drastic as to be ludicrously beyond the reach of ordinary believers then or now. The Jerusalem Christians did not immediately inundate the city's realtors and pawnbrokers with lands and goods. They simply made their possessions available to other believers. As needs became apparent, they were willing to reduce their "private" property to meet those needs; and as they did these things, they found a common fund to be an indispensable tool.

Why should the Jerusalem Christians not live like this? Their leaders had just spent three years with the Holy One. They had watched him deal with money and possessions. They had heard him as he had repeatedly talked about a style of economics which would be a new expression of the old law of Jubilee. Wasn't it appropriate that they, on the fiftieth day (Pentecost), should do what God had called his people to do on the fiftieth year—make Jubilee? In light of Jesus' teachings, wasn't it fitting that they should experience holiness in the area of provision?

How could they have done otherwise? These "Jerusalem Christians were simply doing what they had been taught."[3] As they did so, they were pioneering a style of Jubilee living that would be echoed, in a variety of ways, by countless of the early churches. Clearly the result was enriching people's lives. The church grew, and they all experienced what Luke called "great grace" (Acts 4:33)—concrete grace.

Enemy Loving in Caesarea

It was noontime. Peter, who had become an influential Christian apostle with an itinerant ministry (Acts 9:32), was staying in a seaside house in the Jewish town of Joppa. A faithful observer of the Jewish hours of prayer, on schedule Peter climbed up to the flat roof of the house to pray. One moment he was very aware that it was almost lunchtime. The next moment he was transfixed by a waking vision.

It was a vision of unholiness. Peter saw a vast tablecloth descending from heaven. On it were reptiles, birds, possibly even pigs. And Peter heard a voice, "Get up, Peter; kill and eat" (10:13, TEV). Peter was revolted by the suggestion: "No Lord; for I have never eaten anything that is common or unclean." "What God has cleansed," the voice responded, "you must not call common" (10:14-15). Three times the vision came back, inviting Peter to break his religious taboos; and three times, despite his hunger, he held firm. What did the visions mean? Peter was not a natural rebel; reflexively he obeyed the Law. Were not its regulations means which God had given to his people to protect them from "commonness," the ways of the nations?

Peter's rooftop musings were interrupted by a shout from the street below. "Is this where Simon called Peter is staying?" As he peered over the edge of the roof, fear gripped his stomach. There was something alarming about the men in the street. Peter didn't know any of them; and one of them was clearly a soldier, a member of the Roman occupation force which was his nation's enemy. From rumor and personal experience, Peter knew a lot about Roman brutality. His instincts advised caution.

But then the tablecloth visions flashed into his mind again. Was there some connection between them and the men in the street? In recent months the Spirit had been doing some curious things. When Christians had fled to Samaria to escape the Saul-led persecution in Jerusalem, the Spirit had anointed the enemy Samaritans. Peter knew. He had been there (Acts 8:17). Then there was the experience of Saul, that tireless persecutor of the Jerusalem church. A blazing experience of holiness had knocked him off his camel and given him a mission—to bear witness to the *nations*, "that they may turn from darkness to light ... and ... receive ... a place among those who are made holy by faith" (Acts 26:18-19). This had staggered Peter. Was God really going to use zealous Paul, not to exclude the nations, but to incorporate them into the fire that God was igniting to bring "light to the nations" (Isa. 42:6)?

Peter's hurried thoughts were cut short by inner prompting of God's Spirit. "Accompany [these men] without hesitation; for I have sent them" (Acts 10:20). So Peter went down to talk to the strangers. With the men still in the street, Peter stood in the doorway and listened to their message. A surprising one it was, too. Their master, Cornelius, was, of all things, a Gentile soldier, an officer in the Roman occupation forces. That was enough to put Peter on his guard. But, the messengers continued, Cornelius was deeply sympathetic to the Jewish faith; he was a "just God-fearer." Furthermore, he, like Peter, had had a vision. An angel had instructed him to send to Joppa for Peter, to invite him to his house, and to listen to what he had to say (10:22).

How was Peter to respond? For him the stakes were high. He was a leader of a Messianic renewal movement which was constantly in hot water with pious Jewish people. He had taken risks enough already. Why should he compound his problems by consorting with Gentiles—enemy soldiers at that? He would certainly become ritually defiled, and who could predict what fate would befall him among the Roman legionnaires?

Remembering his visions, Peter pondered the matter. Then he took a risk. Making one of the pivotal decisions in holy history, Peter invited the messengers to be his guests (10:23). And the next morning, along with some members of the Joppa congregation, he set out on the two-day walk to the Roman city of Caesarea, where Cornelius—along with the Roman procurator and countless soldiers—was stationed.

In Caesarea, things quickly came to a head. In eager expectation, Cornelius had prepared for the event by inviting his relatives and close friends (many of them probably soldiers). Peter had also prepared himself. He had prayed about his vision and had concluded that God wanted to break through the barriers of holiness. No longer could any person be called "common or unclean"; no longer could any nation be viewed as outside the boundaries of God's nation (10:28). After listening to Cornelius's story, Peter in some detail told him and his friends the good news of Jesus. He, the Jewish Messiah, is Lord of all! (10:36).

While Peter was speaking, the power of holiness interrupted him. The Holy Spirit fell on everyone there. The Jewish Christians who were with Peter were amazed (and possibly alarmed) by this, but the evidence before them was beyond dispute. In the Spirit the outsiders were praising God and speaking in tongues. Enemy outsiders! Peter knew what he had to do. Recognizing the initiative of God's holiness, he commanded that his nation's enemies be baptized into God's holy nation (10:44-48).

From his past experience, Peter knew that when God reveals his holiness things change. On Pentecost God had led his people to practice Jubilee. And now, in Caesarea, he was leading them to pioneer in another area—by including the outsiders, by loving their enemies. How ironic of God to choose the most fearful of outsiders, an enemy officer, to make his point!

A Nation of Exiles

In the episodes in Joppa and Caesarea, God may have made his point. But to people further away, in Jerusalem, for example, it seemed less clear. We have focused our telescope on the breakthroughs, but we cannot continue to follow the story in detail. Instead, our balloon must zoom upward so we can get a general impression of what was going on. From a greater height we can observe further breakthroughs, such as Paul and Barnabas's decision, "Behold, we are turning to the nations" (Acts 13:46). We can also take note of the conference in Jerusalem, in which Paul and the Jerusalem leaders (including Peter) struggled long and hard about the composition of God's nation (Gal. 2:9-10; Acts 15).

Through the struggle—and there was a great deal of it— something new was emerging. Peter himself expressed it best in a letter that he wrote from Rome to congregations in Asia Minor (now northwestern Turkey). Some of the recipients of Peter's letter were Jewish in race and heritage; rather more of them were non-Jewish. But together they were forming something new.

> You are a chosen race, a royal priesthood, a holy nation, God's own people.... Once you were no people but now you are God's people. (1 Pet. 2:9-10)

In these congregations, as in many places in the Mediterranean world, Jews and Gentiles were coming together to be something that, before Jesus, the Jews alone had been—"a holy nation." Indeed, they had now become a multiethnic "chosen race." Despite their differences, in Jesus Christ they were one people, "fellow citizens . . . [in] the household of God" (Eph. 2:19). But "God's people," as he was now shaping their life, would not have a national life like other nations. In their "holiness" they would be pretty unusual.

For one thing, they would not have a land. They were called to be a *scattered nation,* to live in "dispersion" (1 Pet. 1:1). When Peter used this term, it was by no means a new one. In the centuries since the great deportations which ended the monarchies of Israel and Judah, countless Jews had lived away from their land, in what they called "the diaspora." Many Jewish people in time adjusted to this scattered existence; and Jeremiah, as we have noticed, had seen this as a way forward (Jer. 29:5-7). But for most people diaspora living seemed to be something second best. A nation needs its land.

For the members of God's "holy nation" in Jesus Christ, however, diaspora living would be normal. Wherever Christians lived, they would be "aliens and exiles" (1 Pet. 2:11). Like Abraham and Sarah, they would be "strangers and exiles on the earth" (Heb. 11:13). Everywhere they would be at home, but nowhere would they be fully at home. For they would be "seeking a homeland," anticipating a better country, looking for "the city which is to come" (Heb. 11:14-16; 13:14). As Paul put it, they would be "citizens of heaven" (Phil. 3:20 NEB).

God's holy people, having experienced a new Exodus in Jesus, would be a nation in the wilderness. Until God's kingdom comes fully, they will not have a land. But as an unencumbered nation, they are uniquely equipped to be a nation on the move, taking risks, achieving breakthroughs. In this new nation, it is not only Jew and non-Jew who have found equal status; it is slave and free, male and female (Gal. 3:28). For them, God their King has prepared a way of living that will be holy—different from the nations among whom they will be living. As Peter admonished his friends in Asia Minor, "Maintain good conduct among the nations" (1 Pet. 2:12).

This conduct, by the standards of the nations, will be unusual. According to both Paul and Peter, it is characterized by a resolute *refusal to conform* to the ways of the nations. "Do not be conformed to this world," Paul urged the Roman Christians, "but be transformed by the renewal of your mind, that you may prove what is the will of God, what is good and acceptable and perfect" (Rom. 12:2). Instead of the idea of perfection, Peter used the language of holiness.

> As obedient children, do not be conformed to the passions of your former ignorance, but as he who called you is holy, be holy yourselves in all your conduct. (1 Pet. 1:14-15)

In *all* your conduct. Peter and Paul, like their Master Jesus, had a vision of holiness that would encompass all of life. They had learned how this worked out in the crucial areas of provision (Jubilee economics) and protection (enemies become insiders). Let us watch as this nation of aliens and exiles develops its holy lifestyle, deviant as Jesus was deviant.

Holy Ones:
Living Like Jesus

Throughout the Roman Empire, the early churches were true to the tradition of sharing which the Holy Spirit had begun in Jerusalem on Pentecost. It was a pattern of life which they saw as an expression of their conformity to the Holy One, Jesus. In the areas of primary human need—provision and protection—what was their life like?

To begin with, the early Christians, like the dissident prophets of the Old Testament, were severely critical of rich people. In this, James, the leader of the church in Jerusalem, was most severe. Judgment was about to come on the rich. "Come now, you rich, weep and howl for the miseries that are coming upon you." They had become wealthy by unjust means—by underpaying their workers and cheating their farm laborers. As in the Exodus, the Lord had heard the cries of poor people and was about to come to end their exploitation (James 5:1-6). Paul's warnings were also urgent. He was keenly aware of what wealth would do to rich people; it would ensnare them with its allurements, plunging them to destruction. For "the love of money is the root of all evils" (1 Tim. 6:9-10).

For these early Christians, the word that best expressed the problem that they were facing was *pleonexia*, which has generally been translated "covetousness" or "greed." They had learned to be concerned about this from Jesus himself. "Watch out!" he had cautioned his disciples. "Be on your guard against all kinds of greed; a man's life does not consist in the abundance of his possessions" (Luke 12:15, NIV). If the Holy One had warned against covetousness, the holy ones—saints—must try to root it out of their lives.

But what was covetousness, and how did it work? At its core, covetousness was discontent. It was wanting more than was necessary. It was a craving that took on a spiritual force and became an alternate god. "Covetousness," Paul stated matter-of-factly, "is idolatry" (Col. 3:5; Eph. 5:5). In its discontent, it destroys people. It shatters their relationship with God. It also disfigures their relationships with other people: it takes from them what is theirs (see 2 Cor. 9:5); it defrauds them (1 Thess. 4:6). For good reason, Paul brackets covetous people with robbers (1 Cor. 5:9-10).

In the early Christian communities, there was a revulsion at covetousness. Covetous people, Paul was convinced, would have no inheritance in the kingdom of God (1 Cor. 6:10). For covetousness was as likely to blow them off the kingdom course as sexual immorality. Both were therefore matters on which the church would exercise its discipline (1 Cor. 5:9-11). Just as much as in sexual matters, the attitude to possessions is an area in which God wants his holy ones to be sanctified, to be unlike the nations (1 Thess. 4:3-7). He wants them to be economically holy.

Economic Holiness

God's economic program for his holy ones was based on two principles. The early Christians knew that these were not new ideas. They heard about them in the stories and teachings that they kept repeating about their Master, Jesus. But it is clear that at least one of them, Paul, traced these principles much farther back—to the Exodus. For God had not given up on his "manna principles". Sufficiency and equality, contentment and sharing—these were the basis of the economic life of the early Christians.

Contentment *(autarkia)* was the believers' antidote to covetousness. It was not a position of poverty or need; it was a position of enough.[1] Contentment was God's two-handed provision, both for the individual and for the neighbor. "If we have food and clothing," Paul wrote, "with these we shall be content" (1 Tim. 6:8). But not just enough of these basics for oneself; there must also be enough to give. The reason to work, according to Paul, is to "be able to give to those in need" (Eph. 4:28). God meant his people to "have enough of everything [so that they] may provide in abundance for every good work" (2 Cor. 9:8). Contentment was a road to freedom: "Keep your life free from love of money, and be content with what you have" (Heb. 13:5). And God's people could live in the freedom of this enough-ness because of a reality that he had shown them since the Exodus. To the early Christians, God renewed the promise that he had made to Joshua as he headed into the uncharted terrain of the wilderness: "I will never fail you nor forsake you" (Josh. 1:5; Heb. 13:5). Because God was a faithful provider, the believers would be free to live a risky life of contentment in sufficiency.

But not a life of *self*-sufficiency. When pagan Greeks used the word "autarkia" (contentment) they meant an individual possessing resources enough to stand alone.[2] But the postresurrection disciples of Jesus knew that they could only experience contentment in sufficiency if they also were committed to a second principle—*koinonia*. This Greek word, often translated "sharing" or "fellowship," means "making common." All Christians knew koinonia in the gospel; they had fellowship in spiritual blessings, in Christ's sufferings, in the Holy Spirit, in their eucharistic meals, in their common life with other believers.[3] Clearly, koinonia was a many-faceted reality which enriched all aspects of the early Christians' life.

It was only natural that koinonia had to do with economics as well. Fully a third of the occurrences of the word in the New Testament have to do with financial sharing. "Do not neglect to do good and to share what you have," the epistle to the Hebrews exhorted (13:16). Paul said something very similar to the Roman Christians: "Contribute to the needs of the saints" (Rom. 12:13). What did these exhortations mean? Was Paul telling the Romans to remember to put something in the collection basket? Or was he telling them to do something more unconventional?

Grace and Reequalization

As we have noticed, in the post-Pentecost Jerusalem church there was more than a whiff of Jubilee in the air. But was the "making common" which they experienced a failure, so much so that no other church wanted to go down the same road? To answer this question we do not have as much evidence as we would like. But one thing may help us—Paul's efforts on his third missionary journey to raise money among the Gentile churches for the largely Jewish Christians in Jerusalem.[4] To this subject, Paul kept returning in his letters (Rom. 15:25-32; 1 Cor. 16:1-4); and in one of them, 2 Corinthians, he wrote no less than two chapters about it (8-9).

Briefly, this was the situation of the Christians in Jerusalem in the mid-50s A.D. In the two decades since Jesus' resurrection, their church had grown rapidly. Among the new believers there was a wide variety of people—pilgrims, proselytes, even some temple priests. Inevitably there were also needy people, especially widows (Acts 6:1-7). All of them were heavily taxed by the Roman authorities. We do not know whether, as the decades went by, the Jubilee economics of the Jerusalem church impoverished its members. No biblical writer claimed that it did; indeed, as we shall see, Paul, in seeking to rally the resources of Gentile Christians to meet the needs of their brothers and sisters in Jerusalem, specifically recommended measures of Jubilee-like economics. The facts that we do know are these: in the late 40s there was a severe famine in Judea (Acts 11:27-28).[5] Despite the relief which the Antioch church sent at once, by the middle of the next decade there were still many "poor among the saints at Jerusalem" (Acts 11:29-30; Rom. 15:26). And Paul, perhaps partly to remind the Jerusalem Christians that there were Gentiles in the worldwide church as well as Jews, was determined to help out.

To do so, Paul decided to raise a collection. From the churches in Macedonia, Galatia, and Achaia he asked for money—money which he, along with other emissaries representing the churches, could carry personally to Jerusalem. On the first day of each week, believers should set aside as much money as they could for this project, voluntarily but generously (1 Cor. 16:2-3). To encourage the Corinthians to give more, he extolled the generosity of the Macedonians; and in Macedonia he was full of the praises of the Corinthians (2 Cor. 8:1-4; 9:1-2)!

What was Paul's thinking behind this project? In the remarkable chapters in 2 Corinthians (8—9), he spells it out in some detail. The theme of these chapters is *grace*. In one form or another the word occurs no fewer than ten times in these chapters. God has been gracious. So also has the Lord Jesus Christ. In a profound sentence which has become an essential part of Christmastime carol services, Paul exults:

> For you know the grace of our Lord Jesus Christ, that though he was rich, yet for your sake he became poor, so that by his poverty you might become rich. (2 Cor. 8:9)

God's grace, and the grace of the Lord Jesus, were gifts to the Gentile Christians. But these gifts required a response in kind. God had given to them abundantly, "so that you may always have enough of everything and may provide in abundance for every good work" (9:8). Because Jesus had been gracious, the saints should likewise participate in the collection—which Paul calls "this gracious work" (8:6, 19). The holiness theme is here: the believers were to be gracious as God in Christ was gracious.

Concretely gracious. To show how they should be gracious, Paul expounds his understanding of an interdependent worldwide church. At the time of his writing to them, the Corinthians were prospering while the Jerusalemites were in need; later the situation might be reversed. "As a matter of equality," the Corinthians should draw from their abundance to help their brothers and sisters in Jerusalem. On another occasion, resources might flow in the other direction. "Then," says Paul, "there will be equality" (8:13-14 NIV).

To drive home his point, Paul appealed to the history of God's people. Right after the Exodus, when the people were in the wilderness, God gave them manna. And, according to the passage from Exodus which Paul quotes (16:18), the manna had two principles: "He who gathered much had nothing over, [equality], and he who gathered little had no lack [sufficiency]" (2 Cor. 8:15). Now, in the wilderness following the new Exodus in Jesus, God's people were to live by the same principles.

Paul's aim was not to make his friends feel guilty; nor did he want to bind them by quotas. All giving was to be voluntary, motivated by the grace of God. "God loves a cheerful giver" (9:7). Nor was Paul attempting something legalistic or mechanistic; he was not establishing an international common purse. But he was appealing to the deepest reality which the believers had experienced, the reality of God's grace. And to this grace, which they had experienced concretely, he was asking for a concrete response. God is a generous provider. In his grace he will ensure that his people "may always have enough of everything" (9:8). He will increase the "harvest of [their] justice" (9:10). Can they respond, in thanksgiving, worship, and obedience, by giving to God through establishing equality among his people (9:12-13)? If so, they will participate generously in what Paul calls "the koinonia of the service to the saints" (8:4; literal).

Paul's Jubilee-style approach to economic relations between churches helps us understand his instructions to individual churches. As Evangelical New Testament scholar F. F. Bruce has commented, "That the affluent should supply the deficiencies of the needy was as desirable between churches as it was between members in any one local church."[6] Let us return to Romans 12:13. A conventional translation reads, "Contribute to the needs of the saints." But, in light of the experience of the Jerusalem church and of Paul's principles in 2 Corinthians 8—9 which reinforce the Jerusalem experience, this is more likely to mean: "With regard to the needs of the saints, practice making all things common!"[7] If so, this helps explain why, in writing to the Christians in Thessalonica, Paul was so eager to establish another principle: "If any one will not work, let him not eat" (2 Thess. 3:10). In a community in which widespread financial sharing was taking place, some people must have found it tempting to become layabouts. Sponging was no more holy than self-sufficient economic individualism. But there was an alternative! In his concrete grace, God was helping his people to pioneer a lifestyle of contentment and sharing.

Protection: Living in the Diaspora

If Jesus' postresurrection disciples were discovering new approaches to the perennial problem of provision, how about their protection? How should they deal with their enemies? How should they cope with persecution? How should they view their government? They, the "exiles of the Dispersion" (1 Pet. 1:1), would not find these to be easy questions. But it is instructive to watch them working toward answers which would be consistent with their status as a "holy nation."

For some of Jesus' followers—the members of the churches in Palestine—circumstances remained quite similar to those which Jesus himself had faced. Their land was still occupied by the world empire of Rome. Their fellow citizens increasingly resisted the occupation as an offense to God and a denial of his kingship. The result was war. After a period of growing tension punctuated by occasional insurrections, in A.D. 66 hostilities broke out between the Jewish people and the Romans which lasted for four years and led to the destruction of Jerusalem. In the Palestinian setting, Jesus' command, "Love your enemies," thus had a meaning which was unmistakeably relevant to the political situation. Despite this, identifying with their friends and relatives by joining in the armed struggle against their nation's enemy must have been a temptation to some believers. Jerusalem-based Christian writers such as James cautioned against violence and warned that "the anger of man does not work the justice of God" (James 1:20; 4:1-3). When the revolution broke out, the church maintained its nonviolence by fleeing northeastwards from Jerusalem to the town of Pella.[8]

The Palestinian background was obviously very much in the minds of the other apostles. Peter, for example, as a good Galilean, would have known in great detail about the abrasive edge of Roman rule. And Paul, as a youthful Pharisee, would have found the Romans' tampering with religion to be an offence against God's holiness. For both of these men, good Jews as they were, the Roman occupation of the Promised Land would have been deeply objectionable.

But within a few decades of Jesus' resurrection, Peter and Paul had traveled to other parts of the empire and were helping churches to face situations very different from that of Palestine. Unquestionably Jesus' dispersed disciples were still aliens. In their holiness they were living differently from their neighbors. As a result, they were still subject to pressure and persecution. But the societies around them were quite unlike that of

Palestine; they were pagan, not Jewish, and were more remote from military action. Furthermore, for most early Christians the military profession was simply not an option. Recruitment was generally voluntary, and the Jews among them were forbidden to serve in the Roman legions.[9]

The societies in which the Christians were now living varied considerably. In the cities of Asia Minor to which Peter wrote in the early 60s, there had for some time been restiveness at Roman rule. There were also long-standing social tensions. The urban lower classes, for example, had a heritage of industrial turmoil and revolutionary agitation. Significantly, many of the believers in Asia Minor came from this part of society.[10] And when Christians began to live in a distinctive manner, their neighbors showed considerable readiness to resort to taunts, discrimination, and worse; Peter's letter is saturated with references to such acts.[11]

In Rome, to which Paul wrote his great letter, there was also recent history of turbulence.[12] Christians had come early to Rome, where they met in the synagogues of the substantial Jewish community. When they talked about Jesus, tensions boiled over. As a result of riots "impelled by Chrestus,"[13] in A.D. 49 the emperor Claudius expelled the more vociferous Jews on both sides of the argument about Jesus' messiahship, including the Christian tentmaking couple Priscilla and Aquila (Acts 18:2-3). Within a few years the exiles (including Priscilla and Aquila [Rom. 16:3-5]) began to trickle back to Rome, especially during the early years of Nero (who in 54 succeeded Claudius). There were still tensions. The lower orders were angered by the way they were taxed, and a threatened tax revolt forced Nero to consider revamping the Roman system of taxation.[14] Furthermore, the Christians, now meeting separately from the Jews, were under continual pressure. As one of Paul's first Roman acquaintances informed him, "Everywhere [the sect] is spoken against" (Acts 28:22). In such an atmosphere, it was possible for Nero, in the mid-60s, to blame the Christians for the burning of Rome and to execute many of them—most likely including their leaders Peter and Paul—as arsonists.[15]

So Jesus' disciples were now in a variety of political and social situations. Their communities, living in a new way without withdrawing from the old society, were under pressure. Nowhere was persecution far off. How should they, in these circumstances, relate to their neighbors and to the state?

A Foreign Policy for a Holy Nation

Put simply, it was a question of foreign policy. In the church, God had brought together enemies—Jew and Gentile—to comprise a "holy nation." This nation was not supposed to be conformed to the world, but it was very much enmeshed in the world. The "holy nation" therefore had to decide how it was to relate to the "nations" which surrounded it and were often hostile to it (1 Pet. 1:14; 2:9, 12; Rom. 12:2).

To decide how they were to do this, the postresurrection disciples looked to their Master Jesus. Their approach to him is interesting. It was not a legalistic approach; the early Christians showed considerable freedom in mixing and matching quotes from his teaching. But everywhere, their desire was clear. They wanted to be true not only to what Jesus said but to what he was and did.

In constructing their foreign policy, the Christians listened to Jesus, and drew from his teaching several principles which they repeated frequently. One of these was a potent warning. Don't retaliate! "Do not repay anyone evil for evil" (Rom. 12:17; 1 Thess. 5:15; 1 Pet. 3:9; citing Matt. 5:39). In Romans 12, Paul elaborates upon this. "Do not take revenge, my friends," and "Do not be overcome by evil" (12:19, 21, NIV).

On the other hand, the Christians heard Jesus giving them encouragement toward positive alternatives. "Always seek to do good to one another and to all" (1 Thess. 5:15, citing Luke 6:27). Peter's letter is full of admonitions to do "good works"

(1 Pet. 2:12, 15). He and Paul also encouraged the beleaguered disciples to bless those who were harassing them (3:9; Rom. 12:14). Also a familiar refrain was the admonition to live at peace. "If possible, so far as it depends upon you, live peaceably with all" (Rom. 12:18; 1 Pet. 3:11, citing Mark 9:50). Although they were not to avenge themselves, they could rely on God to give appropriate punishment to their nation's enemies (Rom. 12:19).[16] Unlike many of their contemporaries, they were not to be participants in anti-Roman armed struggle; instead they were to be "zealots for the good" (1 Pet. 3:13).[17]

Indeed, these Christians, like their Master Jesus, were to *be subordinate*.[18] "Be subject for the Lord's sake to every human institution," Peter urged his readers; and Paul, in a famous passage, said virtually the same thing (1 Pet. 2:13; Rom. 13:1). These new Christians were to go on living as "free people," but "without using [their] freedom as a pretext for evil"—which could include anti-Roman agitation (1 Pet. 2:16). Subordination would be a necessary part of the stance of the holy nation toward the nations.

But what does subordination mean? It means accepting a pattern of power, an order of authority. A hierarchical term, subordination means living in a situation—and not withdrawing from it—in which someone else has more power than we do. It means recognizing their authority, accepting that they are in their position of responsibility to do a task that is important to God. The governing authorities—emperors, governors, and the rest—have been "ordered" by God (Rom. 13:1; 1 Pet. 2:13). They are his instruments to encourage good behavior and to judge, punish, even avenge bad behavior (Rom. 13:3-5; 1 Pet. 2:14). Jesus' disciples are to recognize Caesar's God-given authority and to render to him what is his. They are to pray for the authorities, and to give them (according to their due) honor and taxes (1 Tim. 2:2; 1 Pet. 2:17; Rom. 13:6-7).[19]

By urging subordination like this, Peter and Paul were not giving carte blanche to the Roman authorities. Rome, after all, was a pagan, persecuting empire. Significantly, Peter and Paul did not urge the believers to "obey" the authorities as a slave obeys a master.[20] Clearly they assumed that at times their fellow believers, like the earliest Christians (Acts 5:29), would have to be disobedient. The allegiance they owed to God was life-encompassing, vastly larger than the allegiance they owed to Caesar (cf Mark 12:17).

Furthermore, there was one thing the authorities did that the Christians were not to take part in. The government is "an avenger of wrath" (Rom. 13:4, literal); but the command to Jesus' disciples is, "Beloved, never avenge yourselves" (12:19). This is not because they are private citizens; it is because God is the avenger of his holy nation. As he told his nation through Moses, "It is mine to avenge; I will repay" (Deut. 32:35, NIV). Imitators of God in so many other areas, the believers were forbidden to imitate his vengeance.[21]

Being subordinate, doing good, not retaliating or avenging themselves—this was a curious foreign policy. But for God's holy nation, it signified a distinct, Jesus-like alternative in the world of nations. And, if we give it a bit of thought, we will realize that it had deep roots in Israel's past.

Living in Babylon, Living in Rome

Almost seven hundred years before Peter and Paul wrote their letters, another world-empire, Babylon, was amassing its forces for a final assault on the capital of Israel, Jerusalem. Many Israelites were sure that this would be the end of God's holy nation. But the dissident prophet Jeremiah disagreed. He had no illusions about Babylon's violence or paganness. But shocking though this might seem to conventional-minded Israelites, God had a purpose in Babylon's rise. Three times Jeremiah asserted that Babylon was God's "servant" (Jer. 25:9; 27:6; 43:10). Nebuchadnezzar, the Babylonian king, was the bearer of "the sword" of Yahweh; he was the instrument of Yahweh's "fierce anger" (25:38).[22]

In this setting, Jeremiah's message to the panic-stricken Israelites was demanding but simple. Relax! God is using the
Babylonians, an unholy nation, to judge his holy nation. God's
people are not to respond by becoming Babylonians; nor are
they to match the Babylonians in military might. Instead they
are to be subordinate (38:2, 20-21). Trust the Lord and sur-
render! Stop trying to control the situation, but don't give up
your values. In due course, things will change. Babylon, which
at the moment is judging others, will be judged (Jer. 50—51).
But until then, God's people are to "seek the *shalom*" of
Babylon. Indeed, they are to pray that Babylon may have this,
for Israel will not find its own shalom except in the most
surprising of places—the shalom of its unholy enemy (29:7).

Did the parallel with Babylon point a way forward for the
Christians in their dealings with Rome? For some of them—for
Peter and the John of Revelation, clearly, and possibly also for
Paul—it did. For them, unlike most modern commentators,
Babylon did not signify bad government; it signified the
governing authorities of the "nations." Nor was Babylon a term
of abuse. Babylon was a neutral term, describing authorities
that could be basically beneficent but that could also be unjust
and persecuting. And Rome, like Babylon many centuries
earlier, was a world empire which God could use.

Peter was explicit about this. He was fully aware of the good
that Rome could do in furthering justice, and he urged his
fellow believers to be subordinate to it (1 Pet. 2:13-14).
Nevertheless, he called it "Babylon" (5:13).[23] He well knew
that the emperor's officials were summoning Christians to appear in court and would shortly be inflicting a "fiery ordeal"
upon them (3:15; 4:12); yet he exhorted the believers to "honor
the emperor" (2:17). In the book of Revelation, John predicted
that things would get still worse. Babylon (Rome) would
persecute the believers more and more severely, becoming
"drunk with the blood of the holy ones" (Rev. 17:6). Her
misuse of power and her economic luxury would also become

intensified (18:3). As the believers endured and prayed, God himself would preside over the fall of the Babylonian (Roman) Empire (13:10; 18:2).

Unlike Peter and John, the apostle Paul did not explicitly compare the Roman Empire with that of Babylon. But his comments about the Roman authorities in Romans 13 are astonishingly parallel, not only to what Peter was to say in his epistle, but to what, many centuries earlier, Jeremiah had said about Babylon. The authorities were "God's servant"; and as such they were authorized to "bear the sword" and to "execute [God's] wrath" upon the wrongdoers (Rom. 13:4; cf. Jer. 25:9, 38).[24]

In light of this, how were Christians to view the imperial authorities? Of course they were to be subordinate. More than that, they were actively to pray for the authorities (1 Tim. 2:2). And, most characteristic of all, they were to give them respect and honor (Rom. 13:7). In a series of admonitions, Peter put the matter succinctly:

> Honor all people. Love the brotherhood. Fear God. Honor the emperor: (1 Pet. 2:17)

That the Christians were to treat the emperor with respect is obvious. But several other things are clear as well. The Christians were to have loyalties of a different kind to their own nation, "the brotherhood," which they were to love, and to their nation's King, God, whom they were to fear. Furthermore, the believers were to treat the emperor with honor. But then, they were to treat "all people" with honor—it's the same word. The same egalitarian thrust—treating "all people" like kings—is present in Paul's instruction to Timothy that "prayers, intercessions, and thanksgivings be made for all people, for kings and all who are in high positions . . . (1 Tim. 2:1-2).

Everybody—that was the point. For the Christians' overriding concern was a missionary one. Their nation was one that had expanding boundaries. In God's design, outsiders and enemies, even people who now persecuted them, were destined to be fellow citizens. Why pray for the emperor? According to Paul, so that the church may live a quiet and peaceable life, for God "desires all people to be saved" (1 Tim. 2:2-4). Why should Christians behave well among the nations? So that the nations may see their good works and be drawn to God's holy nation (1 Pet. 2:12). Holiness, Peter deeply believed, was attractive. Patience and nonretaliation in the face of abuse—this deviant way was Jesus' way. Nothing was more likely to draw the nations to him than lives that looked like his (1 Pet. 2:20-21; 3:1, 15-18).

Growing Up

The confidence of these early Christians is astonishing. On the one hand they could be realistic about their apparent obscurity. Paul knew very well that not many of his fellow believers "were wise by human standards; not many were influential; not many were of noble birth" (1 Cor. 1:26, NIV). But it was these nobodies, whose lifestyle was so deviant, who were going to be implements in God's hands as he went about changing the world. Having tasted the holiness of God's Spirit, they were the firstfruits of the future. Through them, the church, God was going to declare his wisdom to the "rulers and authorities" (Eph. 3:10, NIV).

For that reason they couldn't withdraw from the world. It would be disastrous if they did so, and Paul urged them to continue to rub shoulders with "the immoral ... the greedy and robbers, and the idolators." If they didn't they would have—unthinkable thought—"to go out of the world" (1 Cor. 5:10). But Paul, like Jesus, knew that holiness was contagious. An unbelieving husband, for example, is "made holy" through his Christian wife (1 Cor. 7:14; see also 1 Pet. 3:1-6). Armed with this contagious power, the early Christians seem to have participated as much as possible in the economic and social life of the Roman Empire. Many were artisans, and by the 50s some even were found in Caesar's household (Phil. 4:22).[25] But the early Christians knew from hard experience that holiness could also provoke hostility. Paul was aware that the "aroma of Christ" could seem a stench to people committed to a deathwards course (2 Cor. 2:15). Peter's experience was similar. He knew that it was his fellow believers about-face toward holiness that had caused them to be rejected by their neighbors ("the nations") (1 Pet. 3:14-17; 4:3-4).

But whatever their experience and their role in society, all of them had the same vocation—to follow Jesus, the Holy One. The only reason their movement was moving at all was that he was among them, pulsating with life and leading them forward. He was their Lord, and they "lived in him" (Col. 2:6). And as they did so, they came to be like him.

The early believers had a number of words for this process of coming to resemble Jesus. One term, which Christian theologians have later used extensively, is "sanctification," which means making holy. At times, the early Christians emphasized that God, through Jesus' sacrifice of his blood and through his Holy Spirit, had already made them holy (Heb. 10:10; 13:12; Rom. 15:16; 1 Pet. 1:2). After all, their status was that of saints—holy ones. At other times, the Christians were very aware how incomplete was their transformation into the image of Christ. How much the "holy ones" still needed to be changed for them to be like him! Sanctification was thus a process as well as a status. The believers were to "strive for peace with all people, and for holiness" (Heb. 12:14); they were to offer their bodies in "slavery to justice leading to holiness" (Rom. 6:19, NIV).

But there is another term which the early believers used which is easier to understand than sanctification; it is *growing up*. The Greek word which they used is *teleios*, which is often translated "perfect." But since it had to do with reaching a goal, the word generally meant "maturity" rather than flawlessness. Jesus had told his disciples that when they had learned to love their enemies they would be mature—perfect as their Father was perfect (Matt. 5:48). Now his disciples used the same term. In the confidence that Jesus himself was the perfect image of the Father, they urged each other to grow up into the image of the Son who also was an enemy lover (see Col. 1:28). This, indeed, was the calling of the church's leaders. It was not only to exercise their gifts to equip the holy ones for service; it was also to enable them to "become mature, attaining to the whole measure of the fullness of Christ" (Eph. 4:11-13, NIV). To protect the church's resemblance to Jesus, they needed at times to exercise a form of discipline upon members who were departing from his way. When members succumbed to immorality, covetousness, or idolatry, a disciplinary process might be begun. If neither a conversation nor a more formal warning succeeded in restoring right behavior, exclusion from fellowship might ensue. In that extreme circumstance, a significant word was pronounced: *Anathema*. This is the word which, in the Greek Old Testament, was used to translate the Hebrew word for holy war—*herem*.[26] God hadn't given up on his determination to protect his nation's holiness. But after the coming of his Son, the methods which he authorized were no longer the same. Excommunication, not killing, was now the ultimate penalty. In fact, the *anathema* of exclusion was something which holy war could never be—something therapeutic, whose goal was reconciliation (2 Cor. 2:5-11). And at all times, the leaders had to keep setting their bearings by Jesus, who was God's demonstration of what it means to be grown up!

Following the Pioneer

To be a Christian, in sum, was simply to follow Jesus. Accepting his acceptance and forgiveness, the disciples began to walk in the steps of the Master (1 John 2:6). And to imitate him. The holy ones were to become like the Holy One; and as they learned to behave like him, they discovered what it meant to be grown up. Their attitude to strangers was to be rooted in the way Jesus had treated them: "Welcome one another . . . as Christ has welcomed you" (Rom. 15:7). Their approaches to economics and to conflict were also to be modeled on him (2 Cor. 8:9; 1 Pet. 2:21). And frequently the apostles used the very word *imitate*.[27] They didn't do this to encourage a slavish copying of Jesus' lifestyle. Celibacy and carpentry were not the main point! But they were concerned that the believers be attuned to Jesus, putting his teachings to work and facing suffering as he had faced it (Phil. 3:10).

To do this, they had to remember him. The Christian churches lived by passing on the traditions of what Jesus had been like. As stories about Jesus' life and teaching circulated, they collected them and wrote them down. The four Gospels are indications of how important it was to Jesus' postresurrection disciples to remember their Master. They also remembered him in their worship. In the Holy Spirit, the disciples sensed that Jesus was with them. When they met they told and retold the story of his life and triumph over death. In their love-feasts and eucharists they likewise remembered him (1 Cor. 11:24). As they, at their communion services, brought their gifts to their congregation's common fund, they were continuing a tradition that went back to their Master.[28]

But the story wasn't complete yet. Jesus' postresurrection disciples knew that, however rich their heritage in the past experience of God's holy nation, God was propelling them into the future. This was frightening, for their lives were intensely insecure. To be a Christian was to be a risk-taker. Every day they could expect that God's Spirit would do creative things in making Jesus' presence real. But this required faith, which wasn't always easy.

They had a source of encouragement, however. From Jesus, through the Holy Spirit, they had learned to know God as Abba (Rom. 8:15). They knew that they were God's children, loved and secure. Sufferings—the buffetings and rejections that always come to genuine nonconformists—awaited them. But as they headed into hardships, they knew that they were following someone who had been there before them.

Jesus, whom they had known in the flesh, they confessed to be "the image of the invisible God" (Col. 1:15). So secure was he in Abba's love that he could not be manipulated—not by physical threats or appeals to his greed or ambition. Even death could not destroy his faithfulness to the Father's way. But Jesus was alive! He had conquered death! He was the "pioneer," the scout, who freed his followers for life—creative, deviant, holy life—because he delivered them from the fear of death (Heb. 2:10, 15). In him, and only in him, they were a holy nation, a nation of holy ones. There is an alternative, because Jesus has shown the way.

Part IV
Coming Closer Home

CHAPTER
13

Between the Times

By this time we may feel somewhat exhausted. Our balloon has been comfortable enough, but we've covered so much distance that we're travel weary. Our minds may soon go on strike: if we see one more exciting event they will refuse to take it in! And the discouraging thing is that we've only come to A.D. 60 or so. We're still over nineteen hundred years from home. How can we make the gigantic leap between the "holy ones" of the New Testament and our own time?

It won't be easy. To help us understand the difficulties, our balloon—rising to an immense height—will once again be useful. But after some high flying early in this chapter, we will be leaving our balloon behind and getting down to earth. For the story that we've been retelling must connect with our own lives. Unless it does so, we may have been self-indulgent and escapist.

The Bible's story *can* connect with our lives. Its main actor, the Holy One, did not retire at the end of the Book of Acts! He has seen to it that holy history has continued. And its continuation is in many ways similar to the history that we've found in the Bible. The same God is at work; his project of a re-created creation, of a Holy City, continues to unfold. And the human participants are much the same. So the story has its downs as well as its ups.

As I write this, I cannot—much as I would like to—retell the rest of this story. I can only give a general indication of its overall shape so that we have some sense of where we are in the story and why. But I do want us to realize this: the story is not yet finished, and whether you and I like it or not, we are going to be a part of it. The great challenges of every era—issues of protection and provision—are familiar to us by now. At every stage of our story they have recurred. But now, today, as a result of decisions that Christians have made, they are present in acute form. How will we respond? Before we decide, we will attempt to orient ourselves, and then to make connections between the first and the late twentieth centuries A.D.

Distinctive Christians

But is it worth the trouble? After all, we're busy, responsible people. As Christians in the Western world, we're doing our best to make a contribution to our society that is visibly Christian. But at the same time we may have a deep sense of futility. Looking objectively at ourselves, we may see people whose way of living—in the areas of provision and protection, at any rate—is pretty much like everybody else's. We have become like the nations; we have lost our holiness. How could we have helped doing so?

We couldn't have! Decisions that have shaped our civilization were made many centuries ago, long enough back to give a seemingly irresistible momentum to the forces that control us now.

But it wasn't always so. For several centuries after the death of the apostles, the Christians in the Roman Empire and beyond lived in a distinctive way. They were aware that they were citizens of a new nation, of a transnational nation. One of the earliest post-New Testament writings put it like this. For the believers "every foreign land is their fatherland, and yet for them every fatherland is a foreign land."[1] When people came to faith and wanted to be baptized, they were invited to change their lifestyle as well as their national identity. Justin, a Christian teacher who was martyred in Rome almost a century after Peter and Paul, described what it meant to turn around and follow Jesus:

> After being persuaded by the Word, we renounce the demons and now follow the only God through his Son. We who formerly rejoiced in fornication now delight in self-control alone. We who employed magic arts have now dedicated ourselves to the good God of creation. We who loved ways of acquiring wealth and possessions more than anything else, now bring what we have into a common fund and share with everyone who is in need. We once hated and murdered one another and would not show hospitality to those not of the same tribe because of their different customs. But now after the coming of Christ we eat with others, pray for our enemies, and attempt to conciliate those who hate us unjustly. . . . The teachings of Christ were short and concise, for he was no philosopher, but his word was the power of God.[2]

This description of Christian conversion contains familiar things, doesn't it? Then as now, becoming a Christian involved renouncing sexual immorality and occult practices. But Justin and his brothers and sisters knew that following Jesus meant other things as well. It meant deciding to take a Jesus-like approach to the critical issues of protection and provision. Christians were to love their enemies. For three centuries no Christian writer justified killing in warfare, and many of them forbade it categorically.[3] Christians were also to participate in a redistribution of their possessions according to need; for early

Christian congregations the common fund was a living reality.

Theologians kept alive the rationale for the common fund that we have seen in the writings of Paul, based on the "manna principles" of sufficiency and sharing.[4] A fascinating archaeological discovery shows how important economic sharing was in the life of the church. In the port city of Ostia just outside of Rome, third-century believers made a use of their congregation's building that speaks loudly about their priorities: they devoted as much space to storing goods to be redistributed as to their formal worship services.[5] These early Christians were different—different from the "nations" of their day, and different from most of us; but they lived in a way that showed that they had hope. Despite persecution, which at times was severe, the church grew.

Everybody a Christian

But in the fourth century A.D. things changed. A severe persecution ended in 312 when the Emperor Constantine was converted. The genuineness of his conversion has always been debated, but nobody contests one thing—that his conversion was quite unlike that which Justin described. Constantine gradually gave up his worship of the sun god, but he did not change his approach to wealth or war. Nor did the majority of courtiers and ordinary citizens who, as the century progressed, flooded into the church. Theologians called "Church Fathers" valiantly struggled to teach the converts; many of them protested at the dilution of the church's witness. By the end of the century it was clear that there was no stopping short of a society in which there were no non-Christians. An imperial law of 391 made it official. *Everyone* in the empire had to belong to the church, or else! Persecution, by Christian officials, was the fate of those who for conscience' sake remained pagans.

What a watershed this was! And it had an unnerving precedent in biblical history—the Israelites' decision to have a king "like all the nations." That decision, according to evangelist Roger Forster, was "a second best to what God intended for his people."[6] So, in my opinion, was the conversion of the Roman Empire by law and force.

What were the results of the "Christianization" of the Empire? Lacking space, we cannot assess these in detail. It is clear, of course, that there were positive results for the Christians. The threat of persecution was lifted from them—so long, that is, as they toed the line in their opinions. Furthermore, the Christians could now participate fully in the public life of the empire. In due course, the great "Christian" civilization of medieval and early modern Europe sprouted from seeds sown in these fourth-century developments. This was a pretty glorious "second best," we might think; and its heritage of spirituality and scholarship is a rich resource for us to draw upon.

But there were also costs. One of these was the removal of holiness from ordinary life. In the fourth century, in an epidemic of "sanctification," churchmen and statesmen affixed the label of "holy" to places, objects, and times. Within the walls of magnificent church buildings, awe-inspiring rites were developed which were to communicate a sense of the holy to the people.[7]

In fact, the people themselves were now being classified in a new way. In the early days of the church all believers had been both priests and "holy ones" (saints). But no longer. A late fourth-century document carefully distinguishes between priests and the laypeople, and revealingly refers to the latter as "passengers" and "brute creatures."[8] In similar vein, the "saints" had now become special Christians, who obeyed "the teaching given by the perfect Master to those who rose above human nature."[9] Into the deserts and monasteries the potential saints went to keep alive the practicality of Jesus' teaching. A flowering of spiritual writing ensued. But the new developments were tinged with sadness. What *all* early Christians had accepted as a part of their discipleship was now removed from everyday life. Holiness was no longer social; it had been specialized. Ordinary believers were to admire it but not to copy it. It was beyond their reach.

This led to a second cost—the construction of new standards for Christian behavior. Jesus' teachings on loving the enemy and sharing possessions were now viewed as extra-cost options to be practiced by "holy" people specially called to lives of strenuous religious observance. Ordinary believers, in contrast, had to have new guidelines—ones which were realistic, not too demanding. To develop these new codes of behavior, fourth-century Christians turned to the "nations," to pagan philosophers.

From the Stoics, the Christians learned that it did not matter how much property one had; what mattered was one's attitude towards it. Rich Christians were admonished to have a detached attitude to their wealth, "having property as though one had it not."[10] From the Stoics, the Christians also borrowed the criteria for going to war which made up the core of the "Just War" theory.[11] Thoughtful Christians such as Augustine of Hippo elaborated these theories with biblical and theological reflections.

The post-Constantinian approaches to wealth and war had their benefits: they led to charity to the poor and the founding of hospitals to care for the casualties of society; they also provided some restraints upon the conduct of warfare. But they had lost sight of what the early Christians had tried to do. No longer were they trying to end poverty, establish equality, and bring on earth a new nation of peace whose life together would be evidence of God's will for all of humanity.

This points to a third cost—the Christians no longer viewed themselves as a nation. No longer did they see themselves as aliens or "exiles of the Dispersion." They were Galatians, Cappadocians, Bithynians, at home in their societies (1 Pet. 1:1, inverted!). How could they have been otherwise? Everybody was a Christian; the law required them to be. Whole bodies of people were converted as a bloc. Evangelization was carried out by state power, often at sword point. As the masses were baptized, pagan altars were destroyed and churches were built.

In London, England, on the eastern edge of Regent's Park, I have seen a monument which says it all—a reproduction of the Jelling Stone, erected in 980 in Jutland (northern Denmark) by King Canute's grandfather Harald:

> Harald King made this memorial after Gorm his father and Thyra his mother: that Harald who won for himself all Denmark and Norway and made the Danes Christians.

And made the Danes Christians. Of course, these Danes would have more sense of solidarity with other Danes than they would with other Christians! In the post-Constantinian world, it was no longer faith that determined the primary national loyalty of Christians. It was genes and geography.

Justifying the Inevitable

So Christians lost much of their distinctiveness. As a logical consequence of the innovations which came in Constantine's century, they came to be like the nations. No longer did they view themselves as a people who were different. To be sure, things that had been trademarks of a distinctive way of living remained; but only the forms remained—the life-giving substance was gone. For example, jubilees have continued to be declared—in the Middle Ages to raise money for St Peter's basilica in Rome, and more recently to celebrate the anniversary of a queen. But when sensitive individuals have heard an echo of Jesus' teachings on wealth or war and tried to do something about it, they—for the protection of the public—have often been removed from ordinary life. Society can tolerate monks, and it knows what to do with heretics. But the idea that Jesus had wanted *all* of his followers to live like him was intolerable. Renewal groups who dared to think such thoughts— Waldensians, Anabaptists, Quakers—were persecuted and

pushed to the margins of society. Respectable people stig-
matized them as "sectarians" who had nothing to say to the
"real world."

Meanwhile, the real world proceeded pretty well untouched
by the Christianity which it professed. In the cool appraisal of a
leading historian of the late Roman empire, Professor A. H. M.
Jones, this was certainly true in the areas of economic justice
and the treatment of the poor: "It is difficult to assess whether
in these matters the general level of morals was lower than it
had been under the pagan empire, but it seems to have been
no higher."[12] In the countries affected by the Calvinist
Reformation, things may have improved somewhat, as the
reformers tried to reawaken a vision for economic stewardship
and the rehabilitation of the poor.[13]

But in the area of warfare, the Reformation if anything made
things worse. The scale and virulence of killing mounted. After
a thousand years of Just War teaching, how like the nations the
Christians were![14] As the great Dutch international lawyer
Hugo Grotius commented in 1625,

> Throughout the Christian world I observed a lack of restraint in
> relation to war, such as even barbarous races should be ashamed
> of; I observed that men rush to arms for slight causes, or no
> cause at all, and that when arms have once been taken up there
> is no longer any respect for law, divine or human; it is as if, in ac-
> cordance with a general decree, frenzy had openly been let loose
> for the committing of all crimes.[15]

The centuries went by, and new forces of tremendous power
appeared on the world scene. These "isms"—industrialism,
modern nationalism, individualism, socialism, secularism, Marx-
ism, political and economic colonialism—were all developed
in "Christian" Europe; and all have been immense motors for
change. At every stage, they have brought both good and ill.
For example, the same forces that exploited the "third world's"
natural resources and crippled its industry have enabled Chris-

tianity to become truly a world religion. Indeed, the greatest numerical strength of the Christian church is now in the southern hemisphere.

But, from a Christian perspective, the striking thing about the changes that have occurred is this: they have been happening faster and faster, with a momentum that appears to be irresistible. And increasingly it is clear that several of the changes are time bombs, ticking away under civilization as we know it.

Time Bombs

The first of these is economic—the momentum leading to *unrestricted growth*.[16] We cannot expect a pagan society to govern its life by biblical ideals such as sufficiency. But when people flout biblical ideals long enough they get in trouble. As we allow production to thunder ahead, few stop to ask what kind of economy it is, domestically or internationally, that this growth is producing. This may in part be because the answers to our question are frightening. Our pell-mell rush toward more is leading to exhaustion: exhaustion of the world's ecosystem; and also exhaustion of the world's nonrenewable natural resources. And what do we do with these scarce resources? The world expends 20 percent of them upon economically unproductive products (weapons). And what we don't use on weapons, we, in the first world, absorb into our own consumer societies. What right do we have—a mere 25 percent of the world's population—to gorge ourselves on 80 to 95 percent of these nonrenewable resources?[17]

Unrestricted growth is already tearing our world apart, for our pagan society is also flouting the biblical ideal of equality. In the first world, unguided growth has produced lasting sectors of unemployed and demoralized people. There are also, even in Europe and North America, millions of poor people (in the U.S. in 1984, no fewer than 35 million), whom the French have begun to call the "fourth world".[18] This comes at a time when Europeans have a "butter mountain" and some Africans try to decide whether they ought to eat once every three days or every four.[19] As never before in history, debt is crippling the economies of poor nations; some of them are spending almost all of their export earnings simply to service their debt.[20] Such levels of debt are unsupportable; and as nations bargain to reschedule their debts and threaten to cancel them, tremors go through the Western banking and political communities. A time bomb is ticking. Even in the West unrestricted growth is "unsustainable, unsatisfying, and largely illusory."[21]

A second time bomb is *militarism*. Throughout history most countries have had factories that could make arms. In times of national crisis, these have been converted into the production of weapons. In times of peace, however, most societies have demobilized the majority of their troops and reconverted their arms factories to production for peaceful purposes. Until the past forty years, that is. Since World War II, a historical novelty has become an unquestioned part of our lives—a massive, growing industrial system devoted solely, and permanently, to the production of weapons. This "military culture" has come about slowly, on two sides of the globe, because two great empires each fear that its security is being endangered by its rival. The unprecedented destructive power of the nuclear bomb has increased this sense of insecurity.

The militarization of our societies has had catastrophic consequences. Immense funds have been spent—since 1945 the nuclear powers have spent $3-4,000,000,000,000,000 on atomic weapons alone.[22] These funds—along with the even more immense sums which they and many other countries have spent on conventional weapons—have been diverted from genuine human need to military production. For example, between 1979 and 1984 the United Kingdom increased its military spending by 20 percent in real terms. The increase in the U.S.'s expenditure was vastly greater. And during this period most rich countries were trimming away at their already scandalously meagre budgets for aid to the poorer countries.

How can these momentums be slowed? By a "nuclear winter," certainly.[23] But by anything less catastrophic? It is hard to see how. As Bob Goudzwaard, a Dutch Christian economist, has noted,

> We live in an age of imprisoned expertise.... The expertise of technicians is imprisoned in the principle that what technology can do it *must* do.[24]

A good example of this is the development of space weaponry. Just when an agreement to limit nuclear weapons on the earth is coming to seem feasible, a new frontier of fear and expenditure is appearing in space. This, according to the *Wall Street Journal*, is the "business opportunity of a generation."[25] With such economic motors at work, it is hard to see what can divert the technology to peaceful projects.

Language can be revealing. Insurance companies offer such religious-sounding benefits as "refuge for life." The salesmen of the newest space armaments similarly use the vocabulary of faith. These weapons, they assure us, offer humanity "enormous hope." It is hope of "assured survival." In fact, these weapons could "save millions of lives, indeed humanity itself."[26] Good tidings indeed! But in whom do we trust? How many gods have we got? Are we able to detect the idolatry around us? When churchmen echo the comfortable words of the arms salesmen, we are encountering religious syncretism in advanced form. And deep down—as we glance furtively at the headlines and watch the incessant militarization of our societies—few of us are reassured. Our society is experiencing the "disappearance of hope."[27] And the time bomb of militarism ticks on.

There is nothing new about this, of course. The two time bombs represent—in heightened form—the same primary human needs that we have seen throughout our story: provision and protection. They are real needs. But any civilization, even one in which Christians play a leading part, gets in trouble when it goes to limitless lengths to satisfy these needs. As Christian historian Sir Herbert Butterfield commented a generation ago:

> The gravest political mistakes of the last forty years in one country after another have been due to fear and overanxiety. . . . We are flying in the face of Providence if we demand too great security for the future.[28]

The institutions and machines that we construct for our security become ends in themselves. Their appetites for investment and ingenuity are insatiable. Dwight Eisenhower may not have seen the spiritual realities behind the web of institutions that he called the "Military-Industrial Complex." But Paul would have done. In the first century, he referred to similar realities—both physical and deeply spiritual—as 'principalities and powers." And modern Christians, in wrestling with these realities, are increasingly using a term familiar to all Bible readers—*idolatry*.[29]

We face formidable forces. We must use language to match. Whatever we call them, the tools that we have trusted for our salvation are becoming our masters. We are imprisoned, trapped. The slogan "There is no alternative" is a pathetic commentary on our age. Our march toward destruction seems irreversible.

CHAPTER
14

Journey
into Holiness

We are living in a remarkable time. It is a time of crisis. There is danger, immense danger. But there is also opportunity. To us, as to Jesus' first followers, comes the call: "The time is fulfilled, and the kingdom of God is at hand; repent and believe in the good news" (Mark 1:15). But how can we repent? How can we believe, responding faithfully to the coming kingdom in a time when time bombs are ticking? In a simple illustration (Matt. 7:13-14), Jesus gives us a clue.

Two Roads

Jesus pictures the world as a wide road. Masses of people, emerging from a wide gate, are streaming along it, walking comfortably along a level surface. They are going in a familiar direction. Their parents have walked in the same direction; and at the moment, their friends and neighbors are at their side. Surely it is obvious to head in this direction. Common sense, majority opinion, the experts all agree—there is no other route worth taking. People of many traditions are walking side by side. But, says Jesus, they are heading toward a precipice. The easy road leads to destruction.

There is, Jesus says, another road. One gets to it by going through a narrow gate. And the road itself is hard. It cuts across the broad road, and is heading in a different direction. Very few people are walking on it, and those who are doing so are not finding it easy. Others view them as an inconvenience. "Everybody" knows that the wide road makes sense. Why cut across the accepted path? You're bumping into people! You're disturbing them, unsettling them in their views! Do you think you know better than people have always known? But, says Jesus, the hard way leads, not to the precipice, but to life.

In Jesus' time, the broad, realistic road led to conflict with the Romans and destruction of Jewish civilization. Jesus wept, for the people of Jerusalem didn't know "the things that make for shalom" (Luke 19:42). But he offered them an alternative road, one that was difficult but that would lead to life. It was an alternative of holy living.

Today Jesus is offering us the same alternative. Once again, there are the realists—people who patronize and reassure. Surely the broad road doesn't lead to destruction; good Christians have been taking it for centuries. Precisely. That's why it's so hard to do something new. But there is nothing that is more dangerous than the obvious. The pressures of tradition, "informed opinion," military-industrial complexes, principalities and powers, and the rest are intense. But it is these forces and institutions, and the realists who run and justify them, that are keeping the world on course for the precipice.

Jesus is calling his disciples today to turn their backs on conventional wisdom and to follow him. His way crosses the currents of our time. It is a narrow way, and difficult; it promises no assured results. Neither withdrawing nor compromising, it guarantees conflict. But it offers the possibility of something new. Jesus' way is a living alternative, a holy way.

Exodus People

How do we begin? How can we "set our hearts on pilgrimage" (Ps. 84:5 NIV)? There is no easy formula. But, as we become Exodus people, we will discover that several things are necessary.

First, we must be *open to change*. Most of us instinctively draw back. Just like the Pharisees of Jesus' day, we resist the kingdom of God because we have a vested interest in keeping things as they are. We have the point of view of settlers. We're quite at home in our homesteads, and we warn off anyone who criticizes the way we manage our patch!

But Jesus calls us to leave our homesteads and become pioneers.[1] By leaving, we are following him, following Abraham and Sarah. We are discarding the false securities that have prevented us from fully trusting him and loving our neighbors. And we are expressing our hope. In God's strength, change is possible; the New Creation is a promise which God can keep. We are sure of this, so sure that we will base our lives upon it.

But what will it mean for us? Until we set out we cannot know. Each of us—individuals, families, prayer groups, churches—begins at a different place. Depending upon where we are, the consequences of pioneering will become clear in a differing order. This is not important. What *is* important is that we, as fully as we know how, commit ourselves to be faithful to Jesus and head from security into risk. John Wimber said it well: "Risk-taking in the New Testament is spelled F-A-I-T-H."[2]

Second, we must be *willing to keep changing*. Having left familiar territory, pioneers find themselves in situations that settlers never encounter. Most of us, as settler Christians, are shy of taking risks. As much as possible, we control all aspects of our lives. We plan for every contingency. We have faith in God for life after death, but for life before death we do everything we can to make our own arrangements. If we're in charge of our lives, we don't need to change and grow.

Pioneers, on the other hand, are constantly facing insecurity.

This is unsettling, and can cause fear. Fear is significant. Unfaced and unnamed, fear is the enemy of F-A-I-T-H. But when we name our fears—to ourselves, to other people, to God—they can help us grow. Each fear can tell us a great deal about ourselves, and can show us areas in which we need to ask God to heal us and deepen our faith. Furthermore, a specific fear might indicate an area in which God is calling us to be obedient in a new and risky way.

So our insecurity is significant. We must not run away from it, or hunt for excuses—in a new place—to join the crowd heading for the precipice. The process is the point! It is vital that we stay on the crossroad, difficult though it may be. As we do so, we must not become proud of our progress. For God's grace is the power source of the humble and dependent. "My grace is sufficient for you, for my power is made perfect in weakness" (2 Cor. 12:9). If we are to be open to his work in our lives we must be "vigilant to remain insecure."[3]

Third, we must be *committed to a long journey*. Our Exodus will not catapult us immediately into the promised land. On earth we will be exiles, whom God calls to keep moving. As we move through the wilderness, we will meet obstacles. We will discover new areas of sin in our lives, new ways in which we are complicit with forces of evil in the world. Much though we want to repent of these, we may find some of them inescapable. But God's call is to a journey, not to perfect purity en route. The air that we breathe is his grace and forgiveness.

Despite our failings, step by step God will lead us onward. And as we go, his Son's promise rings in our inner ears: "I am with you always" (Matt. 28:20). The Holy One, who is our goal, will also be our companion.[4] As we journey with him from security into risk, we will "share his holiness" (Heb. 12:10).

Holiness on the Journey: Living Force

All aspects of holiness! Without any of them, the pioneer life sooner or later becomes impossible, and—whether we are willing to admit this or not—we become settlers in a new place. But God is committed to our journey. And so that we can actually move towards his goal for humanity, the Holy City, he wants to equip us with holiness.

The first aspect of holiness, as we have seen, is *living force*. The living God does not reveal himself lightly. But to people today as throughout history, he continues to give an experience of the one who is "high and lifted up" (Isa. 6:1). Our preparations—whether through charismatic worship, contemplative prayer, a dream, or an inspiring sermon—can open the way for him to speak. But often he reveals himself surprisingly, in unexpected places and in shocking forms. His power and grace can take us aback, dumbfounding us with love and causing to well up within us both dread and hilarity!

When Jesus at his baptism met the Father as living, loving force, he received marching orders—to a journey of service and suffering. Our journeys, by the same token, may start with an experience of his love. Or we may experience this en route, when we're burned out after having done everything in our strength to attain the goal—and failed! Whenever this happens, the Father calls us by name; he teaches us to call him Abba; he loves us. When Jesus looked at people, they saw love in his eyes—and they could change. For his love dispels fear. In the Holy Spirit, we can know the overwhelming reality of being sons and daughters of the Father. We can be secure, secure enough to respond to Jesus' call into insecurity: "Follow me!" Provision and protection may, according to the psychologist Maslow, be our "primary human needs."⁵ But how much more there is to life than these! Indeed, it is God's love—deeply experienced as a living force—that energizes us to see provision and protection in a proper perspective and to take a distinctive approach to them.

When we are without strength for the next leg of our journey, or when we are facing a blank wall and can see no faithful way forward, we discover that God's living force is power as well as love. God is a continuing Creator. In his concrete grace, he opens to us possibilities that amaze us. Sometimes, as we take risks in our approach to protection and provision, his surprises can be literally life-saving![6] Once we have encountered God as living force, we will be ready to recognize these as miracles—"cross-currents that change the previous drift of inevitability, and direct the whole towards a new and different end."[7]

A word of caution may be necessary, however. For there is something about the experience of God's living force which, in its fascination, can become an end in itself. This is a temptation which we must reject. God won't allow his beauty to linger simply for us to appreciate it emotionally or aesthetically. In the Bible, God's self-disclosures were never for their own sake. They were always to equip his people for change. When God reveals to us his living force, he is inviting us to keep moving, to stay on the road that leads to his Holy City. If we refuse his invitation, our experiences of holiness will not recur. We can sing our choruses louder and longer; we can contemplate with ever greater abandon. But if we do not allow God to go on changing us, we will not experience his living force. Deep in our selves we will know the dryness of his silence.

Separateness

The second aspect of holiness is separateness. As we have seen, at a very early date, God forbade his people to be like the nations. Throughout history his policy for them has been one of nonconformity. It still is. But at every stage, God's people have found it hard to live separately while remaining in the thick of things.

There are two obvious ways of dealing with this difficulty. One is to maintain separateness by withdrawing. In Jesus' time the Essenes chose this route. Several centuries after Jesus, Christians began to withdraw from society as well. To hold on to values that all early believers had affirmed, a minority of dedicated Christians from the fourth century onward gave up on direct participation in the life of the empire and became monks. At a later date, renewal movements were forced to withdraw as well. Distinctiveness was possible, but only, it appeared, on the edges of society. Often these groups were tolerated; on occasion they were even valued. But only as long as they kept their distance and refrained from issuing a call to *all* Christians to follow Jesus faithfully. And it didn't take long before some monastic and renewal groups discovered the seduction of cocoon-like separateness.

More common than withdrawing has been a second approach—*surrendering separateness*. Most Christians have felt that it is important that believers occupy the commanding heights of every society for the good of society. Of course this requires compromise, but only with the values of a society which is basically Christian anyway. Since the nations of the West have been Christian, it hasn't seemed to matter if the believers become "like the nations."

Until recently, that is. Of late, Christian critics have been sensing that something has gone wrong. The late Francis Schaeffer has detected in Western Christians an abandonment of spiritual principle—"sheer accommodation to the world spirit of this age."[8] Evangelical statesman John Stott has noted a gravitational pull leading Christians to lose their distinctiveness:

> Probably the greatest tragedy of the church throughout its long and chequered history has been its constant tendency to conform to the prevailing culture instead of developing a Christian counter-culture.[9]

Sociologist Os Guinness has pictured Christians as being lost in a "labyrinth of worldliness."[10] What they do on Sunday may be distinctive, but their faith has nothing to say to what they do from Monday to Saturday.

As the time bombs tick, this problem has become acute. As

we have seen, God has called his people to be distinctive in *all* areas, even in the areas which most immediately affect our security—provision and protection. And in these areas, Christians tend to be just like other conservative citizens—prudent, cautious, afraid of a rocking boat. If Christians have had any distinctiveness, it has often been a distinctiveness of conservative temperaments, and our desire to be different has been nostalgia for an idealized past.

God has an alternative, which is neither withdrawn nor "wet." He expressed it in Jesus. Jesus alarmed people who were afraid of change. He was obviously in the midst of things; and yet he was invitingly different. And Jesus prayed that the Father would protect his followers so that they could *be like him in the world* (John 17:15). How hard it is to be "apart from society and open to it at the same time"![11] Such an accessible separateness is possible only to those who are refreshed by the living water of God's holiness. And these people must keep their eyes fixed on Jesus.

Godlikeness

The only separateness that has anything to say to our time is a separateness that is a reflection of God. Godlikeness is our third aspect of holiness. How essential it is! Without it, we would not suspect that our journey was necessary. Without the Holy One, we would lack both a destination—his Holy City—and a direction for our life as we go. And it is Jesus who, as the "image of the invisible God," reveals to us what godlikeness is all about (Col. 1:15).

How tempted we Christians are to overlook Jesus. It is not that we do not tell people good news *about* him—his love for oppressed and sinful people, his sacrificial death, his resurrection in power. But Jesus himself—the man whose peculiar holiness so threatened the rulers of his day that they had to kill him—this Jesus we are tempted to forget. And that is disastrous for us. Unless we spend time listening to Jesus and watching him work, our understanding of holiness will be crippled.

This is not a new problem for Christians. Signs of it were already present in the great fourth-century statement of faith called the "Apostles' Creed":

> I believe ... in Jesus Christ his only Son our Lord, who was conceived by the Holy Ghost, born of the Virgin Mary, suffered under Pontius Pilate....

There were thirty-three years in between his birth and his crucifixion; in three of these he was engaged in the most important public life in history. Is it not important to believe something about these years?

If we glide over these years, we get the most curious, historically incredible depictions of Jesus. He was, a Cambridge don informed us recently in a series of broadcast talks, "a man who directed others to turn away from the preoccupations of human society."[12] This is an odd view, which still characterizes much Christian preaching in the West. But although it credits Jesus with being King, it doesn't pay attention to his kingly acts or listen to his royal wisdom. And it restricts his rule. New Christians are advised to change their private habits but not their public behavior. So in the crucial security areas of protection and provision, Christians continue to behave just like everyone else. Considering what they have been taught, it's not their fault that their consciences have been cauterized. What an effect this tradition has had! An English Evangelical airman testified:

> I was at Christmas Island in the 1950s, and saw the British nuclear test explosion. I never felt any qualms prompted by the Holy Spirit from it, whereas I have in other areas—like drinking.[13]

How unfair to Jesus, and how dangerous for the whole world, when we see nothing more in Christlikeness than an attitude that is sweet, strong, and free of alcohol and politics.

How far removed this is from the Jesus who strides across the pages of the gospels. This Jesus showed all dimensions of holiness. He didn't divert people's eyes upward, to "the ethereal qualities of immortality."[14] That is not biblical holiness. Rather he radiated holiness into those places that conventional caricatures of "holiness" ignore—the crunch issues of his time, war and wealth. As Savior and Lord, he loved his country's enemies, included the outsiders, and brought justice to poor people. How deeply in trouble we are when we do not allow him to challenge us, and the leaders of our society, to live differently! Remember who it was that built his house upon the sand (Matt. 7:24-27)? It was not the person who refused to accept Jesus as Savior. It was the person who heard Jesus' words and didn't act on them. When the rain fell, that person's house fell—with a bang. How is our house doing?

To grow into the godlike dimension of holiness, let us take off our blinkers. Let us look resolutely at the Jesus of the Gospels. And let us allow him to look at us, lovingly, searchingly. Let us tell and retell his story. Let us memorize his teachings—the law of freedom which followed the second Exodus. Above all, let us watch him at work, for as he responded to the people and crises of his time, he was doing what the Father was doing (John 5:20). He, the Holy One of God, was dramatically demonstrating the Father's holiness. If we are to be holy, we will be drawn to do what he was doing.

Dynamism

Doing, indeed, is the point; it is our fourth aspect of holiness, its dynamism. For in Jesus as throughout the Bible, holiness is on the move. Holiness is a force for change. It mends things and it makes them whole. It "shatters the resistances which humankind sets up against God."[15] As we yield ourselves to its power, it moves us toward the Holy City.

There is no holiness without power. When Isaiah, Jeremiah,

or the early Christians met the Holy One, things had to change. Paul knew this well. "The kingdom of God," he said, "is not a matter of talk but of power" (1 Cor. 4:20, NIV). Its power affects all of life. In Jesus we can see how it works. At his touch, the dynamic wholeness of holiness enveloped physically and spiritually crippled people and healed them. Today, in God's grace, many Christians are once again experiencing the reality of that kind of power. God's Holy Spirit brings change, life, wholeness! How much many of us need to grow in allowing this dynamic power to flow through us.

But the holiness which Jesus brought did more than change individuals. It brought God's power to bear upon the forces that were the time bombs of his society. Jesus didn't weep over Jerusalem because it was full of unhealed blind people; the Jerusalemites were never reluctant to accept healing. He wept over it because its inhabitants, in their spiritual blindness, would not accept what he was saying. They were closed to "the things that make for peace." Love their nation's enemies? Never! Jesus' contemporaries segregated holiness. They were open to its power to heal illness; but they were closed to its power to heal social relationships. And so, within a few years, their Roman enemies destroyed their civilization (Luke 19:41-44). The clocks on their time bombs ran out.

God wants us to experience the fullness of holiness. In calling us to be holy, he is calling us to realign ourselves with the story of Jesus. Jesus is the key to the meaning of the entire Bible; he shows us what the story is about, because he shows us the Father. In word and action, he demonstrates how comprehensive the Father's care is. In his cross, he shows us the depth of the Father's determination to set things right. And he invites us to follow him; he invites us to be a continuation of his story. For that end he wants to empower us with the dynamic energy of holiness. He wants us to be people who look like him—agents of change towards his Holy City.

CHAPTER
15

National Holiness

God is calling us to holiness, to a distinctive life that looks like Jesus. How difficult this is! We feel ourselves isolated. We are squeezed by the pressures of our society into values and lifestyles that are just like everybody else's. They require no faith, and their consequences for the future of the world are choking. When we hear Jesus calling us to be unlike the nations, it is not only non-Christians who do not understand. The incomprehension and disapproval of other Christians is even more distressing. In our weakness, we may well respond to them impatiently and judgmentally. It's exhausting and spiritually precarious to be a holy soloist!

This is a sad situation. It is a distortion of what God wants for his holy people. But we have to be realistic. Our journey will take us, not from where we would like to start, but from where we actually are. When our vision of social holiness isolates us from other people, we must turn to our Father in prayer. We must ask him about ourselves. Do we offend other people because of things within us that are unwholesome and abrasive? Is our vision of holiness flawed? If so—and whose vision of holiness is not flawed!—we must open ourselves to God's healing. But we must also ask God for companions on our journey. Perhaps we should begin by praying, "Lord, give me a companion. And make *me* a companion." As God answers our prayer, building a common life of holy obedience, our prayers can broaden in scope. "Lord, thank you for our prayer group, which is experiencing many dimensions of your holiness. Renew your entire church! Make it to be the *holy nation* you have called it to be!"

The Holy Nation Forgotten

A holy nation. If only we experienced this more, many Christians wouldn't feel so isolated. But for centuries the vast majority of Christians—theologians and layfolk alike—have forgotten that the church can be a holy nation. We have assumed that we live on two levels: the personal level, and the public level. In the first of these, we attempt to live our private lives in as holy a way as possible, and to some extent we can succeed. But things are different in our public life. There we rub shoulders with everyone in our nation, with our entire society. We cannot transfer patterns of behavior from the individual level to the level of society. When we do, the results, "from the political perspective, are quite impossible."[1] Groups behave differently from individuals. Personal holiness is difficult but possible; public holiness is out of the question!

Such ideas are based on a great deal of experience, and they have much to commend them. The American thinker Reinhold Niebuhr stated them in classical form, but he was not being original; he was simply expressing the commonly held assumptions of individualistic Western Christianity. We have our personal rights and we have our social responsibilities—responsibilities to our nation. According to English theologian Keith Ward, we've got to be clear about where our ultimate loyalties lie. We have a "special concern for the survival of our own culture, language, and traditions that [we] do not feel for others ... we have a duty to defend our families and cultures, our communities and countries from destruction, tyranny, and subjugation."[2] The implications for our behavior are clear. In our personal dealings we may forgive debts and reject violence; but when acting as a part of *our nation*—defined in terms of culture, language, and country—we must stand up for its economic and political rights.

Holy Nationhood Regained

But what is our nation? Stupid question! Our passports tell us. We are Argentinian, British, or Cambodian. But is it this simple? As Christians are we not members of another nation—another nation to which we owe primary allegiance? Might there not be a social group, both smaller than our national societies and vastly bigger than them, which God has designed to give social expression to holiness? Christian economist Professor Brian Griffiths evidently assumes not:

> Because the kingdom of God depends for its very existence on an inward supernatural power, it is impossible to translate it into contemporary social, political, and economic institutions.... The real world in which we live is a fallen world and not a community of saints.[3]

There is wisdom here. If we attempt to construct a political platform for an entire national society on the basis of Jesus' kingdom teachings, we will fail. But Griffiths words—which seem to rule out the application of Jesus' teaching on the social plane—contain seeds of something different, more dynamic, more hopeful: "inward supernatural power ... social, political and economic institutions ... community of saints [holy ones]." These words point to a reality that is both social and spiritual, both institutional and holy. And it has a transforming power. In both Old and New Testaments, this reality is the vehicle for God's social strategy. It is his *holy nation*. Formed by his supernatural power, it is "elect from every nation, yet one throughout the earth." This is the nation in which God has designed holiness—all-embracing *social holiness*—to take on political and economic form.

Why is it that we Christians find it so hard to think of ourselves as members of a holy nation? Because we have bad habits—habits which were formed when everybody, in every nation in "Christendom," was a Christian. But that is no longer the case. In the United Kingdom, for example, regular churchgoing by the late 1970s had fallen to 11 percent.[4] Professor Sir Herbert Butterfield saw this decline in historical perspective. "After a period of fifteen hundred years or so we can just about begin to say that at last no one is now a Christian because of government compulsion, or because it is necessary to procure favor at court, or because it is necessary in order to qualify for public office."[5] The old equivalence of church and nation is gone. Almost everywhere (Ireland and Poland are notable exceptions), the mass church is dead. So is the "Christian nation." The conversions to Jesus that one prays for cannot resurrect it.

Is this a reason to despair? On the contrary. According to Professor Butterfield, ours is "the most important and the most exhilarating period in the history of Christianity for fifteen hundred years."[6] It is a time for mission. It is a time for the church to emerge as a community, defined not by cultural coercion but by faith and supernatural power. It is a time when God's holy ones can begin to reclaim their biblical identity. We are Christians. As biblical people, we will be subordinate to a queen or president. But we will obey the King—Jesus. And we will identify ourselves with him and his scattered subjects around the world. With them our bond "is stronger than that associated with national, racial, or ethnic ties."[7]

Our nation—God's holy nation—crosses frontiers. In its common life and institutions, it can give social expression to holiness. In it, Jubilee and enemy loving make sense. It, not the civil authorities, is the bearer of God's cause in history. Our primary way of being socially responsible is not to find new ways of participating in conventional politics, important though that may be; it is rather to find new ways of making God's holy nation a visible, social reality.

Dual Citizenship

But don't we still belong to our "fatherland" as well? Don't genes, geography, and the social solidarity which they have always entailed have a claim upon us? As Keith Clements has written in a moving book, just because secular nationhood is not "the ultimate does not mean it is nothing. Precisely in its very human nature, it has a rightful claim on our solidarity."[8] I agree. It is good to be American. American culture—apple pie, the Super Bowl, soda fountains, Leonard Bernstein—is as beautiful and valid as any other. Both Testaments of the Bible tell us to love our neighbors. And wherever we live, our countries and fellow citizens—maddening though they may sometimes be—will be eminently worth loving.

As Christians, it is right for us to identify with our native lands. There are good biblical reasons for us to be respectful, loyal citizens. Peter urged his friends to honor the emperor of Babylon and to be subordinate to his officials (1 Pet. 2:13-17). No less should we be respectful and as obedient as possible to our government. Dietrich Bonhoeffer was determined to be a good German as well as a loyal member of the communion of saints. His struggle to reconcile these is worth pondering by us all.[9]

But for most of us that is not the problem. Our problem is this: as Western Christians we have had practically no sense of being part of an international, holy nation. There are powerful forces of persuasion and pressure that seek to arouse our emotions as American citizens. No such media bonanzas encourage our solidarity with the network that unites Christian brothers and sisters—Baptist, Catholic, Orthodox, and the rest—in Eastern Europe as well as in the U.S. Even within this country, Christians have not developed an appreciation of the social potential of belonging to each other under the kingship of God.

Two things have resulted. First of all, in a time of international tension, the Christians' primary national loyalty emerges quickly and with great emotional clarity. They, like everyone else, assume that their primary identity is not with other Christians; it is with their fellow countrymen. World War I showed this in flagrant form—in Britain as well as in the U.S. In 1915 the bishop of London exhorted the nation to social holiness:

> I think the Church can best help the nation . . . by making it realize that it is enaged in a Holy War, and not be afraid of saying so. Christ died on Good Friday for Freedom, Honour and Chivalry, and our boys are dying for the same things . . . Mobilize the Nation for a Holy War![10]

So did the German bishops, for German boys were also dying for God.

This isn't simply a thing of the past. At the moment, America is targeting every Soviet city with nuclear missiles—Minuteman, Poseidon, Trident, and the rest. And the Soviet cities have millions of Christian believers in them![11] What kind of wound in the body of Christ would it cause if we used even one of our missiles? But few Christians seem to reflect on that. For we have almost no sense of Christian nationhood. We lapse reflexively into assuming that Americans are "God's people." It is easy to quote 2 Chronicles 7:14: "If my people who are called by my name humble themselves, and pray and seek my face, and turn from their wicked ways, then I will hear from heaven, and will forgive their sin and heal their land."

But it won't do to pray this for America. We can only pray this for those who genuinely are "God's people," the transnational Christian nation. If we Christians don't think of ourselves like that, perhaps it's time that we started to. Our reflexes would have to change. When pushed to declare what our national identity really is, we would be Christians first, Americans (or anything else), second.

The second consequence has already become clear. Because we, as Christians in America, lack a sense of primary commitment to each other and to other Christians around the world, we are doomed to live in an unholy way—like the nations. We go to church as individuals. There we receive spiritual resources to live in the dog-eat-dog life of modern society. How isolated, atomized, and disempowered we are! No wonder we are estranged from holiness. No wonder we live like all the nations. On one point, Reinhold Niebuhr was quite wrong: it is much harder as isolated individuals to live like Jesus than it is in the new society of God's nation.

A Pioneering People

The journey on which God has called us to set out is a journey of discovery. As we travel, we will learn much. We will learn about nationhood. As God's holy nation, we will find out what it means to be a nation without land. We will discover that our deepest solidarity is not with our physical neighbors, who share our accent, education, and taste in tea; it is rather with the believers in Hungary, Haiti, and Hartford, Connecticut—believers who, because of Christ's work, are our brothers and sisters.

What delight there is in this discovery! What excitement there is in discovering the rich history, both common and diverse, which we share with fellow citizens in God's nation that come from every part of the world. And what a firm basis for witness to individuals and to governments this base in holy nationhood will give us! Not everyone will appreciate this. As Scottish Bible teacher Jim Punton commented shortly before he died, if "Christians acted on a real vision of being the nation of God they would immediately terrify governments worldwide." But countless men and women would be drawn to a "worldwide solidarity of justice and love."[12]

How to live as a holy society—this is the second thing we will learn. Because we are so accustomed to living like the nations, we have much to learn. How exciting it will be as we begin to do so. Throughout the Bible, God used creative minorities (another way of saying "holy nations") to move history forward.[13] In the Old Testament, that was how God used Israel among the nations. And for us post-New Testament Christians, that is the calling of Christ to his church.

If we have lost this vision, we can regain it. Like the early Christians, we can be a new society which gives individuals the strength to hold out against the values of a pagan world. We can also give social expression to Jesus' teaching, not just in individual congregations but between congregations and across the worldwide holy nation. "The church is called to be now what the world is called to be ultimately."[14] If we can grasp this vision and live by it in a fearful world, we can be a source of immense hope.

CHAPTER

16

Social Holiness
for Individuals and
Families

But how? This vision of being God's holy nation, living in alternative ways "unlike the nations," trustingly entering into risk because of God's reliable grace—it may sound great but impossible; or it may merely sound suspect! Is it irresponsible idealism to think we might develop a way of living based on such a vision? What specific everyday steps might such a way of living require?

No one can say exactly. And it is not my wish to prescribe details for individuals or groups. But I believe that all of us, separately and in our churches, are called to take steps of faith. Mind you, only one step at a time! Jesus doesn't ask us to be kangaroos as we follow him (but he also doesn't want us to be sloths!). In this chapter, I hope to draw out some principles which can guide us as we make decisions for that next step forward. And I hope that some examples and questions will stimulate us to continue wrestling with the complexities that we face in pursuing a life of holiness.

Salt and Light

When we're trying to think practically, Jesus' words are always to the point. A brief burst of his teaching—which Christians concerned to be involved in society have loved to quote—is particularly relevant:

> You are the salt of the earth; but if salt has lost its taste, how shall its saltness be restored? It is no longer good for anything except to be thrown out and trodden under foot by everybody. You are the light of the world. A city set on a hill cannot be hid. Nor do people light a lamp and put it under a bushel, but on a stand, and it gives light to all in the house. Let your light so shine before everybody, that they may see your good works and give glory to your Father who is in heaven. (Matt. 5:13-16)

"Be salt and light!" Surely this passage, more than any other in the Bible, is a charter for Christian involvement in society.

It is, of course. But it also has become a slogan. Because its meaning is presumably obvious, Christians may not have thought deeply enough about it. Indeed, at times it may have stifled our thinking. But the passage which underlies this slogan is a rich one. It is not simply a charter for involvement; it is a charter for a particular kind of involvement. It is not enough to be involved in society. To be faithful to Jesus, we must be social in a holy way. For the "salt and light" passage is a holiness text.

Why did Jesus give this teaching to his followers? Because he knew that they, as successors to the prophets, would be a persecuted minority living under constant pressure (Matt. 5:11-12). In this position, they would be subject to two temptations. Either they might withdraw from the world like the Essenes had done; or, if they got involved, they might lose their distinctiveness and become just like everyone else. Holiness in the world—this was Jesus' desire for his followers. Withdrawal and compromise—these were how things could go wrong for them.

Jesus foresaw disaster unless his followers were highly visible.

They are light; they illuminate the way for the world. But their light must be set in a place where it really makes a difference; it must be on a stand, and not under a basket! Their city must be on a hill. If it's in a canyon it can't be a model for anyone.

Jesus foresaw another kind of disaster if his followers compromised their distinctiveness. They are salt, and they have to be different to be effective. Only by keeping their saltiness can they fertilize the soil or add spice to the food. When they function like that, the earth becomes a better place and God's kingdom is on the offensive.[1] But if their salt loses its saltiness through being mixed with windblown dust, it becomes useless. It is there, and presumably it is still called salt. But it has nothing to contribute. It can't do what salt is meant to do.

How will Jesus' followers know if they are being salty? Not by measuring their influence on the world, but by monitoring their similarity to their Master and their faithfulness to his teaching. It is men and women of the Beatitudes who are salt. It is men and women whose hearts are pure, who tell the truth, who love their enemies, who trust the Father for provision, who above all else seek God's kingdom and his justice. In other words, saltiness is the distinctive approach to life—all of life, including the sensitive areas of provision and protection—that Jesus taught in the rest of the Sermon on the Mount. This was how Jesus himself lived. Jesus warned that it isn't enough to mouth the right phrases in prayer ("Lord, Lord"), or to exercise the spiritual gifts, if one goes on living like all the nations. Saltiness means putting into practice the will of the Father (7:21-23).

Jesus' followers can do this in two ways. Salt and light operate differently. To be effective, salt must be scattered. In great chunks, it is counterproductive: as a seasoning it is inedible; and as a fertilizer it destroys growth. Jesus' followers, like grains of salt, are willing to risk mingling with society to work there for the change which the kingdom brings.

Light, on the other hand, is a word for gathering, not scattering. When Jesus uses the word "light," he is in fact referring to a cluster of lights. He is alluding to the true nation of Israel which in the Old Testament is the "light to the nations" demonstrating what a holy society is like (Isa. 49:6). And in the Sermon on the Mount, Jesus is calling his followers to fulfil this privileged social function. It is not to an individual on a pedestal that Jesus points; it is to a city set on a hill, a highly visible complex society made up of many individuals.[2]

Jesus' salt and light challenge our lives. Many of us have ignored the challenge entirely, becoming comfortable in our jobs. We have not asked if we are doing holy work, pointing to Jesus and his kingdom. Some of us have tried to choose between salt and light. We have put all our effort into individual questions about saltiness and have been less concerned about the "light" of the church which can function as a model society of justice and love. Others of us, out of fear or long habit, have withdrawn from society, spending all of our time in cells of Christian irrelevance. Whatever the flavor of our unfaithfulness, Jesus invites us to repent. He invites us to become what he is—distinctive, unlike the nations, but like the Father, in the world. He calls us to be holy as he is holy. Our involvement in society must be based on him.

Principles of Holy Living

But what will it look like in practice? In the pages that follow, I can only give a few hints and examples. My suggestions are modest and tentative. But I hope they will be stimulating to us. We certainly need to use our imaginations. For at every level of our lives—as individuals and families, at work, in public life, and in our corporate life within the church—social holiness is elusive.

The reasons for this are familiar. We may adapt ourselves unthinkingly to the customs of the society which surrounds us. We may underestimate the difficulty of a course of action we've chosen to take. We may attempt too lightly to require standards of holy living of people and institutions which are not Christian. Above all, we may forget that we're in hostile territory. If we do these things, Jesus warns us that we won't be salt and that we'll get trampled. But if we persist in wanting to be tasty salt and clusters of hope-giving light, here are a few principles that may help us.

(1) *Our primary citizenship is in God's nation.* As Jesus' disciples we carry the passports of God's holy nation. This nation is made up of men and women drawn from "every tribe and tongue and people and nation" (Rev. 5:9). It spans the globe. It minimizes the political frontiers that carve it into "national" units. Everywhere we citizens of God's nation are living as exiles, in salty dispersion among the "nations"—in Babylon, in societies that live by values in many ways opposed to those of our God and his Messiah. In some of these societies it will be harder to live holy lives than in others; it may be especially difficult in societies which claim to be "Christian." Everywhere we will be under pressure and our attempts as individuals, families, and churches to be socially holy will bring upon us criticism and, at times, exclusion and persecution.

Because we are living under pressure, we need to experience the tangible reality of God's nation, to know the joy of lives lived in freedom and expectancy. We need this simply to survive in a socially holy lifestyle. If we attempt to make a go of it as holy loners, our conventional "Babylonian" neighbors will dismiss us as cranks. And sooner or later we will break down and conform. To remain distinctive we desperately need each other's support. But then that's the way God has designed us to live—he has made us to be social beings. We are to be light as well as salt, and we can arrive at maturity only in the company of others.

The Bible is not just the story of holy individuals; it is the story of a holy nation whose society is meant to be a demonstration to all humanity of God's will for the world. It is vital that we live together in justice and love. Only if we do so can we urge others—including the institutions of our surrounding societies—to adopt ways of living that we have found to be life-giving.

(2) *We cannot apply social holiness directly to the "nations."* We cannot expect Babylon—its state and its major institutions—to operate by Christian standards. Holy living is risky living, and if people do not know the security of having God as their Father, we cannot expect them to do such countercultural things as love their enemies or share their possessions.

But we will at times find non-Christians who do these things. How can we explain our experience that humanists and adherents of other world religions are at times more in tune with Jesus' way than some Christians? Perhaps by Jesus' repeated reminder that God's kingdom is made up of surprising people (e.g., Matt. 8:11-12). This should keep us humble and receptive to others. And it should make us willing to collaborate with non-Christians. After all, we work side by side with them in our jobs; why can't we do so in organizations working for things that Jesus cared about—justice and peace? As we do so, we will need to be candid about our values and motivation. Truth-telling is more important to us than the "gains" that might be made by cutting corners. In dealing with our opponents we will be respectful and nonviolent.[3] And we will want to communicate—both visually and verbally—that Jesus is our reason for acting and the source of true life.

(3) *We should take part in Babylon and try to influence it.* We may sense God's call to participate in the social and governmental structures of our countries (Babylon). In many countries, there is ample opportunity for us to do so. Modern government is complex and varied, and there are many levels at which we can make distinctive contributions. But at all times we must be alert. We must remember that we are participating, not to perpetuate things as they are, but to change them. Furthermore, we must bear in mind the holiness which God ultimately requires—even of nations. Reequalization of

resources and the forgiveness of enemies may seem difficult, even impossible. But these represent God's concerns, and they are the direction in which he will move human history.

If we, having a vision of God's kingdom and knowing his grace, can propose policies which are "stepping-stones" between what we now have and the holy society that God desires, we can be usefully involved in governmental and corporate structures. But, as Evangelical social strategist A.N. Triton reminds us, "We cannot join in all aspects of society."[4] Remember, we are a minority movement. It is not our calling to run the world. It is our calling to follow Jesus, to do those things that are in keeping with his life and teaching and are a fulfilment of the Law and the prophets. If we participate without reference to these, our contributions will be unholy. We will not be salt in the world.

We can also influence the corporate and governmental structures of our time from outside. Where there are Christians in these institutions, we can address them as brothers and sisters in terms of our common allegiance to Jesus and his way. Where these institutions are run by non-Christians, we must express our concerns to them in secular language, but with respect, fully conscious that they are "servants of God" (Rom. 13:4). At times we may, like Jesus and Jeremiah, choose dramatic forms of witness.

In cleansing the temple, Jesus used a nonviolent, direct way of communicating to the establishment of his day. The message got through, and his enemies—challenged on their home ground—immediately began to plot his destruction (Mark 11:18). Whether we use words or actions to get our point across, our message will often be one of warning. When nations (and corporations) flout God's will for sharing and reconciliation, they get into trouble, and so does the whole world. But we should not simply rail or condemn. Where possible, we should offer well-researched practical alternatives, "stepping-stones" toward policies more in keeping with God's will.

Social Holiness For Individuals and Families

Social holiness is never an easy thing. It requires risk-taking in areas of our lives that are sensitive—the security areas of provision and protection. "For better or for worse" we are committed to the welfare of those closest to us. We have learned the well-established patterns of our society for providing that welfare. It may be easier for us as individuals and families to take steps of risky obedience than it is for churches or nations. But even on the smaller scale it is hard to break loose.

What can we do? Only what God calls us to do. But he certainly is calling each one of us into some new area of insecurity. He wants us to rely upon him practically, not just theoretically. As we explore new areas of sharing and reconciliation, he will demonstrate his faithfulness to us.

We might, for example, start by asking ourselves some questions about money and possessions.

—Why are we saving money?
—Are we saving in a way that contravenes justice and peace (for example, through investments in South Africa or the arms industries)?
—Does our savings mask our need to trust in God's provision?
—Do we really need life insurance?
—How much insurance do we have on our personal effects?
—Should we have less valuable stuff anyhow?
—How much does advertising influence what we think and do?
—Does our stockpile of possessions mean that we don't have to be dependent on God for provision?

We might also think more closely about how we live.[5]

—Why do we live where we do?
—If we have a choice, could a move enhance our obedience

to the life and principles of God's kingdom?

—Could we cope with the consequences if our moving house brought isolation, urban violence, culture shock?

—If we intentionally lived near other Christian people, could we form a "cell of light" that could help us cope? Could a cluster of Christian households improve the tone of an entire neighborhood?

—Do we plan our menus by unexamined habit, responding to advertising or following the latest trend?[6]

—Could simplifying our diet free money to give for food for the hungry?

—Could we go a whole year without buying new clothing in order to contribute our normal budgeted amount to a hard-pressed development agency?

—Would we consider bypassing a promotion at work in order to stay in the community where our church is located and where we are learning how we can give and receive?

—How do we counter society's pressures to accumulate more and more possessions?

—How do we teach justice and peace to our children? Do we let them play with war toys?[7]

—How can we say *no* to the stereotyping of outsiders and to the demeaning language of racism and sexism?

Any of these questions may lead us to take a first step, a small step toward the life of holiness that God is asking of us. Our little steps will not be earthshakingly significant. Are they worth the trouble? Will they have a useful effect? We can't tell, can we? But our individual steps forward can be important. God began his story with individuals—Abraham and Sarah— who responded to his call by doing something daft. Similarly our small steps can set a new direction for our lives, and lead us to further steps as God keeps us moving.

God has a way of surprising us. Our attempts to be faithful often have a significance that we can't see at the moment. Our coming to understand an outsider ("immigrant") because we live near to him or her may change more than just our own attitudes. The money that we no longer spend on an insurance policy or an expensive new car might combine with the financial giving of others to enable our church to employ a new community worker. And in any event, the time bombs ticking under our society are going to force us all in the West—sooner or later—to lower our living standards. Wouldn't it be exciting if Christians came to discover now that life lived by the "manna principles" can be rich and full? Wouldn't it be wonderful if God's holy nation rediscovered its true role as a nation of pioneers?

On Not Insuring Yourself

Friends of mine recently decided not to invest in a life insurance and savings policy. They are modest about their decision. They know that what they've done is not necessarily what everyone in their position should do. I agree. But I still think that their approach may speak to us all, possibly as a sample of the way that we might ponder the choices that we face. So at my request, they allowed me to reproduce their process of searching for God's guidance.

We almost signed the policy. It wasn't that expensive, only $25 per month, closed for ten years. We assumed we needed it to cover a bank loan that we've got. But that wasn't really so; it was more of an excuse. As we thought about it, the costs of the policy began to mount in our minds. It would tie up a large amount of our money over a long period of time. How else would we use the money? Couldn't we give it to the church, which certainly needs it? Or to the charity that we're committed to?

And how about Abba as our Protector and Provider? Of course he does his protecting and providing work through human means, but what are the most responsible ways of organizing these? He calls us to take risks, and living in risky dependency is the way most likely to show forth his power and reality to others in the world. But we couldn't discuss this with others, could we, and say we have financial protection? Most of our friends couldn't think of affording a policy like this one. What right would we have to talk about it, especially when we have so much more financial security than most people anyway?

What does the Bible say? It says a lot of things, but these particular passages in our lectionary readings have been speaking pretty directly to us:

> Learn not the way of the nations, nor be dismayed at the signs of the heavens because the nations are dismayed at them, for the customs of the peoples are false. (Jer. 10:2-3)
>
> I remember the devotion of your youth, your love as a bride, how you followed me in the wilderness, in a land not sown. Israel was holy to the Lord, the first fruits of his harvest. (Jer. 2:2-3)
>
> [Jesus is] the pioneer of [our] salvation.... He partook of flesh and blood, that through death he might destroy him who has the power of death, that is, the devil, and deliver all those who through fear of death were subject to lifelong bondage. (Heb. 2:10, 14-15)

Firstfruits. How do we live so we really are firstfruits of God's new thing? Pioneers. To be that, some people have to take risks and go out on a limb ahead of others. It's not that we're being in any way superior. It's just that for us at this time we can't accept this insurance policy and keep a clear conscience. It's also not that we're saying that life insurance is wrong. But this is the area where we believe God is asking us to express practical trust.

"But what about the children? Now you must be responsible." We're always uneasy when people say this kind of thing. Is it an excuse to conform? What about the children of people who can't afford insurance? It looks like God will care for us, but he isn't big enough to look after them, too. We don't believe that: God hasn't changed his character! But this is the greatest stumbling block for us. The children—that is where we get insecure and fearful. Therefore perhaps we need to trust all the more. And after all, how little we're doing. Our decision about the insurance is simply one act, a symbolic act of trust toward God. As we start our family life, we're trusting him for the children as well. It's a very small step. But only by starting in that direction can we be open to the next steps that he will show us for our future.

Social Holiness in Our Work

If it's hard to be distinctive in the way we live as individuals and families, it's just as difficult at work. Of course, we will experience this in many ways. If we live in East Germany, we may have no difficulty getting work; but we may find that certain areas—such as politics—are ruled out for us. In the West, for some of us the big problem is that we can't find any work at all. Or, we may have retired from the workaday world with energies yet to invest. Some of us have work alright, but the work seems meaningless. Or other things about our work may trouble us. It may be a taskmaster absorbing 98 percent of our best energies. We could do with more time for ourselves and less pay, but that is not a choice. Our firms may have investments or contracts that seem wrong to us. . . . .

And so we need to learn to formulate the questions, to find ways of thinking through the implications of our principles of holy living for the world of work. Are there small steps of faith that put us on the narrow path to a deeper trust in God as the one who provides for us in this vital area?

Here are some questions to use as starters, to prime our thinking.

—If I am unemployed, can I expand my understanding of "work" so that I can use my time and energies positively for God's kingdom? What will I do if the only jobs that come my way are in an industry which is producing something that I cannot square with God's purposes?

—If I am at home, and am financially supported by another person (my spouse?), can I take a more vigorous part in the chain of life-support for oppressed and marginalized people around me?

—If I am at work, can I bring kingdom qualities to my relationships? Can I be a peacemaker, one who brings the outsider into the circle, one who resists evil with good?

—What does Sabbath mean to me? The Bible doesn't prescribe an annual holiday, but it does call for a Sabbath day holy to the Lord. Can I trust God for provision and meaning even if I'm not working all the time?

—If I'm on my way up in my firm or department, does that mean that I am too easily conforming to the system? Are there times when I have been squeezed into its mould?[8]

—Whose finger would I rather have on the nuclear trigger, a Christian's or an atheist's? Or who would I rather have performing an abortion or doing research with human embryos?[9] Does it make any difference?

—If I'm involved in politics, do I agree with one theologian that "the essential characteristics of a successful politician are precisely the opposites of the essential characteristics of a good Christian"?[10] If this seems unduly pessimistic, given the wide variety of political and governmental jobs available in most Western countries today, is it possible to be involved in many of these in a Jesus-like way: "to take upon oneself the cross, give up force and splendor"?[11] Can we, as one English Christian Member of Parliament put it recently, make an essential contribution through "flinging open the doors—to reduce the number of dark corners to render our stewardship of power as visible and accountable as can be"?[12]

—If my conscience is pinching me about staying in the job I have, can I deal with these questions?

a. Is what I'm doing promoting justice and shalom? Is it helping the poor or hurting them? Could I imagine Jesus doing my job?

b. Do I have close Christian contacts in a local church, or

am I more and more associating with people at a similar professional or technical level? Do I discuss the doubts I have about my work with anybody?

c. Do I ask for the prayers of my fellow Christians as I struggle with my questions? Have I ever thought of bringing my big life decisions to my prayer group for their counsel and discernment?

—If I quit my job for conscience' sake, how will I provide for myself and my family? How can I give to the church? Won't I be wasting my training or my time? Who will share the good news with people at work?

—Is it fool's courage to think up an alternative type of job? Have I really explored the alternatives that are available?[13] If I would rather use my expertise working for an organization trying to change the system (like the New Alchemy Institute on Cape Cod, which is developing new approaches to environmental issues, or Washington's Center for Defense Information) instead of a military industry, can I actually find a job? Can I cope with the cut in pay and the hassle? It's so much easier to work within the system!

Principles for Involvement in Work

Are there any general principles that can give us positive guidance as we approach our work, regardless of whether we're a professional, a manual worker, or a person who is unwaged, retired, or communally supported? Can we view work in its larger sense, not only as the effort that brings the pay envelope but particularly in its contribution to God's project? I suggest the following:

1. *We must choose what we do.* As strangers in Babylon, we Christians are in a minority in virtually every society that we live in. In the U.S. at the moment, it may in many parts of the country be the "done thing" to go to church; but the percentage of the populace that is open to following Jesus in a

costly way in all areas of their lives is small. Our resources in personnel are therefore scarce. We can't possibly do every task in American society. But we can choose to do distinctive things that point toward the Holy City.

2. *Jesus is Lord! So we will not concede any area of life to Satan.* As Jesus' followers, we may not be able to do certain tasks and be faithful to him, his teachings and his priorities. Space weapons, for example, may seem to us to be utterly contradictory to Jesus' way—a theft of resources from the poor and a means of perpetuating human hatred and the dominance of the strong. If so, we may not be able, in good conscience, to be involved in research on space weapons, or eventually in production as well.

But Jesus is as much Lord of space as he is of everything. Indeed, there is no area of creation or human experience of which he is not the key to a proper approach for his followers. We must be careful, however. It is easy to talk glibly about the lordship of Christ but for that lordship to be theoretical, not real. How can we tell? By using this yardstick: does the "lordship of Christ" agree with the teaching and action of the Jesus of the gospels? If it does so, we are on safe ground. If not—if we separate the "lordship of Christ" from the Jesus who shows us the Father at work in his world—we are fooling ourselves. We may still talk about Christ as Lord, but the content of his "lordship" may be determined by pragmatism or nostalgia. And however much we may rail against the Christians who disagree with us as "humanists" or worse, the policies that we recommend will very likely be worldly and despairing. Jesus the Messiah is our hope; there is no other foundation (1 Cor. 3:11). Even in the stubborn, problem areas of our life—wealth and war—he points the way forward. As Mennonite theologian John Howard Yoder has wisely commented, "If Jesus Christ is Lord, obedience to his rule cannot be dysfunctional."[14]

So let's not withdraw from areas of life that humans are distorting for un-Jesus-like ends. On the contrary, let's stay involved in them, thinking and acting as agents of change. As we reclaim these areas for Jesus, he—and not the spiritual opposition—will be effective Lord there.

This is a tough assignment. It will require men and women of spiritual strength, backed up by supportive congregations. In every major area of human concern, some of us will be called to understand the issues and master the details. This may mean learning the ins and outs of the proposed space weaponry, and thinking through their implications for the world's political stability and economic resources. Or it may mean gaining a thorough understanding of the international debt crisis, or amassing every statement made by a major politician about the Non-Proliferation Treaty.[15] It may mean asking questions in a research project that no one has thought of asking before: an Evangelical Christian has recently completed a Ph.D. thesis on the effects of nuclear warfare on British agriculture.[16] Or it may mean helping policy formers emerge from their tunnel thinking, for example, by exploring new approaches to common security, including nonprovocative nonnuclear defense, in Central Europe.[17]

People who represent the well-established ways of the nations may dismiss us and reject our attempts to find new ways. We will need criticism, and will need to listen to our critics carefully. Are they offering us genuine insights and well-warranted correction? Or are they responding with the kind of knee-jerk hostility which Jesus received from the establishment of his time? We must not be deterred by a fear of making mistakes or by rejection. For the time bombs are ticking, and the world desperately needs followers of Jesus who will respond to them by thinking new thoughts and living in new ways.

3. *We must work on alternatives.* In every major area of human concern, some of us Christians must work on distinctive ways of doing things. Many orthodox answers manifestly aren't working. Pioneers are needed, walking in the steps of Jesus toward new ways of doing things that can offer hope.

In Palestine and Ireland, for example, soldiers, guerrillas, and politicians continue to back the use of military force as if it could lead to a solution of the crises there. But in both lands the irrelevance of violence is increasingly evident; it cannot lead to the reconciliation which alone can bring peace and prosperity to the people. In both lands, there are signs of hope. Individuals are crossing barriers, at times at great personal expense. In Northern Ireland, real hope has at times come from surprising sources—such as Will Warren, an English Quaker printer who decided to retire (of all places) in the deprived Bogside area of Derry. As a nonpartisan channel of communication between rival paramilitary forces, he helped save many lives.[18] But groups can often do more than individuals. Communities of Christians are springing up in areas of intercommunal conflict or urban blight, where their deviant ways of living pose questions and offer practical aid. And hope. As recent events in the Philippines have demonstrated, nonviolence offers a way forward; violence is a dead-end. Theologians can contribute to this as well. In Ireland and elsewhere, the way forward may be through a rediscovery of forgiveness—a "politics of forgiveness" in which neither party can be suppressed or wished away.[19]

In business, increasing numbers of people are disillusioned by impersonal corporate structures. And they are doing something about it; they are organizing their firms in an alternative way—as workers' cooperatives.[20] In a strife-ridden industrial world, Christians and non-Christians alike are attracted to a form of business that offers the possibility of both productivity and peace. And many Christians are committed to cooperatives for another reason: it seems to them to be the closest modern equivalent to biblical patterns of property holding and societal cooperation.[21] Sabbath, Jubilee, equality, enoughness—all seem closer to a cooperative (or even to a partnership) than to a multinational conglomerate. Some partnerships, in fact, divide their profits in commercially eccentric ways, setting aside portions of their profits for organizations working for reconciliation and development.[22]

In struggling with the international debt crisis, Christians in politics and international agencies could work toward new approaches which are reflections of their biblical understandings. They might, for example, propose a measure of modest Jubilee—that the U.S. and other Western governments forgive the debts of the poorest nations. Of course, the money would have to come from somewhere. How many guns do we really need? In 1983, 34 sub-Saharan African nations owed the U.S. government the total of $1.95 billion—slightly less than the cost of one Trident nuclear submarine.[23]

Stepping Stones

None of these solutions is ideal. None of them would produce a world order based on "enoughness" and equality, reconciliation and shalom. But each represents a step in the right direction. Each could function as a "stepping-stone"[24] leading from the unimaginative mental rigidity of our current orthodoxies toward something that offers hope. Each is an attempt by Christians to think of an alternative approach; each shows that in the bible, and especially in the themes of Jesus' life and teaching, there is creative potential that is to be found nowhere else.

Could these attempts be fitted together to provide a coherent approach to our time-bomb threatened world? Bob Goudzwaard has chosen to devote his energies to the political and economic life of his native Netherlands; but the larger picture—of the whole world under God's lordship—has always been in his mind. Out of his experience and concern has come the following proposal:

a. That we in the West reorient our assumptions to a level of enough. Unending economic growth is unrealistic and unsustainable. For many of us this may mean a fall in living standards.

  b. That we cut our spending on weapons. Current "defense" efforts are increasing our insecurity and crippling the world's economy. At first this might increase unemployment, but it would free scarce resources for constructive purposes.

  c. That we spend the money that we were no longer spending on armaments on two things: (1) canceling the debts of the poorest countries and relieving them of interest payments, on one condition—that they cut their own military expenditures; (2) creating new jobs—more than were lost in the military industries—in our own countries in areas (housing, hospitals, urban renewal) that meet genuine human need.[25]

Each part of this proposal is controversial and would need to be discussed in detail. I do not have the space to do that here, nor do I have the competence in every area. But I do not need to. Abundant research has already been done on each part of Goudzwaard's proposal. Some of this research has been done by Christians. When we as Jesus' followers today devote our expertise to thinking about such ways—and to implementing them—we have begun to find a valid form of involvement in society. We are neither withdrawn or compromised. We are the salt of the earth.

CHAPTER
17

Social Holiness
for the Church

It's hard to stay salty. The pressures that society places upon us are intense. We get tired of walking on a narrow way. It's exhausting to be an inconvenience to sensible people and to feel out of step. Our self-respect can be beaten down by the ridicule of others. Ultimately we will burn out or sell out. We cannot make it on our own.

That is why God has designed that we be light as well as salt. He wants us to be gathered as well as scattered. When we are conscious that we do not stand alone, when we are joined together with other followers of Jesus in a society living in a new way—*then* we can begin to survive in social holiness.

This place of Christian solidarity is called the church. Whatever its organizational structures, the church is primarily people. It is people who know God as their Father and are therefore committed to each other as sisters and brothers. It is people who, because of the work of the Holy One, know that they are a holy nation. We may live in Babylon, but our primary sense of identity is not Babylonian. So we can experiment. We can attempt to live in ways that might be impossible for everyone in Babylon but which are right for our nation.

Secular minds recoil at the thought of living by Jesus' kingdom teachings, but for us in the church these teachings are practical and life-giving. Loving the enemy, incorporating the outsider, serving the weak, re-equalizing wealth—all of these require conversion, faith, and God's supernatural power; but as Christians these are the air we breathe. The life of our true nation is based on them.

God has a way of living for us that is holy. And like all holiness, other people experience it as both repugnant and deeply compelling. But however others respond, the way God calls us to live represents their true destiny, for holiness is where he is going to take his world. Let's get a few glimpses of what a church that lives in this way may look like.

Five Characteristics of God's Holy Nation

National solidarity.

This has two aspects.

a. We are not alone. Many people experience the society of our political nation as fragmented and heartless; they have an overpowering sense that they are isolated, that nobody really cares. Some sense this in times of personal crisis. Others (many old people, single parent families, people without work) are aware of it all the time. God's holy nation, in contrast, is a place where people can know that they belong. In God's nation we are valued, not for what we might become, but for what we are. In the security of love, we can discover that it is safe to be ourselves. We can be receivers as well as givers; we can grow from where we are instead of from where we would like others to think we are. It is safe to change.

b. We experience national loyalty to an immense nation. God's nation spans the divides that are threatening the future of the world—north vs. south, east vs. west, black vs. white, inner city vs. suburbs. We may know this, but it is vital that we base our knowledge in practical experience. Commitments to people and groups that are far from us can be unreal and therefore dangerous. So it is vital for us to build personal relationships with people and congregations in the other parts of our holy nation. We can twin-link our churches with congregations in Central America or the inner city; we can be pen friends with believers in Eastern Europe; we can give up a luxury holiday in the sun for the privilege of sharing the lot—however briefly—of Christians who are under pressure; we can contribute to the costs of poorer Christians visiting our churches. And, within God's nation, we can make a minimal commitment: "Let the Christians of the world agree that they will not kill each other." [1]

Provision: Economic sharing.

God's nation has a different economic policy from the other nations. As its citizens, we have a vision of equality and sufficiency; we are committed to be contented with what we have and to receive as well as to give. We have a vision of a nation in which there will be no poor people, and we are willing to share our possessions to make that vision a reality. Within our congregations, we, like the early Christians, may find a common fund (called a "Jubilee Fund" or a "Koinonia Fund"?) to be a means of meeting immediate need and of equalizing our wealth. And of reaching others with good news. A group of Christian students at the University of Surrey who decided to do something Jubilee-like—pooling their grants and giving what was left over to poor people—found that their actions were instrumental in attracting Marxists to Jesus.

Between rich parts of God's nation and poorer parts, we can consider measures to equalize resources. In recommending such measures, Christian thinkers are not espousing "pure Marxist theology"; they are simply following in the tradition of institutions as biblical as the Jubilee and Paul's collection

(2 Cor. 8).[2] As we, both in our local churches and throughout
our worldwide nation, move to make this vision practical, pit-
falls will appear at surprising places. Through sin and bad
habits we will fail. But as we experiment with new forms of
faithfulness, God, the God of provision, will come to our aid.
He will bless us with miracles: the miracle of just economic
structures and relationships; the miracle of the "spontaneous"
arrival of desperately needed food and money; perhaps even—
as happened in the mid-1970s to a Texas prayer group and
their poor friends across the border in Mexico—the miracle of a
humanly inexplicable multiplication of food.[3]

Protection: Enemy Loving

Both locally and throughout his worldwide nation, God
grants citizenship to widely differing people. As God's people
we must therefore learn to live together. Reconciliation must
be high on our list of priorities. To achieve these, we will have
to learn to listen better, and to communicate in ways that don't
threaten one another's integrity. Significantly, the apostle Paul
cites "speaking the truth in love" as the sign of holy living
(maturity in Christ)(Eph. 4:15). As we learn to do this, and as
we learn to share our possessions, we will become a people of
peace.

But we will also face other peacemaking tasks. Living in
urban areas will raise acute questions of insecurity and require
us to make difficult decisions.[4] At times, our stand as God's nation for social justice may offend some of our neighbors. So also
may our attitude to nuclear weapons. We know that, as a holy
nation, there is no kind of bomb that can defend us. Persecution cannot stamp out the church—the Roman imperial authorities and, more recently, the Chinese communists have discovered this—but a nuclear war can.[5] Of course, it takes faith
to live without the bomb; and a non-Christian nation may not
want to take that risk. On the other hand, in view of nuclear
proliferation and escalating firepower, it takes some kind of

blind faith to live with the bomb!

We can urge our non-Christian nation to adopt a more modest, less threatening foreign policy. And at all times the love of Christ will compel us to bear witness to what we know. As we tell of God's faithfulness and warn about the direction that events are moving, some of our neighbors and fellow Christians will find us offensive. That cannot be helped. But reconciliation is our calling. As we seek to build bridges to those whom we offend and who offend us, God's call will echo in our hearts: "Do everything possible on your part to live in peace with everybody" (Rom. 12:18, TEV).

Involvement in Pilot Projects.

God's nation has values and priorities which are different from those of the other nations. We therefore can do things that Babylonian society views as odd, unimportant, or impossible. Throughout Christian history there are numerous examples of this. It was the church that pioneered in schools, hospitals, and mental health care. So also it did with the hospices for the terminally ill. And within the past few years, churches have been taking the lead in other areas. I can list only a few. In several countries, sheltered workshops for mentally handicapped adults were first established by Christians. And more recently, Christian lawyers have worked hard to find ways in justice. They have established mediation and conciliation services which help civil litigants to listen to each other and to settle their disputes out of court. "Victim-Offender Reconciliation Programs," which do the same kind of thing in criminal cases, have been equally beneficial.[6] On the border between Nicaragua and Honduras, Christians have functioned as a kind of "international peace guard," standing nonviolently between warring parties and praying for peace.[7] In doing these things, Christians are not trying to replace the national governments. But out of their experimental work, new ideas and programs may emerge which governments may want to adopt.

Commitment to Public Witness.

The church, as God's holy nation, is not the same thing as any nation state. But it intensely desires the good of the countries in which it finds itself. It can contribute to this welfare in many ways. In part, it can do so through its knowledge, contacts, and sensitivities. When it is functioning as it should, it is giving its life among poor people whose concerns it will represent. Furthermore, as a transnational body, it will be in touch with enemies with whom our governments are unwilling to communicate. In the early 1980s, American Christians usefully maintained contact with Vietnamese people, while English Baptists took the lead in reestablishing contact with Argentinians after the Falklands/Malvinas war.[8] As a nation of "pilgrims and strangers," Christians will be especially sensitive to the plight of other minorities—racial and religious—in our societies.

Should Christians speak out on issues of public policy? Should congregations and denominational bodies speak as well as individual Christians? I believe that they should, for the church has a unique perspective. In part, this is a historical perspective. The church exists to remember, ponder, and continue the story of God's dealings with men and women. The Bible is just as important to us in interpreting the contemporary world as any newspaper or TV program. Our perspective is also shaped by our sociology. As a body which spans every nation, our point of view is not limited by any poltical party. And yet the church is in the world. Its separate existence is *for* the world. As its members grow in holiness and become like God, they will love the world more and more. Thus, because of their perspective and because of their love, they will speak and act in response to human hurt. Sunday trading and children's fantasy games are legitimate topics for Christian bodies to be concerned about. So also are the areas of alienation in our world—race and class, war and wealth.

Christians must not speak lightly. Before we say anything we must study carefully and discern rigorously. We must never ask the state to do something that we ourselves, as individual Christians and congregations, are unwilling to put into practice. On occasion, expert Christian groups may have special competence to give detailed advice on matters of policy. Some Christian groups—notably the Quakers—have also made important behind-the-scenes contributions to international reconciliation. And, in humility and modesty, there are two things which all Christian groups may have to offer.

One is a sensitivity, growing out of their meditation on holy history, to what God is doing today. In 590 B.C., most Jerusalemites couldn't see what was happening; Jeremiah could. A similar blindness was afflicting Jesus' contemporaries. So also today. Ours is a day of official optimism; everything, we assume, will work out alright. But Christians, sensitized by holy history, will be more perceptive than that. In sorrow we will recognize that judgment is looming. Now, as throughout history, God's judgment is appropriate. It is not that he is saying to us, "You've been playing with matches, so I'm going to give you a caning." He rather is saying, "You've been playing with matches, bigger and better matches; and, unless you stop doing that, you're going to burn the house down."

A second contribution that we can make also comes from the Bible. It is vision. God's thoughts about how we humans should live are not our thoughts. And if we're willing to listen to him, if we have room in our hearts for revelation, God can speak to our situation with a simplicity that is breathtaking. In the Old Testament law, in Jesus, in the life of the early believers, a pattern of living is advocated and enacted which is good news. Jubilee makes sense; the current economic world order doesn't! Equally, at a time when our world is spending more on armaments than the entire income of the poorer half of humanity,[9] it isn't loving the enemy that sounds absurd.

Making political sense of Jesus' teaching is a demanding task. But it is one that some political commentators—including one of West Germany's leading TV journalists—are attempting.[10] Should it surprise us, as Christians living in this desperately dangerous time, that Jesus can shed more light on our situation than anybody else? It is our privilege, as his followers, to point humanity to him, his insights, and his way.

The Worship of God's Nation

As God's holy nation, it is worship that keeps us on course. Our worship of God will be intensely personal; it *must* be. Unless we know that we are loved and forgiven, and unless we can offer to God our own love and thanks, our attempts to be a faithful people will be fruitless. But equally, unless we are responding to God's call to be faithful, our worship will be barren. There can be no social holiness unless we as individuals encounter the Holy One. And our life together as his holy nation—as the light to the nations—is rooted in our experience of the one who is light.

What happens when we come together in his presence? For one thing, we recognize the one who is in charge. "The Lord is King," we declare as we gather. "Jesus Christ is Lord!" In making these statements, we may not realize that we are saying something political. But we are. We are expressing our ultimate loyalty. We are acknowledging the authority of the One who has a final claim upon our lives because he has given us life. When it comes to the crunch, we will obey him rather than any human (Acts 5:29). For it is he, our King and our Ruler, who is the true "Father of his country." Our national life, as his holy nation, is based upon his unchallenged authority.

Second, when we gather we remember and give thanks. "O give thanks to the Lord, for he is good; for his steadfast love endures for ever" (Ps. 136:1). And a story unfolds. It is the story of our King and his nation. It is a long story, spanning thousands of years. It is a story of kingly power flashing forth to liberate oppressed people and to make them a nation. It is a story of a gracious God providing and protecting, giving a law to guide his nation in a distinctive lifestyle. It is a story that culminates in a Man, Jesus of Nazareth, who is the image of the invisible God and who has borne the punishment for our wrong turnings. And the story continues in a nation whose citizens, filled with the Holy Spirit, carry the person and lifestyle of Jesus to the world. The story is tragic: humans reject God to become like other nations. The story is glorious: God shows his faithfulness, forgiveness, and power.

But most importantly, the story is *our* story. God in his mercy has given us a people and a living past. By telling the story we stay on course. And the story goes on. In our lives as individuals and in our experience as a nation, God continues to show his acts of concrete grace. He forgives us and heals us. He provides for us and he protects us. He frees us to live like his Son. He cares for us. Even in times of suffering and apparent defeat, he is faithful. And we give thanks. When we tell of his acts, those of the distant past and those that have just happened, we praise him.

But when we forget his acts, we go astray. When we doubt his capacity to protect and provide, we become like everybody else. So we've got to keep telling his story; and he, in turn, will keep on working—loving us, caring for us, giving us a nation of sisters and brothers. He is good; we praise him and give him our thanks!

Third, when we gather we express our needs. Because we have a rich history, we can do so in trust. At every stage, our life will be precarious. God has called us to walk in a way in which our only security will be in him. We often cannot foresee how God will provide for us and protect us. But we base our behavior on the belief that he will do so. When we in the past have ventured into insecurity he has been faithful; he will be so in the future as well. So we offer ourselves, and the things that we care most deeply about, to God with confidence based upon experience. Our intercessions come at the intersection of our past and our future. We pray not only for our own nation but for "all people," including those "in high places" (1 Tim. 2:1-2). We also pray that God, who has blessed us, will bless the people we find most difficult—our enemies and persecutors (Luke 6:28). At times these will be our rulers.

Finally, we gather to meet God. How important this is, and how elusive. For the Holy One cannot be programed. He, our Sovereign, is not simply at our beck and call. In our day as throughout history, his self-disclosures of living force are unpredictable and mysterious.

But at least one thing is sure. We are far more likely to meet the Holy One when we are living in faithful insecurity than when we are clinging to human security. God's power is not made perfect in us when we are powerful; it is when we are weak (2 Cor. 12:9-10). This is difficult for many of us Europeans and Americans to realize, for we have immense cultural, economic, and military power. How ironic that the current nuclear buildup may have an unexpected and positive spiritual by-product: it has given us our first real sense of powerlessness.

But when we are weak, God can show his strength. When our attempts to be faithful have brought us to the end of our resources, he can manifest his holiness. And how wonderful it can be when we awake, in the depths of our being, to the realities that we talk and sing about. Our songs take on a new meaning, because they express our real experience. When we don't know how we're going to cope, then "A Mighty Fortress Is Our God" becomes our trusting exclamation. When we are making costly choices to obey the Lord rather than other lords, then "O Worship the King" states our deepest resolve. When we are struggling to find ways to practice Jubilee, do we have any good songs to sing? I know of a few, but we need many more. When we are taking steps of risky obedience, we might even choose to sing Psalm 46:10 according to the original meaning of its Hebrew words. Instead of "Be Still and Know," we will sing—"Lay Down Your Arms, for I Am God."[11] It is in our weakness (and nowhere else) that we will know his empowering and become his instruments.

The Larger View

We have come to the end of this book, but not to the end of our journey. It is therefore right that we should climb aboard our balloon for one last overview.

Look! From a great height, things take on a true perspective. As we look back, we can see more than we used to be able to see; the past has become much clearer to us. It is God's story, which began at the source of time and which continues up to now. It has, we know, already come to a climax, in God's revelation of himself in flesh and action in his Son Jesus of Nazareth. His human intervention in history was brief, but it was decisive. And his strategy was the only one that could definitively break through into newness; John the Baptist expressed his premonition of it when he called Jesus "the Lamb of God" (John 1:36).

How about the present? If we lean out and crane our necks, we can see it. It is the small swath of territory immediately beneath us. Things are happening there which look important; immense destructive forces are at work—oppression, war, preparation for bigger war. But amidst the confusion we can also make out a band of purposeful people who seem to have a significance out of proportion to their numbers. It is not that they are strong. In various ways all of them are crippled, so they are helping each other along. They are surviving solely by a strength that comes from outside themselves. And yet they are on the move. They may be limping, but they are sure of their direction. And we can hear their song soaring up to us— "Jesus shall reign!"

Where are they going? As we look ahead, gazing into the distance, we can dimly make out the future which is their destination. Shining on the horizon, it is the holy city in which all of life reaches its goal. God is its glory. Its illumination is the

Lamb who is Jesus (Rev. 21:23). Our look into the future fills us with hope. God's story, we can sense, has an end of transcending joy. And until Jesus comes again to bring things to a conclusion, history will proceed with purpose, for God is not finished with his world.

God himself is the main participant in this story. He will bring the holy city. So we can relax. Everything doesn't depend on us, on our holiness, or our exertions. But somehow we can also sense that we—weak though we are—are important. Our task is demanding but simple: pressing on toward God's future, we "follow the Lamb wherever he goes" (Rev. 14:4). Relying upon the power of the Holy Spirit, we continue, in our personal lives, in society, and in our life together, the earthly life of the Holy One, Jesus. As we do this, we are becoming an "insurgent type of Christianity."[12] We are a force for life and change.

Intensely aware of the past, our orientation is nevertheless toward the future. As the "first fruits for God and the Lamb" (Rev. 14:4), we—though we seem to be insignificant—are "the presence of the future in the conditions of history."[13] So the social holiness which we are experiencing now is important. It is an anticipation of the "justice and peace, and joy in the Holy Spirit" (Rom. 14:17) which will characterize all of life in the holy city. Jesus is Lord! By our life together, we are announcing—hopefully, defiantly, invitingly—that our God, who has been faithful in the past, will continue his work in the future. God's project will end triumphantly. God himself will do it!

Notes

Chapter 1

1. For this expression and much more, I am indebted to Walter Brueggemann, *Living Toward a Vision: Biblical Reflections on Shalom* (Philadelphia: United Church Press, 1982), p. 54.

Chapter 2

1. I first encountered this term in Jean-Paul Audet, *The Gospel Project* (New York: Paulist Press, 1969).

2. Theologians have had differing perspectives on the holy city. Some of them, especially in the Eastern Orthodox tradition, view the holy city as a restoration of things as God originally meant them to be: holiness is reality "purified and restored to its original state" (Paul Evdokimov, "Holiness in the Orthodox Tradition," in Marina Chavchavadze, ed., *Man's Concern with Holiness* [London: Hodder & Stoughton, n.d.], p. 147). Calvinist thinkers, on the other hand, tend to see the holy city as the summation and purification of human history and creativity (Richard J. Mouw, *When the Kings Come Marching In: Isaiah and the New Jerusalem* [Grand Rapids: Eerdmans, 1983], pp. 5-6). The two positions, it seems to me, are compatible. As Reformed philosopher Nicholas Wolterstorff has written, the shalom which

God intends for all aspects of his handiwork will be "the eschatological counterpart of creation" *(Until Justice and Peace Embrace* [Grand Rapids: Eerdmans, 1983], p. 130).

3. In quoting the biblical text, I almost always have rendered the Hebrew word *tsadaq* and the Greek word *dikaiosune* as "justice" rather than "righteousness." Justice is a word which is less "churchy," more ordinary, more earthy than righteousness. But God's justice is not identical with or limited to the meaning of the word justice in contemporary English usage. It is richer, more varied, and more concerned for the rightness of relationships (see Robert D. Brimsmead, "The Scandal of God's Justice," *The Christian Verdict*, 6, pt. 1, pp. 3-4.

4. Karl Barth, *Action in Waiting* (Rifton, N.Y.: Plough Publishing, 1969).

5. Stanley Hauerwas, *The Peaceable Kingdom: A Primer in Christian Ethics* (London: SCM Press, 1984), p. 62. Previously published (Notre Dame, Ind.: University of Notre Dame Press, 1983).

6. To pious Jews this was scandalous, so scandalous, in fact, that the scholars who later translated the Old Testament into Greek simply omitted these disturbing passages. Upon reflection, we should be sympathetic with their pious concern to edit the unthinkable out of holy writ. We would have just as much difficulty if a modern-day Jeremiah called the current Soviet leader Mikhail Gorbachev (and not our Western leaders) "my servant"!

Chapter 3

1. Rudolf Otto, *The Idea of the Holy: An Inquiry into the Non-Rational Factor in the Idea of the Divine and Its Relation to the Rational*, 2nd ed. (New York: Oxford University Press, 1958), pp. 6, 10.

2. Gerald Finzi, writing at the time of the composition of *Dies Natalis* (1939), q. Diana McVeagh (Argo ZRG 896 [1979]).

3. Evdokimov, "Holiness," p. 148.

4. Wolterstorff, *Until Justice and Peace Embrace*, pp. 69-70. See also Brueggemann, *Living Toward a Vision*.

5. Mary Douglas, *Purity and Danger: An Analysis of Concepts of Pollution and Taboo* (London: Routledge and Kegan Paul, 1966), p. 54.

6. Hans Wildenberger, *Jesaja*, I (Biblischer Kommentar, X/i) (Neukirchen/Vluyn: Neukirchener Verlag, 1965-1972), p. 249.

7. Frank Lake, *Listening and Responding* (Clinical Theology Association, First Year Syllabus, No. 1 [n.d.]), p. 9.

8. Abraham H. Maslow, *Motivation and Personality* (New York: Harper & Row, 1954), p. 82.

9. Ibid., pp. 83-98.

10. Bob Goudzwaard, *Idols of Our Time* (Downers Grove, Ill.: Inter-Varsity Press, 1984).

11. John Wesley, Preface to *Hymns and Sacred Poems* (1739), in his *Works*, XIV, 321, quoted by Howard A. Snyder, *The Radical Wesley* (Downers Grove, Ill.: Inter-Varsity Press, 1980), p. 88.

Chapter 4

1. Otto, *Idea of the Holy*, p. 6.
2. The meaning of Exodus 13:18 is unclear.
3. Millard C. Lind, *Yahweh Is a Warrior: The Theology of Warfare in Ancient Israel* (Scottdale, Pa.: Herald Press, 1980), p. 23.
4. Some scholars have objected that it didn't happen like this. The biblical writers, they have contended, may have credited Yahweh with the victory at the Red Sea. But this was a "theologizing" and sanitizing of what really happened, written many years after the event. This victory, like later Israelite victories at Jericho and elsewhere, were really attained by brute force and military prowess. I have trouble with this objection for two reasons. In the first place, unlike some scholars I have no philosophical difficulties in accepting that miracles can actually occur—in the present day as well as in biblical times. Second, even scholars who accept a critical dating of the text of the Pentateuch, view the hymn of Moses and the people in Exodus 15 as very early (e.g., F. M. Cross, *Canaanite Myth and Hebrew Epic* [Cambridge, Mass.: Harvard University Press, 1973], p. 123). And this hymn, which tells the story of "the central event in Israel's history," describes an unassisted miracle by Yahweh.
5. Brevard Childs, *Exodus: A Commentary* (London: SCM Press, 1974), p. 237. U.S. edition: *The Book of Exodus: A Critical, Theological Commentary* (Philadelphia: Westminster Press, 1974).
6. On the significance of murmuring, see chapter 5 below.
7. Lesslie Newbigin, *The Other Side of 1984* (Geneva: World Council of Churches, 1984), p. 49.

Chapter 5

1. For profound comment on the Exodus, see John H. Yoder, "Exodus and Exile: The Two Faces of Liberation," *Missionalia*, 2, i (April 1974).
2. Martin Noth, *The History of Israel* (New York: Harper, 1958), p. 3.
3. Christopher J. H. Wright, *Living as the People of God: The Relevance of Old Testament Ethics* (Leicester: Inter-Varsity Press, 1983), p. 83.
4. Gordon J. Wenham, *The Book of Leviticus* (The New International Commentary on the Old Testament) (London: Hodder & Stoughton, 1979), p. 320. U.S. edition published by Eerdmans, 1979.
5. André Neher, *L'Essence du Prophetisme* (Paris: Presses Universitaires

de France, 1955), p. 162.

6. Carl von Clausewitz, *On War*, transl. Michael Howard and Peter Paret (Princeton University Press, 1976), I, i, 24; John Howard Yoder, *The Original Revolution* (Scottdale, Pa.: Herald Press, 1971), p. 104.

7. I have taken the "holy war" seriously because Christian friends have, for many years, assured me that God in the Old Testament approves of war. So I have been concerned to see what sort of warfare it was that God approved. I have noted two things. First, the form of warfare—the "holy war"—of which the Old Testament approves, is dramatically different from other warfare ancient and modern. It requires intentional weakness in anticipation of God's miraculous assistance. It also requires genocide. Both of these cause difficulties—practical and moral—for most Christians today. Second, as we shall see in Chapter 6, the form of Old Testament warfare that most closely resembles modern warfare—that fought by the kings and their armies—is condemned by Old Testament writers. Both Samuel and the later prophets saw it as apostacy (e.g., 1 Sam. 8). Why do modern Christians dismiss as "unique" the forms of warfare of which Yahweh approved, and espouse uncritically (and purportedly with Old Testament justification) the form of national warfare which Yahweh saw as a rejection of himself and an adaptation to the ways of the nations? Do we turn to the Old Testament for revelation or for self-justification? The Old Testament, to be sure, does not advocate systematic nonviolence. But it does not teach any other theory of warfare (the just war or otherwise) that modern Christians can live with comfortably, either. For adherents of Christian nonviolence, at any rate, the issue is settled not by the Old Testament but by the one towards whom the Old Testament was pointing—the Messiah Jesus who, in living and teaching a different approach to national enemies, was the Father's perfect revelation of himself.

8. Donald W. Blosser, *Jesus and the Jubilee (Luke 4:16-30): The Year of Jubilee and its Significance in the Gospel of Luke* (Ph.D. thesis, University of St. Andrews, 1979), p. 23.

9. Recent scholars have been more inclined than their predecessors to view the Jubilee laws as both ancient and influential in Israelite life. See A. van Selma, "Jubilee, Year of," in *The Interpreter's Dictionary of the Bible*, Suppl. vol. (Nashville, Abingdon Press, 1982), p. 497.

10. Isaiah 38:6; 2 Kings 19:7; 1 Samuel 7:10; Joshua 10:11; Judges 5:21.

11. Cross, *Canaanite Myth and Hebrew Epic*, 156; William Foxwell Albright, *The Archaeology of Palestine and the Bible* (New York: Fleming H. Revell Co., 1935), pp. 109, 121.

12. James B. Pritchard, ed., *The Ancient Near East: An Anthology of Texts and Pictures* (Princeton, N.J.: Princeton University Press, 1958), pp. 190-191.

Chapter 6

1. Pritchard, *Ancient Near East,* pp. 188-189.
2. See also 10:18; 12:6f.
3. Lind, *Yahweh Is a Warrior,* p. 100.
4. See Neher, *Essence,* p. 291.
5. Cf. 1 Samuel 16:14.
6. E.g., Joshua 8:1-2; Judges 20:23; 1 Samuel 23:9-12; 2 Samuel 5:23.
7. See also 1 Samuel 27:2; 2 Samuel 15:18; 20:7.
8. Roland de Vaux, *Ancient Israel: Its Life and Institutions,* 2nd ed. (London: Darton, Longman and Todd, 1965), p. 220.
9. E.g., 1 Chronicles 19:6f.
10. E.g., David's capture of the Jebusite city of Jerusalem (2 Sam. 5:6).
11. Yigael Yadin, *The Art of Warfare in Biblical Lands in the Light of Archaeological Discovery* (London: Weidenfeld and Nicolson, 1963), p. 283.
12. De Vaux, *Ancient Israel,* pp. 229-230.
13. 1 Kings 5:13-15. There is some apparent confusion in the text as to whether Solomon impressed Israelites into his corps of forced laborers, or whether (as 1 Kings 9:20-22 seems to suggest) he obtained his "forced levy of slaves" solely from the remnants of the Canaanite peoples whom the Israelites had displaced. In view of the sheer size of the conscripted labor force and of later developments—the revolt of the people of Israel against Solomon's son Rehoboam in which they stoned to death the "taskmaster over the forced labor" (1 Kings 12:4, 18)—it is clear that the corps of forced laborers was not drawn entirely from non-Israelites.
14. De Vaux, *Ancient Israel,* pp. 72-73.
15. Ibid., p. 73.
16. Claus Westermann, *One Thousand Years and a Day: Our Time in the Old Testament* (London: SCM Press, 1962), p. 101.

Chapter 7

1. See also Jeremiah 6:17; Ezekiel 33:7; Hosea 9:8.
2. Claus Westermann, *Basic Forms of Prophetic Speech* (London: Lutterworth Press, 1967), p. 95.
3. See also Jeremiah 2:34.
4. De Vaux, *Ancient Israel,* pp. 229-231.
5. This, as always, was both a theological and a military question. See 2 Kings 2:12; 6:17.
6. See also Isaiah 31:1; Jeremiah 2:36-37; Ezekiel 17:17; Hosea 8:7-10.
7. See also Isaiah 2:7; Hosea 8:14; 10:13-14.
8. For other prophetic passages making this interconnection, see Jeremiah 2:26-37; Hosea 8:4-14.

9. Sir Herbert Butterfield, *Christianity and History* (New York: Charles Scribner's Sons, 1950), p. 58.

10. See also Jeremiah 27:6; 43:10. This was as hard for later Jewish scholars to accept as it must have been for Jeremiah's contemporaries. The translators who rendered his Hebrew text into Greek (in the Septuagint) in each case simply omitted the phrases designating Nebuchadnezzar as Yahweh's "servant."

11. I first encountered this expression in André Trocmé, *The Politics of Repentance* (New York: Fellowship Publications, 1953).

12. Moshe Weinfeld, *Deuteronomy and the Deuteronomic School* (Oxford: Clarendon Press, 1972), pp. 151-155, cited by Lind, *Yahweh Is a Warrior*, pp. 164, 213. For comparable passages, see 1 Kings 15:11; 22:43; 2 Kings 18:3.

13. A partial list includes: 1 Kings 20:13-21; 20:28-30; 2 Kings 6:8-19; 7:3-8; 19:14-37 (see parallel 2 Chronicles 32:20-22; Isaiah 37:14-38); 2 Chronicles 13:13-16; 14:9-13. See also the chronicler's comment on King Uzziah: "He was marvelously helped, till he was strong" (2 Chronicles 26:15).

14. The correctness of this rendering, which is similar to that of the TEV, is vouched for by commentators: A. A. Anderson, *The Book of Psalms*, New Century Bible, (London: Oliphants, 1972), I, p. 360 published in the United States by Eerdmans, and Artur Weiser, *The Psalms* (Philadelphia: Westminster Press, 1962), p. 373.

Chapter 8

1. Neher, *Essence*, p. 291.

2. In the passages that deal with the *Man*, there is some ambiguity as to whether they refer solely to an individual, or whether they refer to the entire Israelite nation. With many scholars, I assume that the prophets' emphases vary from passage to passage, but that in sum they were referring both to the individual and to the nation. Indeed, in the thinking of the prophets, these two were intertwined: the purpose of the individual was to show what the entire nation should be like.

3. For comment on this Dead Sea document, Melchizidek 11Q, see R. B. Sloan, *The Favorable Year of the Lord: A Study in the Jubilary Theology in the Gospel of Luke* (Austin, Texas: Schola Press, 1977), pp. 45-46.

4. See Joshua 11:9; 2 Samuel 8:4, and chapters 4 and 5 above.

Chapter 9

1. Lesslie Newbigin, *The Open Secret: Sketches for a Missionary Theology* (Grand Rapids, Eerdmans, 1978), p. 99.

2. This chapter and the next owe much to Marcus J. Borg, *Conflict, Holiness and Politics in the Teachings of Jesus* (New York: Edwin Mellen Press, 1984).

3. Josephus, *Jewish War*, II, ix, 4.

4. F. F. Bruce, "Render to Caesar," in E. Bammel and C. F. D. Moule, eds., *Jesus and the Politics of His Day* (Cambridge: Cambridge University Press, 1984), p. 254.

5. Josephus, *Jewish War*, II, xvii, 6.

6. Josephus, *Jewish War*, II, ix, 4 (trans. G. A. Williamson [Harmondsworth, Middx.: Penguin, 1959], p. 157).

7. Joachim Jeremias, *Jesus' Promise to the Nations* (London: SCM Press, 1958), p. 43.

8. *Encyclopaedia Judaica*, 7, p. 411, s.v. "Gentile."

9. *Jewish Encyclopedia*, new ed., 5, p. 621, s.v. "Gentile."

10. Leader of the Jewish revolt against Antiochus IV, the Syrian ruler of Palestine, in the 160s B.C.

11. Josephus, *Antiquities*, XVII, x, 9-10.

12. See, for example, the Pharisee Gamaliel's summary in Acts 5:35ff.

13. Borg, *Conflict, Holiness and Politics*, p. 57.

14. Richard J. Cassidy, *Jesus, Politics and Society: A Study of Luke's Gospel* (Maryknoll, N.Y.: Orbis Books, 1978), pp. 121, 197.

15. Rabbi Eliezer ben Hyrcanus, q. Jeremias, *Jesus' Promise*, p. 41.

16. Borg, *Conflict, Holiness and Politics*, p. 66.

Chapter 10

1. The confession that Jesus was the Holy One was, however, centrally important to his disciples after his resurrection (Acts 2:27; 3:14).

2. This commissioning from the Father was drawn from a royal psalm and a "servant song" (Ps. 2:7; Isa. 42:1).

3. The "Waiting Father," according to a sermon of Helmut Thielicke, is the main point of the parable of the "prodigal son" (*The Waiting Father* [New York: Harper & Brothers, 1959], pp. 26-29).

4. The Greek word *aphesis*, translated here as "release" and "liberty," occurs in the Greek Old Testament in all of the passages having to do with the Jubilee and sabbath years, e.g., Leviticus 25:10, 11, 13, 28; 27:17; Deuteronomy 15:1, 9; Isaiah 61:1; Jeremiah 41:8 [MT 34:8]; Ezekiel 46:17. Some of Jesus' contemporaries linked the prophetic passage which Jesus was quoting, Isaiah 61:1-2 (along with a phrase of Isaiah 58:6) with the Jubilee (Blosser, *Jesus and the Jubilee*, p. 92). For discussion of the relation of Jesus' Nazareth sermon to the Jubilee, see John H. Yoder, *The Politics of Jesus*

(Grand Rapids: Eerdmans, 1972), pp. 34-40; J. Massyngbaerd Ford, *My Enemy Is My Guest: Jesus and Violence in Luke* (Maryknoll, N.Y.: Orbis Books, 1984), 55-60; Sloan, *Favorable Year*, passim.

5. Jeremias, *Jesus' Promise*, p. 45.

6. The meaning of the Greek words is quite clear here. Because translators have found it hard to imagine that Jesus cared about the religious dimensions of social issues, they have considered almsgiving to be a deed of piety rather than of justice-making and reequalization. Hence their attachment to their customary mistranslation.

7. Blosser, *Jesus and the Jubilee*, p. 283.

8. This interpretation is broadly in harmony with that of F. F. Bruce, "Render to Caesar," p. 260: "Jesus' counsel of non-resistance to Rome was on all fours with Jeremiah's counsel of submission to Babylon."

9. A number of writers continue to maintain that Jesus, in commanding his disciples to love their "enemies," had only personal enemies in mind. This interpretation might make sense if Jesus had been speaking in a prosperous American suburb, but he wasn't. He was speaking of a "politico-religious tinderbox," a land brutally ruled by an occupying army. When Jesus said "enemies," everyone knew who he was talking about—and it wasn't simply the cantankerous person next door! Most recent scholars who have carefully looked at this question agree: Jesus was telling his disciples to love their nation's enemies, the Romans. For careful studies of this issue, see Martin Hengel, *Victory over Violence* (London: SPCK Press, 1975); William Klassen, *Love of Enemies* (Philadelphia: Fortress Press, 1984); Cassidy, *Jesus, Politics and Society*. For a brief survey of the issue, see Willard Swartley and Alan Kreider, "Pacifist Christianity: The Kingdom Way," in O. R. Barclay, ed., *Pacifism and War: When Christians Disagree* (Leicester: Inter-Varsity Press, 1984), pp. 40-43.

10. Yoder, *Original Revolution*, p. 108.

11. The same coming together of holiness themes occurs in the parallel passage in the Sermon on the Plain (Luke 6:27-36).

12. The translation which best captures the meaning of Matt. 5:48 is that of the NEB: "There must be no limit to your goodness, as your heavenly Father's goodness knows no bounds."

13. Some people have used this whip to indicate that Jesus was no "pacifist." The passage clearly indicates that Jesus was, on occasion, willing to use force against property. A careful translation of the verse (John 2:15), such as that of the NIV, however, indicates that Jesus did not use the whip against the sellers and money changers. (And even if he had used the whip against the people, there is a considerable difference between whipping people and

killing them.)

14. E. Earle Ellis, "How the New Testament Uses the Old," in I. Howard Marshall, ed., *New Testament Interpretation* (Exeter: Paternoster Press, 1977), p. 211. U.S. edition published by Eerdmans.

Chapter 11

1. Paul Minear, *Images of the Church in the New Testament* (London: Lutterworth Press, 1961), p. 137. U.S. edition, Philadelphia: Westminster Press, 1970.

2. "The early church sought to apply jubilee principles to its socio-economic life; indeed, Luke seems deliberately to describe its achievements in terms that echo the sabbatical promise in Deuteronomy 15 that God would richly bless an obedient people" (Wright, *Living as the People of God*, p. 101).

3. Virgil Vogt, *Treasure in Heaven: The Biblical Teaching About Money, Finances and Possessions* (Ann Arbor, Michigan: Servant Books, 1982), p. 79.

Chapter 12

1. John V. Taylor, *Enough Is Enough* (London: SCM Press, 1975), p. 45.

2. Colin Brown, ed., *The New International Dictionary of New Testament Theology* (Exeter: Paternoster Press, 1975-1978), III, p. 727. U.S. edition: Grand Rapids, Mich.: Zondervan Press, 1976-1978.

3. Philippians 1:5; Romans 15:27; 1 Peter 4:13; 2 Corinthians 13:14; 1 Corinthians 10:16; 1 John 1:3, 7.

4. On this, see Keith F. Nickle, *The Collection: A Study in Paul's Strategy*, Studies in Biblical Theology, p. 48 (London: SCM Press, 1966).

5. Joachim Jeremias, *Jerusalem in the Time of Jesus* (London: SCM Press, 1969), p. 140.

6. F. F. Bruce, *1 and 2 Corinthians*, New Century Bible (London: Oliphants, 1971), p. 223. U.S. edition, Eerdmans.

7. Vogt, *Treasures*, p. 82.

8. Eusebius, *Ecclesiastical History*, III, v, p. 3.

9. Jean-Michel Hornus, *It Is Not Lawful for Me to Fight: Early Christian Attitudes Toward War, Violence and the State*, revised ed. (Scottdale, Pa.: Herald Press, 1980), p. 17.

10. Bo Riecke, *The Epistles of James, Peter and Jude*, The Anchor Bible (Garden City, New York: Doubleday, 1964), pp. 73, 96.

11. 1 Peter 1:6, 7; 2:12, 20; 3:6; 3:15-17; 4:4, 12, 19.

12. For general background, see Raymond E. Brown and John P. Meier,

Antioch and Rome (London: Geoffrey Chapman, 1983), chap. 6.

13. A corruption of "Christ," from Suetonius, *Claudius*, 25, 4, quoted by Brown and Meier, *Antioch and Rome*, p. 100.

14. J. Friedrich, W. Pöhlmann, P. Stuhlmacher, "Zur historischen Situation und Intention von Rom. 13:1-7," *Zeitschrift für Theologie und Kirche*, 73 (1976), pp. 131-166.

15. Brown and Meier, *Antioch and Rome*, p. 124.

16. The passage which Paul cites here, Deuteronomy 32:35, refers to God's vengeance against Israel's collective, national enemies, not against the personal enemies of individual Israelites. It will not do to distinguish between the personal ethics of Romans 12 and the public ethics of Romans 13. Both chapters have as much to do with the public behavior of God's nation as with the behavior of individual disciples of Jesus.

17. Reicke, *Epistles*, p. 107.

18. Yoder, *Politics of Jesus*, pp. 163-192.

19. I do not mean to imply that there is never a case for tax-refusal by Christians. For a discussion of this issue, see Donald D. Kaufman, *What Belongs to Caesar?* (Scottdale, Pa.: Herald Press, 1969); Willard M. Swartley, "A Study on the Payment of War Taxes," *Sojourners*, February 1979, p. 18-20; Lynn Buzzard and Paula Campbell, *Holy Disobedience: When Christians Must Resist the State* (Ann Arbor, Michigan: Servant Publications, 1984), chap. 8.

20. The Greek word for "obey," *hupakouō*, is different from the word for "be subordinate," *hupotassō*.

21. John Piper, *"Love Your Enemies": Jesus' Love Command in the Synoptic Gospels and in the Early Christian Paraenesis*, Society for New Testament Studies, Monograph Series, 38 (Cambridge: Cambridge University Press, 1979), p. 62.

22. Similarly, Ezekiel conveyed Yahweh's message that "I will strengthen the arms of the king of Babylon, and put my sword in his hand" (Ezek. 30:24).

23. An alternative interpretation would suggest that, for Peter, "Babylon" connoted not just Rome, but any pagan society in which Jesus' followers would be "aliens and exiles" (1 Pet. 2:11; J. N. D. Kelly, *The Epistles of Peter and of Jude* [London: Adam & Charles Black, 1969; U.S. edition, Grand Rapids, Mich.: Baker Books, 1981.], p. 219). This would not alter the basic social strategy that I find Peter to be suggesting.

24. To the best of my knowledge, commentators have not examined the possibility that Babylon lay behind Paul's use of the "servant" terminology for the state (Rom. 13:4). The exegete who comes closest to seeing this emphasis is C. E. B. Cranfield (*The Epistle to the Romans*, International Critical

Commentary [Edinburgh: T. & T. Clark, 1979], II, p. 665), who cites Isaiah 10:5-15, a passage that refers to Assyria but that does not use "servant" language. The Jeremiah passages about Babylon (25:8-38), on the other hand, use not only a pagan nation as God's servant, but also talk about "sword" and "wrath." I would be grateful if competent biblical scholars would test this hypothesis.

25. Wayne A. Meeks, *The First Urban Christians: The Social World of the Apostle Paul* (New Haven: Yale University Press, 1983), p. 73.

26. Rebecca Yoder, "Old Testament *Cherem* and New Testament Sentences of Holy Law," *Occasional Papers of the Council of Mennonite Seminaries*, 1 (1981), pp. 19-34.

27. 1 Corinthians 4:16; 1 Corinthians 11:1; Ephesians 5:1; 1 Thessalonians 1:6; 2:14.

28. For the practice a century later, which is probably in continuity with earlier customs, see Justin, I *Apology*, p. 67.

Chapter 13

1. *Letter to Diognetus*, 5.5.

2. Justin, I *Apology*, 14.

3. E.g., Hippolytus, *Apostolic Tradition*, 16; Roland H. Bainton, "The Early Church and War," *Harvard Theological Review*, 39 (1946), pp. 189-212.

4. Charles Avila, *Ownership: Early Christian Teaching* (London: Sheed and Ward, 1983), pp. 36, 39.

5. Axel Boethius and J. B. Ward-Perkins, *Etruscan and Roman Architecture* (Pelican History of Art) (Harmondsworth, Middx.: Penguin Books, 1970), plates 152-154.

6. Roger Forster, "The Church That Makes for Peace," in Dana Mills Powell, ed., *Decide for Peace: Evangelicals and the Bomb* (Basingstoke, Hants: Marshalls, 1986).

7. Alexander Schmemann, *Introduction to Liturgical Theology* (Leighton Buzzard, Beds.: The Faith Press, 1966), chap. 3.

8. *Apostolic Constitutions*, II, 58.

9. Eusebius, *Demonstratio Evangelica*, I, 8, 29b.

10. Julio de Santa Ana, *Good News to the Poor: The Challenge of the Poor in the History of the Church* (Geneva: World Council of Churches, 1977), p. 77. In their economic thinking, some Christians had been borrowing from the Stoics for some time prior to Constantine (Redmond Mullin, *The Wealth of Christians* [Exeter: Paternoster Press, 1983], pp. 65-66).

11. John Eppstein, *The Catholic Tradition of the Law of Nations* (London: Catholic Association for International Peace, 1935), pp. 57ff.

12. A. H. M. Jones, *The Later Roman Empire, 284-602* (Oxford, Basil Blackwell, 1964), II, p. 978.

13. W. K. Jordan, *Philanthropy in England, 1480-1660* (London: George Allen and Unwin, 1959), pp. 165ff. It was only among the Reformation's radicals, both on the continent and in England, that true ideas of equality developed. See Donald Durnbaugh, ed., *Every Need Supplied* (Philadelphia: Temple University Press, 1974); Christopher Hill, *World Turned Upside Down* (Harmondsworth, Middx.: Penguin, 1975).

14. "It remains an open question whether just war theories have limited more wars than they have encouraged" (Frederick H. Russell, *The Just War in the Middle Ages* [Cambridge: Cambridge University Press, 1975], p. 308).

15. Hugo Grotius, *On the Law of War and Peace* (1625), sect. 28, in Arthur Holmes, ed., *War and Christian Ethics* (Grand Rapids, Baker Book House, 1975), pp. 235-236.

16. Goudzwaard, *Idols of our Time*, p. 52.

17. Oral communication from John Mitchell, director, World Development Movement.

18. Ruth Leger Sivard, *World Military and Social Expenditures, 1985* (Washington, D.C.: World Priorities, 1985), p. 26. For the U.K. in 1984, 7.5 million people—1 in every 7 people—were living in poverty (Joanna Mack and Stewart Lansley, *Poor Britain* [London: George Allen and Unwin, 1985], p. 182).

19. *Newsweek*, November 26, 1984, p. 23.

20. U.S. Bishops' Pastoral Letter (first draft), "Catholic Social Teaching and the U.S. Economy," *Origins*, 14, no 22/23 (November 15, 1984), p. 373.

21. A. B. Cramp, *Economics in Christian Perspective: A Sketch-Map* (Toronto: Institute for Christian Studies, n.d.), VIII/36.

22. Sivard, *World Military and Social Expenditures, 1985*, p. 5.

23. According to influential scientists, a modest exchange of nuclear weapons between the superpowers would release so much smoke and dust into the atmosphere that the earth would be darkened and the earth's temperature would plummet. Many of those who had survived the blast and radiation of the nuclear explosions would die of cold and starvation. See R. P. Turco et al., "Nuclear Winter: Global Consequences of Multiple Nuclear Explosions," *Science*, December 23, 1983, 1282-1292; and the exhaustive study of Mark Harwell, *Environmental Consequences of Nuclear War* (New York: John Wiley, 1986).

24. Goudzwaard, *Idols of Our Time*, p. 95.

25. Quoted in the *Observer*, May 26, 1985, p. 13.

26. *Guardian*, April 4, 1985, p. 14; February 9, 1985, p. 6; *Times*, February 8, 1985, p. 8.

27. Newbigin, *The Other Side of 1984*, p. 1.

28. Butterfield, *Christianity and History*, p. 106.

29. This is as true of Evangelical Calvinists as it is of liberation theologians. See especially Goudzwaard, *Idols of Our Time;* Pablo Richard, et al., *The Idols of Death and the God of Life* (Maryknoll, N.Y.: Orbis Books, 1983). Other writers for whom this has been an important theme are Richard Mouw, Nicholas Wolterstorff, Jim Wallis, Dale Aukerman, Keith Clements, Jacques Ellul, and Karl Barth.

Chapter 14

1. This is a theme of Gerald Coates ("Pioneers or Settlers," *Pioneer*, 1, i [Spring 1983], pp. 8-10); and of Vernard Eller *(The Outward Bound: Caravaning as the Style of the Church* [Grand Rapids, Mich.: Eerdmans, 1980], pp. 11-26).

2. Quoted by Graham Cray, in a sermon in St. Michael-le-Belfrey, York, England, May 5, 1985.

3. Jean Vanier, *Community and Growth* (London: Darton, Longman, and Todd, 1979), p. 105.

4. Alan Jones, *Journey into Christ* (London: SPCK, 1978), p. 4.

5. Maslow, *Motivation and Personality*, pp. 82-98.

6. See René Laurentin, *Miracles in El Paso?* (Ann Arbor, Mich.: Servant Books, 1982); John H. Yoder, *What Would You Do?* (Scottdale, Pa.: Herald Press, 1983), pp. 28-35.

7. Evdokimov, "Holiness in the Orthodox Tradition," p. 159.

8. Francis Schaeffer, *The Great Evangelical Disaster* (Westchester, Ill.: Crossway Books, 1984), p. 115.

9. John Stott, *Christian Counter-Culture: The Message of the Sermon on the Mount* (Leicester: Inter-Varsity Press, 1978), p. 63.

10. Os Guinness, *The Gravedigger File* (London: Hodder and Stoughton, 1983), p. 122.

11. Vanier, *Community and Growth*, p. 75.

12. E. R. Norman, *Christianity and the World Order* (Oxford: Oxford University Press, 1979), p. 78.

13. Quoted in Malcolm Doney, "Faith in the Forces," *Today*, September 1982, p. 19.

14. Norman, *Christianity and the World Order*, p. 2.

15. Wildenberger, *Jesaja*, p. 249.

Chapter 15

1. Reinhold Niebuhr, *Moral Man and Immoral Society* (New York: Charles Scribner's Sons, 1932), p. 270.

2. Keith Ward, "The Just War and Nuclear Arms," in Francis Bridger, ed., *The Cross and the Bomb—Christian Ethics and the Nuclear Debate* (London: Mowbray, 1983), p. 55.

3. Brian Griffiths, *The Creation of Wealth* (London: Hodder and Stoughton, 1984), pp. 62-63.

4. Nationwide initiative in Evangelism, *Prospects for the Eighties: from a Census of the Churches in 1979* (London: The Bible Society, 1980), p. 15.

5. Butterfield, *Christianity and History*, p. 135.

6. Ibid.

7. Richard Mouw, *Called to Holy Worldliness* (Philadelphia: Fortress Press, 1980), p. 66.

8. Keith W. Clements, *A Patriotism for Today: Dialogue with Dietrich Bonhoeffer* (Bristol: Bristol Baptist College, 1984), p. 60.

9. The Clements book, cited in the previous note, is a penetrating study of Bonhoeffer's struggles with nationhood.

10. A. F. Winnington-Ingram, q. by Albert Marrin, *The Last Crusade: The Church of England in the First World War* (Durham, N.C.: Duke University Press, 1974), p. 139.

11. Walter Sawatsky, *Soviet Evangelicals Since World War II* (Kitchener, Ontario: Herald Press, 1981), p. 14; David B. Barrett, ed., *World Christian Encyclopedia* (New York: Oxford University Press, 1982), p. 696.

12. Conversation with Jim Punton, January 29, 1986.

13. According to Christian historian Sir Herbert Butterfield, "the most powerful organizational unit in history—the most perfect instrument for prying open any status quo—is the group of people we call a 'cell' " (*History as the Emancipation from the Past* [London: 1956], p. 17).

14. John Howard Yoder, *The Priestly Kingdom: Social Ethics as Gospel* (Notre Dame, Indiana: Notre Dame University Press, 1984), p. 91.

Chapter 16

1. In contrast to many interpreters, who view the salt primarily as a preservative which keeps things from spoiling, I think it is more likely that Jesus had in mind the more positive properties of salt: seasoning, which makes good food taste better, and fertilizer, which makes good soil more productive (cf. Luke 14:34-35). This, I believe, is in keeping with Jesus' vision of holiness, which was not defensive, but offensive. On this reading of Matthew 5:13, see *New International Dictionary of New Testament Theology*, III, pp. 443, 445.

2. The corporate nature of "light" has eluded most Western commentators (but see John Driver, *Kingdom Citizens* [Scottdale, Pa.: Herald Press, 1980], p. 73, and Eberhard Arnold, *Salt and Light* [Rifton, N.Y.: Plough Publishing, 1967], p. 21, who get it right). It has, however, been obvious to the peasant Bible readers of Solentiname in Nicaragua. See Ernesto Cardenal, ed., *The Gospel in Solentiname* (Maryknoll, N.Y.: Orbis Books, 1982), I, p. 194.

3. Christians can learn an immense amount about these values that we find in Jesus from non-Christians, not least those in the Gandhian tradition.

4. A. N. Triton, *Salt to the World: The Christian and Social Involvement* (Leicester: Inter-Varsity Press, 1978), p. 54.

5. For ideas and testimonies, see Doris Janzen Longacre, *Living More with Less* (Scottdale, Pa.: Herald Press, 1980).

6. For nutritional insight and good recipes, in a framework of kingdom theology, see Doris Janzen Longacre, *More with Less Cookbook* (Scottdale, Pa.: Herald Press, 1976).

7. For helpful hints, see J. Lorne Peachey, *How to Teach Peace to Children* (Scottdale, Pa.: Herald Press, 1981); Kathleen and James McGinnis, *Parenting for Peace and Justice* (Maryknoll, N.Y.: Orbis Books, 1981); Jacqueline Haessly, *Peacemaking: Family Activities for Justice and Peace* (New York: Paulist Press, 1980).

8. For perceptive comments on the difficulties of Christian involvement by someone who knows, see Neil Summerton, "The Just War: A Sympathetic Critique," in Barclay, ed., *Pacifism and War*, pp. 203-204. See also a useful collection of reflections and case histories by North American Mennonites in professional life (Donald B. Kraybill and Phyllis Pellman Good, eds., *Perils of Professionalism* [Scottdale, Pa.: Herald Press, 1982]).

9. See the fascinating debate in the General Synod of the Church of England between the late Raymond Johnston, who saw the research as "wrong in principle and contrary to Christian standards," and Canon Douglas Rhymes, who was concerned that Christians be able to influence genetic engineering (*Guardian*, July 5, 1985, p. 3).

10. Peter Hinchcliff, *Holiness and Politics* (London: Darton, Longman, and Todd, 1982), p. 2. Hinchcliff proceeds to ponder this apparent polarity and the Christian's participation in politics in a profound way.

11. This quote, from a sixteenth-century Anabaptist, comes from John H. Yoder, "Anabaptists and the Sword Revisited," *Zeitschrift für Kirchengeschichte*, 85 (1974), p. 132.

12. Simon Hughes, "Truth to Tell," *Third Way*, March 1986, p. 21.

13. For examples, see George McRobie, *Small Is Possible* (New York: Harper and Row, 1981).

14. Yoder, *Priestly Kingdom*, p. 37.

15. The Greenpeace office in Lewes, Sussex, is commendably doing this (*Guardian*, February 29, 1985, p. 2).

16. *Guardian*, September 29, 1983, p. 2.

17. E.g., the work of Catholic thinker Stan Windass, in Stan Windass, ed., *Avoiding Nuclear War: Common Security as a Strategy for the Defence of the West* (London: Brassey's Defence Publishers, 1985).

18. John Lampen, ed., *Will Warren: A Scrapbook* (London: Quaker Home Service, 1983).

19. See the study packet, including contributions by many Irish and English people and formative theological contributions by Haddon Willmer, available from: Forgiveness and Politics Study Group, 2 Eaton Gate, London SW1W 9BL, England.

20. *The Future of Worker Co-ops in London* (London: Industrial Common Ownership Movement, 1986).

21. A. B. Cramp, *Economics in Christian Perspective*, VIII/38, IX/25; *Christian Arena*, June 1985.

22. Carl Kreider, *The Christian Entrepreneur* (Scottdale, Pa.: Herald Press, 1980), pp. 177-178.

23. *Origins*, 14, no 22/23 (November 15, 1984), p. 381.

24. "Stepping-stone" is a way of expressing, in nontechnical language, what ethicists call a "middle axiom" (John H. Yoder, *The Christian Witness to the State* (Newton, Kans.: Faith and Life Press, 1964), pp. 72-73.

25. Goudzwaard, *Idols of Our Time*, p. 106. For his comments on the multilateral aspects of disarmament, see ibid., pp. 70-75.

Chapter 17

1. John Stoner, "A Modest Proposal for Christian Unity," *One World*, May 1984, p. 18. I personally would want to make a larger commitment as well—not to kill non-Christians, either. For our God "has compassion over all that he has made" (Ps. 145:9). Given a missionary understanding of God's project for his creation, the outsider is always a potential brother or sister.

2. Archbishop of Canterbury's Commission on Urban Priority Areas, *Faith in the City: A Call for Action by Church and Nation* (London: Church House Publishing, 1985), pp. 158-159.

3. Laurentin, *Miracles in El Paso?*

4. Dave Jackson, *Dial 911: Peaceful Christians and Urban Violence* (Scottdale, Pa.: Herald Press, 1981).

5. For a recent illustration of the capacity of the Christian church to grow under persecution, see David H. Adeney, *China: The Church's Long March* (Ventura, Calif., Regal Books, 1985), pp. 140-143.

6. Lynn R. Buzzard and Laurence Eck, *Tell It to the Church* (Elgin, Ill.: David C. Cook Publishing Co., 1982); Ronald S. Kraybill, *Repairing the Breach: Ministering in Community Conflict* (Scottdale, Pa.: Herald Press, 1980). For victim-offender reconciliation, see the lengthy, how-to-do-it manual, *The VORP Book* (available from the PACT Institute of Justice, 106 N. Franklin, Valparaiso, Ind. 46383, USA).

7. For the story of members of "Witness for Peace" under fire, see *Sojourners* October 1985, pp. 7-10.

8. Paul G. Weller, "For He Is Our Peace: Baptist Responsibilities in British-Argentinian Reconciliation," *Baptist Quarterly*, 31 (1985), pp. 66-73.

9. Lester R. Brown, et al., *State of the World 1986: A Worldwatch Institute Report on Progress Toward a Sustainable Society* (New York: Norton, 1986), p. 197.

10. See the manifesto by a leading West German TV journalist, Albrecht Alt *(Peace Is Possible: The Politics of the Sermon on the Mount* [New York: Shocken Books, 1985]).

11. See above, Chapter 6, note 13.

12. Herbert Butterfield, *Writings on Christianity and History*, ed. C. T. McIntire (New York: Oxford University Press, 1979), p. 254.

13. Jürgen Moltmann, *The Church in the Power of the Spirit* (London: SCM Press, 1977), p. 193.

Suggestions for Further Reading

Borg, Marcus J. *Conflict, Holiness and Politics in the Teachings of Jesus* (New York: Edwin Mellen Press, 1984)

Brueggemann, Walter. *Living Toward a Vision: Biblical Reflections on Shalom* (Philadelphia: United Church Press, 1982)

Butterfield, Sir Herbert. *Christianity and History* (New York: Charles Scribner's Sons, 1950)

Cassidy, Richard J. *Jesus, Politics and Society: A Study of Luke's Gospel* (Maryknoll, N.Y.: Orbis Books, 1978)

Clements, Keith W. *A Patriotism for Today: Dialogue with Dietrich Bonhoeffer* (Bristol, England: Bristol Baptist College, 1984)

Goudzwaard, Bob. *Idols of Our Time* (Downers Grove, Ill.: Inter-Varsity Press, 1984)

Hauerwas, Stanley. *The Peaceable Kingdom: A Primer in Christian Ethics* (Notre Dame, Ind.: University of Notre Dame Press, 1983)

Kraybill, Donald B. *The Upside-Down Kingdom* (Scottdale, Pa.: Herald Press, 1978)

Kraybill, Donald B., and Phyllis Pellman Good, eds. *Perils of*

Professionalism: Essays on Christian Faith and Professionalism
(Scottdale, Pa.: Herald Press, 1982)

Kreider, Carl. *The Christian Entrepreneur* (Scottdale, Pa.: Herald
Press, 1980)

Lind, Millard C. *Yahweh Is a Warrior: The Theology of Warfare in
Ancient Israel* (Scottdale, Pa.: Herald Press, 1980)

Longacre, Doris Janzen. *Living More with Less* (Scottdale, Pa.:
Herald Press, 1980)

Longacre, Doris Janzen. *More with Less Cookbook* (Scottdale, Pa.:
Herald Press, 1976)

McRobie, George. *Small Is Possible* (New York: Harper and Row,
1981)

Mouw, Richard. *Called to Holy Worldliness* (Philadelphia: Fortress
Press, 1980)

Newbigin, Lesslie. *The Open Secret: Sketches for a Missionary
Theology* (Grand Rapids: Eerdmans, 1978)

Otto, Rudolf. *The Idea of the Holy: An Inquiry into the Non-rational
Factor in the Idea of the Divine and Its Relation to the Rational,*
2nd ed. (New York, Oxford: University Press, 1958)

Vanier, Jean. *Community and Growth* (London: Darton, Longman
and Todd, 1979)

Vogt, Virgil. *Treasure in Heaven: The Biblical Teaching about
Money, Finances and Possessions* (Ann Arbor: Servant Books,
1982)

Wallis, Jim. *The Call to Conversion* (San Francisco: Harper and Row,
1983)

Wright, Christopher J. H. *Living as the People of God: The
Relevance of Old Testament Ethics* (Leicester: Inter-Varsity
Press, 1983)

Yoder, John Howard. *The Politics of Jesus* (Grand Rapids: Eerdmans,
1972)

Yoder, John Howard. *The Priestly Kingdom: Social Ethics as Gospel*
(Notre Dame, Ind.: University of Notre Dame Press, 1984)

Index of Scriptures and Other Ancient Writings

General Index

Photo by Christopher Phillips

The Author

In 1966 Alan Kreider arrived in London, England, as a young American graduate student doing a thesis on the English Reformation. To his great surprise (and pleasure—he loves England!), he has spent most of the years since then in London. His primary concern has shifted as well—from academic history to the renewal and missin of the church.

His training has been strictly historical: from Goshen College, where he did his undergraduate training, to Harvard

University, where he completed his Ph.D. in 1971. But as he studied history, he repeatedly found himself embroiled in discussions about the Bible and theology. And by 1974, when the Mennonite Board of Missions asked him to begin an assignment in London, the search for forms of Christian thinking and living that were appropriate to neopagan Europe had supplanted history as his major preoccupation.

Since then, working cooperatively with his wife, Eleanor (Graber) Kreider, Alan Kreider has seen the London Mennonite Centre change in focus from a residence for international students into a center for Christian training, thinking, and renewal. Alan and Eleanor have also been committed, as members and elders, to the growth of the London Mennonite Fellowship, the first Mennonite church to spring up in England since Queen Elizabeth in 1575 burned and disbanded a previous congregation. Alan and Eleanor's shared ministry has been most visibly expressed in the speaking which they do together. They have one child, Andrew, born in London in 1967.

Alan has taught history at Goshen College and at London Bible College. The fruit of his academic study appeared in a book on the English Reformation (published in 1979 by Harvard University Press). He has also written numerous articles—both scholarly and popular—on Christian discipleship, church history, and Christian attitudes to war and peace.

A founder member of the Evangelical Peacemakers, Alan has been concerned that Christian peace activists find empowering in Scripture, worship, and prayer. He has been equally excited when advocates of evangelism and renewal discover that God's peace, in the power of the Holy Spirit, is good news for the real world. Alan's slogan is Romans 14:17: "The kingdom of God is ... justice and peace and joy in the Holy Spirit."